KATIE'S MEMOIR

KATIE'S MEMOIR

IT AIN'T ALL ABOUT ME

Katie M. Wallace-Davis

XULON PRESS

Xulon Press
2301 Lucien Way #415
Maitland, FL 32751
407.339.4217
www.xulonpress.com

Library of Congress Control Number: 2022-911698

Paperback ISBN-13: 978-1-66285-164-3
Hard Cover ISBN-13: 978-1-66285-165-0
Ebook ISBN-13: 978-1-66285-166-7

Katie M Price

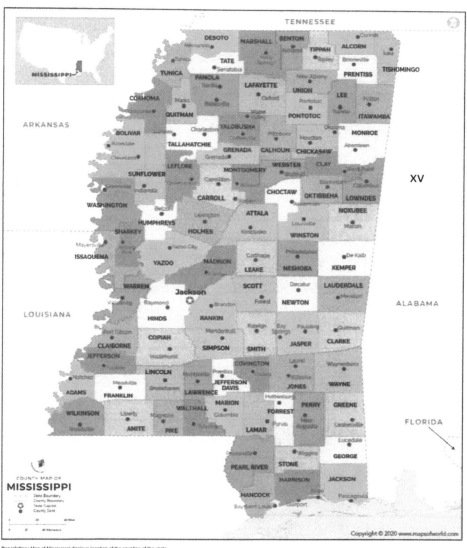

Description: Map of Mississippi displays location of the counties of the state.

Map of Mississippi

TABLE OF CONTENTS

Photo of Katie M Price

Photo of Map of Mississippi

INTRODUCTION xv

BOOK REVIEWS xvii

HONOR THY FATHER 1

Photo of emancipation

Photo of Abar 1870

Photo of Sarah 1880

Photo of Edna Stamps

Photo of Edna Caston 1880

Photo of Edna Caston Stamps 1920

Photo of Eugene Registration

Photo of Eugene and Flora Stamps

OUR STORY BEGINS 14

Photo of Ida Stamps Price and James Price

Photo of Will Price

Photo of William Price 1920 census

Photo of Lula Price

Photo of Lula Price 1920 census

BIG TROUBLE 22

Photo of Baby Katie

CHICAGO MY HOMETOWN 25

Photo of Colored Waiting Room

Photo of State of IL

BEFORE I SLEEP 33
   Photo of James Price

DADDY'S HOME 33
   Photo of James Price in hat
   Photo of James Price World War II Draft Card

ALONE WITH MY BROTHER. 40
   Photo of Jeffery James Price

DADDY DON'T YOU LOVE ME 43
   Photo of Family at Club
   Photo of James Price in hat

BUT HE'S MY BROTHER! 46
   Photo of Photo Jeffery James

OH NO. 49
   Photo of Father Time

THE WEST SIDE OF CHICAGO. 52
   Photo of Chicago city map
   Photo of Uncle John's Fence

TAKING YOUR CHILD TO WORK DAY 58

THE DINNER 66

ALL I COULD DO WAS CRY. 72

AUNT MARY STAMPS BARTWELL AND
UNCLE WALTER BARTWELL. 75
   Photo of Aunt Mary
   Photo of Mary J Stamps in the 1920 U.S. Federal Census
   Photo of Walter Bartwell

UNCLE HILLMAN 80
   Photo of Isiah Stamps {Hillman}
   Photo of Isiah Stamps 1920 U. S. Federal Census

AUNT KATIE MAY STAMPS BUSH. 84
  Photo of Henry Abron
  Photo of Aunt Katie M Bush in Wedding Dress
  Photo of Katie M Stamps 1920 U.S. Federal Census
  Photo of Katie M Bush & Edward Bush
  Photo of Marriage License December 1st 1927
  Photo of Edward Bush U.S. Social Security Death Index
  Photo of Henry Abron U.S. Social Security Death Index

RACE AND REALITY 98
  Photo of Just Women Summer 2017 Magazine Cover
  Photo of Women in Mission article
  Photo of Cornelia Stamps
  Photo of Cornelia Stamps 1920 U.S. Federal Census

EDNA LEE 103
  Photo of Edna Lee
  Photo of Women's Ministry Fall Retreat 2017

JOHNNIE ETHEL STAMPS WILLIAMS. 106
  Photo of John E Stamps 1920 U. S. Federal Census
  Photo of Johnny E Stamps U.S. Social Security Applications

UNCLE LUTHER STAMPS AND AUNT ANNIE STAMPS 110
  Photo of Luther M. Stamps 1940 U. S. Federal Census
      pages 1 & 2
  Photo of Annie Stamps and Katie Wallace and Luther Stamps

THELMA AND JOHN LOVE 114
  Photo of Thelma Stamps Love
  Photo of Thelma Stamps 1920 U.S. Federal Census pages 1 & 2
  Photo of John Love and his Truck

ME AND MRS JONES 121
  Photo of Estella Stamps Jones
  Photo of Estella Stamps 1920 U. S. Federal Census

UNCLE CHARLIE 129
 Photo of Aunt Estella Jones in their Store
 Photo of Aunt Estella and Charlie Jones

WHEN IDA MET SAM 133
 Photo of Samuel Buckingham and Ida Buckingham
 Photo of Cook /County Illinois Marriage Index
  Samuel B Buckingham and Ida Stamps
 Photo of Dave's Hot Dog
 Photo of Katie Price as teenager
 Photo of Katie and Ida

THE SUIT 141
 Photo of Mama in Suit

UNCLE LYMON AND AUNT ELSIE STAMPS 146
 Photo of Uncle Lymon
 Photo of Lyman Stamps 1940 U. S. Federal Census pages 1 & 2
 Photo of Elsie Ross Stamps Photo
 Photo of L C Stamps 1940 U. S. Federal Census
  (Elsie Ross Stamps)

SUNNY 151
 Photo of Sunny (Eduardo Williams)
 Photo of Annie Green Williams from Ancestry family tree
 Photo of Annie M Green Williams

FANNIE MAY PRICE. 157
 Photo of Fannie M Price and Family
 Photo of Fannie M. Price 1940 Census Record
 Photo of Fannie Mae Price Ancestry family tree person
 Photo of Jean Price 1920 Census Record

MY FIRST KISS. 162

SOME ENCHANTED EVENING 165

YESTERDAY 169

Photo of Katie Price and James Wallace (Lamont)

Photo of James Price and Katie Price

Photo of Wallace, Price. Stamps and Lee Families

STOP LAMONT 179

I WAS WITH CHILD 182

I SURVIVED 184

Photo of Erik in 1965

Photo of Erik

Photo of Erik and Katie

RAYFIELD CHANEY 189

Photo of Rayfield Chaney

Photo of Cook County, Il Death Index Rayfield Chaney

Photo of Rayfield and Lovie's family

THE SLEEP OVER 194

I PROMISE 196

Photo of Anne Green

Photo of Daddy James Price

Photo of James Price Marriage License to Sonora Walls

Photo of James Price Marriage License to Lois Ellis

Photo of Lois Ellis Price and James Price

SAY WHAT 205

Photo of Daddy in his gas station

Photo of Daddy's gas station

Photo of Daddy and Rose

Photo of James and Minnie Price

Photo of Jeffery James Price and Minnie Barnes Marriage record

Photo of James and Erma Price after wedding

Photo of James and Jeannie Price Erik and Daddy

Photo of Jeannie and James Price

Photo of Alycea and her Dad Erik Wallace

Photo of Renee and Erik's wedding day with family

Photo of Renee and Erik Reception

OLIVIA NANETTE COSEY WALLACE 218

Photo of Chicago theatre

Photo of Erik and Olivia's wedding

Photo of Wallace children

Photo of All 5 of Erik's children

Photo of Erik and Jessica marriage

Photo of Erik and Jessica's Wallace's Family

KATIE MET ROBERT 224

Photo of Katie Wallace and Robert Davis

Photo of Robert Keith Davis Ancestry person

Photo of Katie and Robert's wedding picture

Photo of Ann Hamman Article

Photo of Katie and Robert in Los Vegas family reunion

Photo of Robert and Mary Davis Wedding photo

Photo of Robert and Debbie Davis family photo

Photo of Robert's extended family

Photo of Robert's sibling family

SOMEDAY WE WILL BE TOGETHER. 233

Photo of Mitzi Ekekhor

MAMA, ARE YOU WHITE?. 236

I OUGHTA BE IN PICTURES 239

Photo of Katina model composite 1 & 2

Photo of 7 UP Photo shoot 1 & 2

Photo of Photo shoot Kelvinator 1 & 2

Photo of Katie & Erik in fashion show

IF I CAN'T HAVE YOU 246

KATIE, YOU HAVE CANCER 249
    Photo of Katie in Turtleneck sweater

MOMENTS REMEMBERED 253

THE FAKE JOB INTERVIEW 256

DON'T TELL ANYONE! 258

THE SOUND OF MUSIC 260

FEAR AND HATE 263

AIRPLANES AND AUTOMOBILES .266

AT LAST 268

LIVING 273

GAY 287
    Photo of Alycea and Tomesha Wallace
    Photo of Herman Wilson
    Photo of Erik L Wallace II

THEY CALL IT SWEET ALABAMA 295

IN THE MIDDLE OF THE NIGHT 296
    Photo of Ida Buckingham Find a Grave index
    Photo of 1920 census Ida Stamps

WILL YOU KNOW MY NAME 301

STORMS 306
    Photo of Jeffery James with Ida {Mama}
    Photo of Celebrating Jeffrey James' retirement
    Photo of Daddy, Mitzi, James and Angela
    Photo of Family of Angela Freeman, Mitzi Ekekhor,
        Jeffery J Price Jr, Takijah Murphy, Kizza Harris
    Photo of Brother and Sister Katie and James
    Photo of James and Katie 2020

BIOGRAPHY 312

INTRODUCTION

My Mama and I have talked several times about authoring a book on the life and times of the Stamps and Price family. I think if she had lived during the time I started this book there would be many different stories. I want the family, friends even friends I have not met yet to know the stories of this family. Some of them may have the same events in their family. Yes, everyone has a story. Not everyone has chosen to share their stories to the world I have.

My Parents and Aunts and Uncles lived in a different time. They had difficulties and any small moves forward was a compliment to them, Their struggle to survive without an adequate education. Their desire to be property owners and entrepreneurs motived those that followed them.

It was very important to my Mama that my brother and I finish school and graduate doing the best that we could. When I looked at the past that was shared with me, I was able to locate my Great Grandparents had a need to know who they were even if I only came to know that my Great Grandparents was born in this country and sad to know that a large part of their life they lived as property.

Some information was told to me by my Mama who sat at the feet of her Grandmother while she shared her life experiences as a slave.

While working for Internal Revenue Service I developed my curiosity but there was not time to spend trying to gather my families information until I retired. To introduced myself to you I would share that I loved to create things, crafts, sewing, crocheting fashion shows and modeling. Always seeking a position of authority. Union Steward, Toastmasters, and singing in the church's choir,. Administrative and Faith based roles. Shared Leader of the Children's Vacation Bible School. I decided to show the pictures of the family so you see that they were real. They cared about each other. Their disagreements never separated them. Some will look at our collection of family photos and the story of that picture may remind them of a conversation they had or the way they made you feel comes to your memory. These pictures speak loudly to me. I hope you find many moments in the reading of this book that will make you think of your own personal experiences.

Katie M. Wallace-Davis, Author

BOOK REVIEWS

This book, part memoir, part family stories, is a remarkable tribute to the writer, Ms. Katie Wallace-Davis, and to those she memorializes within its pages. Each chapter focuses on a particular person or event, or series of events, which span some six generations of Ms. Wallace Davis's family. It dates to her enslaved great-grandparents, whom she knows through her grandmother's recollections and some scant historical records, mainly census data, and continues into the 21st century. Each person recollected comes alive through the author's keen powers of observation and seemingly eidetic recall, as well as fantastic photographs. The photos alone make the book compelling.

The author captures the individuality of each person, including herself, bringing insight and compassion to all, even the worst of the family rogues. Tributes go to several women in the family who were special helpers, role models, and inspiration. Ms. Wallace-Davis also shares a special acceptance and love for those who dare to take risks or to be different; embracing diversity in all its forms is a noticeable sub-theme. There are universal stories here, and Ms. Wallace-Davis reminds us, the readers, that few among us are completely flawed or thoroughly saintly, but all are gloriously human and contribute to the rich tapestry that is life. Through all the stories, the author's heart, humor, faith, and love of family shine through.

The sub-title of Ms. Wallace-Davis's book is "It's Not All About Me," which is quite true; most of the book focuses on others in the family.

On the other hand, one of the most delightful aspects of the book is tracking the author's own development. We learn she was an attentive and curious child—and an ambitious youngster who even set out to become a model, and did!; she was creative and entrepreneurial, designing, sewing, and selling a clothing line; she was a successful career woman and dedicated church woman, the latter leading her to her second husband!; she was and is a devoted daughter, sister, mother, wife, aunt, friend, and more. How she learned and matured, through effort, luck, tragedy, and happenstance, is well documented, The stories will make you smile, laugh aloud, and sometimes cry.

Ms. Wallace-Davis's family history is told in these pages, but so is much of the larger history of Black people in America: enslavement and persecution; emancipation at last, only to be reversed by segregation and marginalization, all enforced through Jim Crow laws and the cultural force of white privilege; the Great Migration with new opportunities; the Civil Rights era with its new protections and opportunities; the ongoing struggle for freedom and equal rights. Accounts of racism permeate the pages, from everyday microaggressions to the murder of family members in a house fire set by anti-miscegenation arsonists in Mississippi. Ms. Wallace-Davis documents all this in a highly personal and evocative way, using well her talents as a gifted storyteller and keeper of family wisdom and lore.

Initially intended as a gift to the author's family, this book is a gift to anyone who is fortunate enough to encounter it. It is especially timely reading for a broad audience at this time in our country, when many are learning, or re-learning, American Black history.

Katie Wallace-Davis is known to be a jovial, interesting Auntie and friend. You will always find her being busy with the work of her hands involved in Book Club, Women's Groups or bringing to light racial matters Thank you Aunt Katie for your creativity and your dedication to genealogy and the telling of your story. Mitzi Ekekhor

It is a pleasure to learn from you, you've shown me so much. You have watched me grow into the man I am. Mom you are passionate about all you get involved in. I have watched you take on the world with God and Grandma. Overcoming all obstacles. All the while teaching me about our family. Showing me how to keep in touch with family and sharing family knowledge I'm honored to be your son and I wish you all the success God has planned for you. Erik L Wallace.

Katie Wallace-Davis is a great grandmother and a captivating storyteller she retired after 45 years in the IRS to focus on her lust for life, liberty, and love. Since 2009 you have been writing your memoirs which are sure to enchant and educate fellow pilgrims. From all social classes.

Erik L Wallace II

—◇○◇○◇—

I'm of the age to remember the ubiquitous axiom plastered on posters, bumper stickers, and sprinkled generously in conversation and comments – "Shit Happens." Yes, it does! It happens all the time and it happens to all of us. Fortunately, we have the resiliency to make the best of each moment and encounter. We learn from them, and they better equip us for what happens next. Other times we're knocked for a loop. Our equilibrium is impaired. It takes us time to recover, negotiating our way cautiously or carelessly. Regardless, whether invoked or not, God is present.

The author has taken the advice of countless persons who said, "The greatest gift you can give to your kids is to share your life stories with them." The stories in this book reveal important life experiences. They act as pegs to hang the precious story of the shit that happens which shapes the way she reacts, thinks, and forced her to change. These stories were compiled to be read by her family and friends to help interpret her and their life journey's. During this process, the author discovered how very much her mama influenced who she is. As a result, she endeavored to draw the line of influence from her ancestors to the present in hope that other family coming after might be intrigued and develop the thread from the past to their own live experiences.

I am so proud of the author for sticking with this project over the years. I am blessed to have witness the struggle and resulting self-discovery she experienced as she pursued giving her gift. I am grateful to her friends and family who've encouraged her and helped transition her desire and words into this book to share with others.

Robert K. Davis, April 2022

HONOR THY FATHER

Grandma Edna died when Mama was young. Mama was the ninth child of ten children. Mama was born April 25th, 1916, when her father Eugene was thirty-six and Edna was thirty-three years old. Based on her birth certificate her Dad was a sharecropper farmer while her Mother Edna did housework. Both of Mama's parents were born in Hines County, Mississippi. Grandma Edna was listed in the census as a Mulatto that could read and write. It did not say the same for my Grandfather Eugene. He was listed as a Negro. Who could read or write. Grandma Edna was the only child of Abar Caston and Sarah Caston. They were born into slavery in United States of America.

Abar and his daughter Edna were both considered as Mulatto, which is a person of mixed white and black ancestry, especially a person with one white and one black parent. This term was derived from the Spanish and Portuguese Mulatto, a common term in Southeastern United States during the era of slavery. My Great Grandparents were the property of a Master. They had no rights to vote they had to live as slaves, for all their lives. Abar shared living quarters with 5 others. The names of those he resided with were Spencer Hell, Julia Hell, Joseph Hell, Henry Hell, Petty Hell, Gabriel Scott, and Abar. The name of the slaveholder was illegible.

Mama mentioned that her Grandmother Sarah used to tell them about her life as a child slave. They would sit on the floor of the porch and listen to her tell the stories of her life, while rocking in a rocking chair.

Sometimes she would be talking and suddenly just stop and just rock, back and forth, lost in her memories.

Abar Caston, born about 1835 (this information was found in the 1870 census) he worked as a farmhand. Great Grandpa Abar passed before Great Grandma Sarah. We do not have any additional information on either of them. Nor dates of death. She was the only mother my Mama had because Grandma Edna was always sick and Great Grandma Sarah took care of Mama until her death. She also helped care for her other grandchildren while her daughter and the other younger children needed her.

The only memory Mama had of her mother was when they put her mother Edna in a box. Her older girls had put a nice dress on her. As it sat in the front room, relatives, friends, and neighbors came over with food and words of sympathy. The children were not allowed to go to the funeral held at Morning Star Baptist Church, because they did not have any shoes or nice clothes to wear. So, before the undertaker came, they gathered around the coffin and said goodbye to their mother at home. Tears were in some of their eyes. Mama did not have a real chance to know her mother. She watched while they put the top on the coffin and nailed it down. She was amazed at the beautiful white horses that backed up the wagon to the porch. Several men in black clothes picked up the coffin and placed it on the funeral wagon. There were no flowers to cover her coffin. Mama stood in silence and watched those white horses walk away. She watched until they were no longer in sight.

It seems that her Daddy had selected his new bride at their mother's funeral. It was often said you should pick your next mate at the funeral of your departed mate. In came Stepmother Flora Bell Stamps who brought her daughter. Mama never knew the reason Miss Flora did not like her, but this new stepmother showed her dislike for all of

Papa's children. She would comb Mama's hair because the other girls did their own hair and Flora would braid Mama's hair so tight that it was painful.

There was not much profit in cotton, but all the children had to pick cotton. Papa was a sharecropper. The children that did not work in the fields had to fix the food for the family. All the children were not allowed to go to school, because it took them away from performing their duties out in the field. A sharecropper must pay the owner of the property half of the money they made when they sell the crop. They also had to reimburse them for the credit they used while the crop was growing.

Many of the neighbor children would tease the Stamps children because the Stamps children wore their old clothes and hand me downs. Also, Mama took a lot of kidding from her siblings. Her navel was an outie, they called her pistol popping Mama. It was always peeking out of her shirt or leaving an imprint on her dresses. She also was often left behind when her siblings left the house, because of her fear of lizards, frogs, and snakes. Sometimes they would not want her to follow them, and they would leave a stick in the road when they left so she would not follow them.

She learned early in life to fight with them and the neighbor girls who messed with her. She had quite a reputation for fighting. Papa also made moonshine, and he taught Mama how to take care of the moonshine and hide it properly from the Revenuers. She was just a child doing this. There was so much happening in the house and my Mama was the one that their stepmother accused. Mama, who was not a quiet violet, told Papa that Miss Flora was not telling the truth. That She did not do what Miss Flora said she did. She ran away from her Papa to keep from getting a whipping. He was swinging his belt and he hit her in the head with the belt buckle, and she went down and was

3

out cold. Grandpa picked her up and put her on the bed. Everyone was upset, and the other children were crying for they thought that Ida was dead, and her Papa did too. She was out for quite a while before they found the smelling salts and put it under her nose. Papa said he was sorry, and was glad Mama was all right.

Early that next morning Papa's oldest daughter Mary, was told about her Papa knocking Mama out, and she came crashing through the front door with a shotgun and found her Papa in the house. She told him she was going to kill him, because she was tired of him hurting her Mama's children. She said she heard what he did to Ida, and she was mad as hell and was not going to take it anymore. Everybody there knew that Mary knew how to use that gun. Papa begged her not to shoot him and said "See Mary, there's Ida; she's all right! it was an accident I did not mean to hurt her. Baby, put down the gun," she did not put the gun down, for she did not have the heart to really kill her Papa. He had hurt Mary in the past. She wanted him to know if she hears anything else about him hurting her sisters, she was going to blow his head off. She backed out of the door keeping the gun on Papa and left.

The Emancipation Proclamation
January 1, 1863

A Transcription

By the President of the United States of America:

A Proclamation.

Whereas, on the twenty-second day of September, in the year of our Lord one thousand eight hundred and sixty-two, a proclamation was issued by the President of the United States, containing, among other things, to wit:

"That on the first day of January, in the year of our Lord one thousand eight hundred and sixty-three, all persons held as slaves within any State or designated part of a State, the people whereof shall then be in rebellion against the United States, shall be then, thenceforward, and forever free; and the Executive Government of the United States, including the military and naval authority thereof, will recognize and maintain the freedom of such persons, and will do no act or acts to repress such persons, or any of them, in any efforts they may make for their actual freedom.

"That the Executive will, on the first day of January aforesaid, by proclamation, designate the States and parts of States, if any, in which the people thereof, respectively, shall then be in rebellion against the United States; and the fact that any State, or the people thereof, shall on that day be, in good faith, represented in the Congress of the United States by members chosen thereto at elections wherein a majority of the qualified voters of such State shall have participated, shall, in the absence of strong countervailing testimony, be deemed conclusive evidence that such State, and the people thereof, are not then in rebellion against the United States."

Now, therefore I, Abraham Lincoln, President of the United States, by virtue of the power in me vested as Commander-in-Chief, of the Army and Navy of the United States in time of actual armed rebellion against the authority and government of the United States, and as a fit and necessary war measure for suppressing said rebellion, do, on this first day of January, in the year of our Lord one thousand eight hundred and sixty-three, and in accordance with my purpose so to do publicly proclaimed for the full period of one hundred days, from the day first above mentioned, order and designate as the States and parts of States wherein the people thereof respectively, are this day in rebellion against the United States, the following, to wit:

Arkansas, Texas, Louisiana, (except the Parishes of St. Bernard, Plaquemines, Jefferson, St. John, St. Charles, St. James Ascension, Assumption, Terrebonne, Lafourche, St. Mary, St. Martin, and Orleans, including the City of New Orleans) Mississippi, Alabama, Florida, Georgia, South Carolina, North Carolina, and Virginia, (except the forty-eight counties designated as West Virginia, and also the counties of Berkley, Accomac, Northampton, Elizabeth City, York, Princess Ann, and Norfolk, including the cities of Norfolk and Portsmouth[)], and which excepted parts, are for the present, left precisely as if this proclamation were not issued.

And by virtue of the power, and for the purpose aforesaid, I do order and declare that all persons held as slaves within said designated States, and parts of States, are, and henceforward shall be free; and that the Executive government of the United States, including the military and naval authorities thereof, will recognize and maintain the freedom of said persons.

And I hereby enjoin upon the people so declared to be free to abstain from all violence, unless in necessary self-defence; and I recommend to them that, in all cases when allowed, they labor faithfully for reasonable wages.

And I further declare and make known, that such persons of suitable condition, will be received into the armed service of the United States to garrison forts, positions, stations, and other places, and to man vessels of all sorts in said service.

And upon this act, sincerely believed to be an act of justice, warranted by the Constitution, upon military necessity, I invoke the considerate judgment of mankind, and the gracious favor of Almighty God.

In witness whereof, I have hereunto set my hand and caused the seal of the United States to be affixed.

Done at the City of Washington, this first day of January, in the year of our Lord one thousand eight hundred and sixty three, and of the Independence of the United States of America the eighty-seventh.

By the President: ABRAHAM LINCOLN
WILLIAM H. SEWARD, Secretary of State.

emancipation

Abar Caston
in the 1870 United States Federal Census

VIEW

📄 View blank form

✏️ Add alternate information

⚠️ Report issue

Name:	Abar Caston
Age in 1870:	35
Birth Year:	abt 1835
Birthplace:	Mississippi
Home in 1870:	Township 3 Range 7, Pike, Mississippi
Race:	Mulatto
Gender:	Male
Post Office:	Summit
Value of Real Estate:	View image

Household Members:

Name	Age
Spencer Hell	25
Julia Hell	23
Joseph Hell	13
Henry Hell	5
Petty Hell	2
Gabriel Scott	51
Abar Caston	35

SAVE ⌄   Cancel

Provided in association with National Archives and Records Administration

Suggested Records ❓

📄 1880 United States Federal Census
A. Caston

Write a

Make a Connection

Find others who are researching Abar Caston in Public Member Trees

Source Citation
Year: *1870*; Census Place: *Township 3 Range 7, Pike, Mississippi*; Roll: *M593_745*; Page: *60A*; Image: *123*; Family History Library Film: *552244*

Source Information
Ancestry.com. *1870 United States Federal Census* [database on-line]. Provo, UT, USA: Ancestry.com Operations, Inc., 2009. Images

Abar 1870

ancestry

Sarah Caston

BIRTH ABT 1850 • Mississippi
DEATH Unknown

great-grandmother

Facts

Age 0 — **Birth**
abt 1850 • Mississippi

Age 28 — **Birth of Daughter Edna CASTON STAMPS** (1878–)
abt 1878 • Mississippi

Age 30 — **Residence**
1880 • Beat 3, Amite, Mississippi, USA
Marital status: Married; Relation to Head of
House: Wife

Family

Parents

Spouse & Children

 A. Caston
1835–

  Edna CASTON STAMPS
1878–

Sources

Ancestry Sources

1880 United States
Federal Census

U.S., Social Security
Applications and Claims
Index, 1936-2007

Sarah 1880

7

Edna Stamps

Children (6)

Mary Julia STAMPS	D: 1900
Katie STAMPS Bush	B: 1904
Cornelia STAMPS	B: 1907

 Edna CASTON STAMPS
B: abt 1878 in Mississippi
D: Mississippi, USA

EUGENE STAMPS
B: abt 1880 in Mississippi

Parents

 A. Caston
1835~

 Sarah Caston
1850~

Edna Caston
in the 1880 United States Federal Census

Detail | Source

Name:	Edna Caston
Age:	2
Birth Date:	Abt 1878
Birthplace:	Mississippi
Home in 1880:	Beat 3, Amite, Mississippi, USA
House Number:	314
Dwelling Number:	314
Race:	Black
Gender:	Female
Relation to Head of House:	Daughter
Marital Status:	Single
Father's Name:	A. Caston
Father's Birthplace:	Mississippi
Mother's Name:	Sarah Caston
Mother's Birthplace:	Mississippi
Sick:	Well
Cannot Read:	Yes
Cannot Write:	Yes
Neighbors:	View others on page

Edna Caston 1880

9

Edna Stamps
in the 1920 United States Federal Census

Name:	Edna Stamps
Age:	37
Birth Year:	abt 1883
Birthplace:	Mississippi
Home in 1920:	Utica, Hinds, Mississippi
Street:	Utica Tallahalah Road
Race:	Mulatto
Gender:	Female
Relation to Head of House:	Wife
Marital Status:	Married
Spouse's Name:	Eugene Stamps
Father's Birthplace:	Mississippi
Mother's Birthplace:	Mississippi
Able to Speak English:	Yes
Occupation:	None
Able to Read:	Yes
Able to Write:	Yes
Neighbors:	View others on page

Household Members:

Name	Age
Eugene Stamps	40
Edna Stamps	37
Mary J Stamps	18
Isiah Stamps	17
Katie M Stamps	15
Cornelia Stamps	14

Edna Caston Stamps 1920

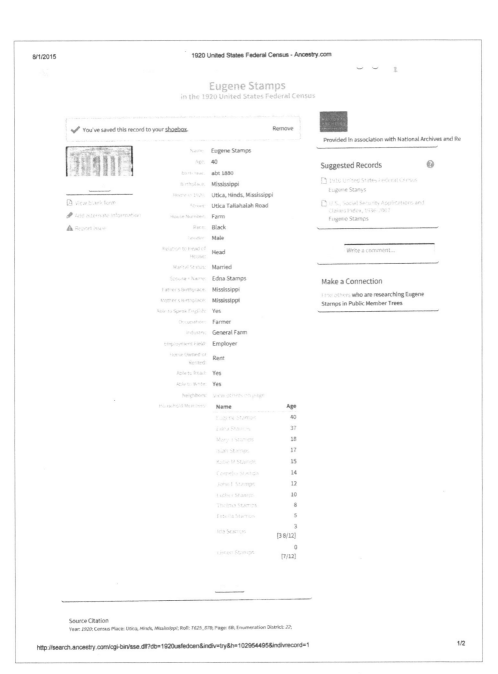

Eugene Stamps
in the 1920 United States Federal Census

You've saved this record to your shoebox.   Remove

View blank form

Add alternate information

Report issue

Name:	Eugene Stamps
Age:	40
Birth Year:	abt 1880
Birthplace:	Mississippi
Home in 1920:	Utica, Hinds, Mississippi
Street:	Utica Taliahalah Road
House Number:	Farm
Race:	Black
Gender:	Male
Relation to Head of House:	Head
Marital Status:	Married
Spouse's Name:	Edna Stamps
Father's Birthplace:	Mississippi
Mother's Birthplace:	Mississippi
Able to Speak English:	Yes
Occupation:	Farmer
Industry:	General Farm
Employment Field:	Employer
Home Owned or Rented:	Rent
Able to Read:	Yes
Able to Write:	Yes
Neighbors:	View others on page
Household Members:	

Provided in association with National Archives and Re

Suggested Records

1920 United States Federal Census
Eugene Stanys

U.S., Social Security Applications and Claims Index, 1936-2007
Eugene Stamps

Write a comment...

Make a Connection

Find others who are researching Eugene Stamps in Public Member Trees

Name	Age
Eugene Stamps	40
Edna Stamps	37
Mary I Stamps	18
Isiah Stamps	17
Katie M Stamps	15
Cornelio Stamps	14
John E Stamps	12
Luther Stamps	10
Thelma Stamps	8
Estella Stamps	5
Ida Stamps	3 [3 8/12]
Union Stamps	0 [7/12]

Source Citation
Year: *1920*; Census Place: *Utica, Hinds, Mississippi*; Roll: *T625_878*; Page: *6B*; Enumeration District: *22*;

http://search.ancestry.com/cgi-bin/sse.dll?db=1920usfedcen&indiv=try&h=102954495&indivrecord=1 1/2

Eugene 1920 image

Eugene Stamps
in the New York, County Marriages, 1847-1849; 1907-1936

Name:	Eugene Stamps
Gender:	Male
Spouse:	Edna Caston
Child:	Katherine Stamps
Film Number:	001014361

Source Information
Ancestry.com. New York, County Marriages, 1847-1849; 1907-1936 [database on-line]. Lehi, UT, USA: Ancestry.com Operations, Inc., 2016.

Original data: Marriage Records. New York Marriages. FamilySearch, Salt Lake City, UT.

Description
This collection consists of county marriage records from various counties in New York. Learn more...

Eugene Stamps New York

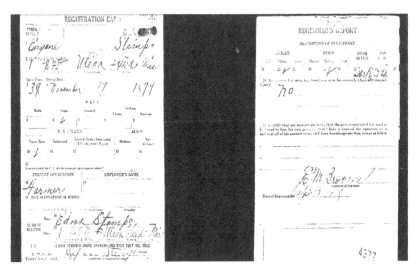

Eugene Registration

Eugene and Flora Stamps

OUR STORY BEGINS

T hey met at a small church in Hinds County Mississippi. The Morning star Daddy was one of the men who sang in the church's quintet. I am not sure if he was an alto he was not the leader of the group but his voice added something to the music. The men in the quintet were great gospel singers they were very popular most of them were single, all of them were tall attractive men. The women loved to hear them sing and were happy about the fact that they were eligible bachlors. Those men could really sing gospel music, all the single ladies wanted to catch one of them.

Mama was very possessive of her man, and she addressed anyone who thought she wanted Daddy, one of her cousins said to a group of women if James, wanted to "stop her train"; she would certainly let him ride." That little group of women roared in laughter, Mama found out what she had said and begin to look for her to teach her a lesson. She wanted her to feel her wrath. If she had found her while she was angry it would have been a physical fight. Daddy would walk Mama back from church to Aunt Neal's house and share Sunday suppers with them. Mama was an excellent cook, Daddy would tease Mama about their age his birthday was the 1st day of February and Mama's was April 25th both of them was born in 1916, Daddy would always claim that he was younger than Mama. Daddy married Mama because he had fun with her and she was a good cook. She also would not have sex with him without being married.

He did not tell his Parents that he was getting married they just went to the courthouse and got married. He brought her home late that evening and introduced her to his Parents, his Mother was beside herself in anger. His Dad thought he had made a good choice. Will Price thought Mama was really cute. But Lou Price did not and told Daddy they could not sleep together in her house. So they didn't, she had Daddy in their room and Mama was where Daddy slept. Mama was afraid to be alone in Daddy's room, she thought they had a strange house they did not use the upstairs and Mama thought she saw the outline of a snake in the walls. She was terrified but it was too dark to leave, so she left at first light the next day before they got up, she went home where she lived with her sister Neal,

Daddy knew where his bride went so he followed her later that day. Mama had a job with the Cross family, she was a domestic. She washed the clothes, dusted, mopped the floor, and washed the dishes, changed the sheets on the bed, and washed and hung them on the clothesline outside and ironed them. She also cooked daily. She asked Mrs. Cross if there was a job for her new husband and there was so he got the job and they stayed in a shack on the Cross' property. They had Daddy's Parents over for dinner, Mama did her best making some biscuits and fried chicken and greens, and corn. Her Father-in-law told Mama her biscuits were so light, he had to hold them down to keep them from flying out of the window. He always knew how to make Mama smile. Papa loved Mama's cooking. It wasn't long after the marriage that James was conceived and born in October 1935 he was the family's pride and joy they always told James that his birth certificate was incorrect the date was wrong because the mid wife did not report the birthday correctly, his name Jeffery James Price Jr. But they just called him James and called Daddy Jean, my brother celebrates both days for his birthday every year our parents were alive they celebrated his birthday on the day they said was correct and Daddy said he was actually there that day.

One thing I remember Mama and Daddy agreed on was the date of James birthday. Daddy and Mama still attended Morning Star Baptist Church. Mama was holding James in her lap, when Daddy's brother, Uncle Bunk, asked Mama if he could hold James she gave James to him, through the open window. He immediately took James to where our Daddy was standing outside the church talking with some young ladies. As Uncle Bunk came close to Daddy, James reached out for Daddy calling" da, da" and the girls were surprised to know that James was married with child. They turned away from Daddy and started giggling with Uncle Bunk. Uncle Bunk broke up that action. Those two were always competing with each other in regard to who was more attractive to the women.

Once during an argument Daddy put a gun to Mama's head and threated to shoot her. Mama begged Daddy not to shoot her she pleaded with him to just let her see their son James one more time her pleads soften his heart and he put the gun away. She wanted Daddy to stay home with her and James. He would have other plans for the evening.

I once asked Mama why did she want to fight the ladies, fight daddy, she said she tried but he would hold her away from him with his long arms and her arms were too short to reach him. She was afraid he would, in anger hurt her. I concluded that he was not ready to be a married man with a family. Lou his mother was right their son was not mature enough for marriage. There also were additional members to their family during Will and Lou's marriage there was a daughter, Fannie Mae Price daughter of Lou and I heard there was a son, a child of Will, during their marriage. My Parents had good and troubled times 5 years later I was conceived and born on Monday August 5th,1940. As soon as I came into the world feet first, the gossip in the family was that I was not my Daddy's child because I had light skin, not a lot of melanin. The midwives said I was not the color of my Daddy, my Mama, or my brother. They repeated this that this child does not look like her Daddy. This spread to the local women. They all wondered who my biological father was. I was light skin with a head full of black curly hair. Daddy did not have any reservations, but shortly after I was born there was big trouble in the family. Daddy did not take his marriage vows seriously and Mama was very serious about her vows to Daddy, he did not stop pursuing women they managed to get along most of the time. I think they were 18 when they married and soon after became parents and that can be too young, 5 years later, when Mama conceived me. But as soon as I was born. There was big trouble for the family.

Ida Stamps Price and James Price

Photo Will Price

William Price
in the 1920 United States Federal Census

Name:	William Price
Age:	39
Birth Year:	abt 1881
Birthplace:	Mississippi
Home in 1920:	Carpenter, Copiah, Mississippi
House Number:	Farm
Residence Date:	1920
Race:	Black
Gender:	Male
Relation to Head of House:	Head
Marital Status:	Married
Spouse's Name:	Lula Price
Father's Birthplace:	Mississippi
Mother's Birthplace:	Mississippi
Able to Speak English:	Yes
Occupation:	Farmer
Industry:	General
Employment Field:	Own Account
Home Owned or Rented:	Rent
Able to Read:	No
Able to Write:	No
Neighbors:	View others on page

Household Members:

Name	Age
William Price	39
Lula Price	27
Jean Price	4

Source Citation

Year: 1920; Census Place: Carpenter, Copiah, Mississippi; Roll: T625_874; Page: 12B; Enumeration District: 56

Source Information

Ancestry.com. 1920 United States Federal Census ;database on-line]. Provo, UT, USA: Ancestry.com Operations, Inc., 2010. Images reproduced by FamilySearch.

Original data: Fourteenth Census of the United States, 1920. (NARA microfilm publication T625, 2076 rolls). Records of the Bureau of the Census, Record Group 29. National Archives, Washington, D.C. For details on the contents of the film numbers. visit the following NARA web page: NARA. Note: Enumeration Districts 819-839 are on roll 323 (Chicago City).

Description

This database is an index to individuals enumerated in the 1920 United States Federal Census, the Fourteenth Census of the United States. It includes all states and territories, as well as Military and Naval Forces, the Virgin Islands, Puerto Rico, American Samoa, Guam, and the Panama Canal Zone. The census provides many details about individuals and families including: name, gender, age, birthplace, year of immigration, mother tongue, and parents' birthplaces. In addition, the names of those listed on the population schedule are linked to actual images of the 1920 Federal Census. Learn more...

William Price 1920 United States Federal Census

19

Photo Lula Price

Lula Price

1920 Census Record

Gender: Female   Race: Black

Age at Time of Census: 27   Estimated Birth Year: 1893

Birth Location: Mississippi Map

Residence: Copiah, MS Map   Can Read: Yes

Can Write: Yes   Father's Birthplace: Mississippi

Mother's Birthplace: Mississippi   Spouse: William Price

Marital Status: Married   Spouse Birthplace: Mississippi

Head of Household: William Price

Relationship to Head: Wife

Members in Household

William Price
39 yrs, Spouse, Male

Jean Price
4 yrs, Child, Male

Suggested Records for Lula Price

1930 Census - 2 records
Lula Price, born in MS, around 1893

1910 Census - 1 record
Lula Price, born in MS, around 1893

Historic Newspapers - 12 mentions
Lula Price located in MS

Lula Price 1920 U.S Federal Population Census

BIG TROUBLE

We sat in the front row right behind the defendant's table and all the other black people there sat behind us. I saw my Daddy's chains taken off. James said, "Hi, Daddy." He responded and smiled at me, but he could not look Mama in the face. I thought he may have been ashamed.

He told his lawyer that his family was here, and the lawyer turned and looked at us. Tennessee's Mother sat behind us, and we heard her tell her companion, "It's a shame that Tennessee would do what she did to this lovely family." I got a good look at the crowd when Mama put me up near her left shoulder. Mama had James in his best clothes, and she dressed me up in a pink dress with a matching pink blanket that her sister sent me from Philadelphia. I had a head full of black curly hair that was peeking out of the blanket.

Daddy was involved in a shooting; the dead girl was named Tennessee. Daddy and Tennessee struggled over a gun. Daddy had pulled it out to get her to let him go home. It discharged and she was seriously hurt. I have always thought of her as being a tall woman with light caramel-colored skin and naturally long hair. She was attracted to Daddy and wanted him to herself and was not ready for him to leave her, so he could return to Mama and his children. That night there were three of them in the car, Daddy, his male friend, and Tennessee. Daddy and Tennessee had some drinks and danced close, grinding on the dance floor. Both were having an enjoyable time and he loved the attention he was getting. The jealousy that was showing on his friend's face, amused him. Tennessee had a relationship with him and was drinking. She only wanted to be with him as she had done many times before, but Daddy said it was getting late, or shall I say early in the morning, and he had something else he wanted to do so he wanted to leave.

At least that is what he told her. She wouldn't hear of it. By then they were getting in the car, but she wanted to go to another club to have some more drinks and get on the dance floor. He told her he was going home to see his kids. (What a break for us!) Tennessee had different plans for the night. She thought he would stay with her for the night, which he had done in the past. Daddy resisted, and she told him "You ain't going home to those kids tonight! I ain't had my fill of you yet!" Daddy told her no, she demanded his time, they became angry with each other, and Daddy pulled out his gun to threaten her. She grabbed it, and in the struggle for the gun, it went off and Tennessee was hurt bad. Blood was everywhere in the car. Daddy drove her to the colored hospital.

She died, and Daddy was arrested and charged with second degree murder. Daddy's Aunt Fannie owned a small grocery and restaurant called "Fannie's." She asked Mama to go to court and take the children, saying this may help Daddy's case. She arranged for the ride to Jackson. Our driver was driving so fast that he lost control of the car and swerved off the road. We ended up in a ditch. No one was hurt. He managed to get us out of the ditch and arrive to court on time. The trial did not last but a few hours.

Daddy was found guilty, and the Judge gave him a five-year sentence for involuntary manslaughter, or he could pay $5,000. Dr. Cross his employer, offered to pay the fine. If Daddy would sign an agreement to be a bond servant for Dr. Cross, for 5 years, which means he would be paying back the loan by $1,000 a year. It could be transferred if he wanted to sell the bond. Daddy refused. He was sent to Parchman Penitentiary where they were harvesting cabbages it was slave labor for the prisoners there were no bars, there were these tall stands that the guards used. The guards were sharp shooters. If anyone tried to escape, they would just shoot to kill. I was less than a year old. Well, Tennessee was right. Daddy did not come home to his kids, that night, or any other night for years.

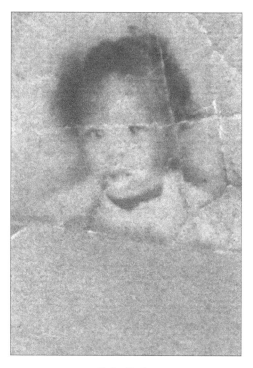

Baby Katie

CHICAGO MY HOMETOWN

Mama had a broken heart. Daddy was in prison. The whole town knew about it. She did not have any help with my brother and me. She would be our only support. It is difficult to work when you need childcare. For now, she could take us to work with her. Mama decided to write her older sister, Thelma, who was living in Chicago. She asked if she could come up north with her two kids. Thelma was married to John Love, and they were doing well, compared to the life they had in Mississippi. Mama wanted to know if Thelma would help her secure work. This was during the second wave of the great northward migration from1940 until 1970. James was getting big, and she was worried for him, being a black male child in Mississippi, living within Jim Crow laws. Thelma said, "Yes, you may come here and bring the children. I am sure we can find some work for you."

Before Mama left Mississippi, James and I were in the big house with her. I was wrapped in a blanket lying in a basket and Mrs. Cross and her blue-eyed blonde daughter Sylvia, who was the same age as James, had several bananas. Sylvia handed one of them to James, which made him extremely happy. He reached out and kissed her on the lips, something he had seen Dr. and Mrs. Cross do every day while he was there. Mama was shocked and told James, "Don't do that!" She rushed to move him away from Sylvia. Mrs. Cross said, "Oh, Ida, don't worry about it; don't let Dr. Cross see anything like it!" Mama was relieved but was careful to not let that happen again. My brother was

5 years old, and I was just months old. So, during the Second Great Northward Migration of 1940, Mama planned to go north to Chicago.

Before leaving, Mama took James to see Daddy at the prison, to say goodbye. Mama had enough money for one ticket. Since she was holding me, I could travel free. She was able to gather a few things together and move to Chicago. She did not have enough money to bring James, so she left James with her sister Neal. She promised, "Just for a short while, until I have a job." She said she would send Neal money for James's expenses. She planned to save enough money for James's ticket. She said goodbye to Mississippi. We rode in the colored car to Chicago, Illinois toward a new life and hope for a better future for her and her children.

The people in our car were carrying watermelons and small animals. Mama held tight to her possessions as we watched the miles away from Mississippi pass by. This was farther than she had ever been from home. When we arrived in Chicago and stepped onto the platform, Mama was happy to see her brother-in-law John Love at the train station. We were on the south side of Chicago near 63rd street. He grabbed her suitcase and showed her where he parked. Our new address was 645 East 61st Street, Chicago Il.

Aunt Thelma was delighted. John and Thelma did not have any children, so, they were happy to help take care of a baby. Mama had no problems finding work and she used every opportunity to work. She needed to pay rent and send money to her sister Neal. She also saved all she could, not allowing herself any luxuries. She cleaned during the week as a domestic and took extra jobs as a server for private parties at night. On weekends she secured a job across the street at the cleaners. She pressed clothes and cleaned the store. She was the one that cleaned our apartment, mopping floors and cleaning the bathroom and kitchen. Thelma and John both were working.

Mama did not read well because she was kept from going to school. She had some difficulties using public transportation. But she managed. She showed me how to work, sick or well. She also occasionally smoked Camel cigarettes. We all stayed in a one-bedroom apartment. Mama and I used the bedroom. We shared a full-size bed, and Thelma and John slept where I later figured out was the dining room. It was the largest room in the apartment. They kept the window drapery closed so it was always dark in there. Their bed was huge in comparison to the bed Mama and I slept in. It was taller, and she had wonderful comforters on it. The windows in their room faced west, and it should have been very sunny in the afternoon. Their room did not have a door, but our room had a door. The only sunlight that came in the apartment was from the window in the bathroom the bedroom windows had a west view, as the living room faced the courtyard with a view of the apartments across the way. The apartments on the end of the buildings had a balcony, but ours were full of dirt from the heavy traffic that came through 61st Street. I was not allowed out there, but I sneaked out there once and they screamed at me to never do that again. We had a galley kitchen; those windows faced east. There was a small table with an attached leaf, and when it was extended, three people could sit down but you had to squeeze into your seat.

On Sundays they lifted the leaf and we managed to get around the table and enjoy our breakfast together. Aunt Thelma would serve pig brains and scrambled eggs with bacon and biscuits, but Mama was always standing up. All the other meals were taken separately. This was a special treat for Sundays only. After I found out what I was eating, I never accepted the pig brains again. There were 3 adults and a baby in that one-bedroom apartment. Mama finally had enough money to send for James. She had been sending money to Aunt Neal weekly for James's expenses. She finally was able to buy a train ticket for James to come north.

Aunt Neal put James on the train with a note pinned to his clothes, showing his name, Mama's name, and our address and telephone number. The Porter was to let James off at the 63rd Street Train Station. When Uncle John met that train, James was nowhere to be found at the 63rd Street Station. Uncle John came home without James, and everybody was upset! Mama was devastated and crying. She was sure she would never see her son again. Then the phone rang. Aunt Thelma answered the phone and waved her arms for Mama to hush as she took the information. A Porter had found James at the station down-town. So, Uncle John left to pick James up at the downtown station. Mama gave Uncle John money to give a tip to the porter.

We were all so happy when they walked through the door. My brother was here! He had a big safety pin attached to a note on his coat. He was my big brother. He had big brown eyes and dark skin. He did not look like me or Mama. John and Thelma were happy to see him too. I was so happy James was there. Mama grabbed him and hugged him tight. He hugged Mama and kissed her on the cheek. We were so happy that everyone had a great big smile on their face. Now we had to get to know James. James had a habit that Mama did not like, for he called her Ida and when they talked about Aunt Neal, James would call her Mama. So, all the adults started to call Ida Mama, until James stopped calling Aunt Neal his Mama. It took a while before he adjusted to his unfamiliar environment. The city was so different from living in the South. Most of the children played in the courtyard. He met the Roundtree's family. James said it was the actor that tried to take his lunch money. James was confined in the courtyard of the building, where the grass soon died.

Mama and I slept in the full-sized bed and James had a cot. There was just barely space to walk between the two beds. Now there were 5 people living in that one-bedroom apartment. My brother and I sat at the kitchen table and did our homework. Since my Mama did not finish elementary school, she was not able to help me, she worked in her father's fields and also worked as a housekeeper for money to help the family pay bills. Since she did not have the opportunity to go to school as we did, she knew that an education would afford us a better life. My brother helped me when I had problems understanding my homework. Mama brought these lined cursive writing tablets. She had us copying in them for hours until we developed excellent cursive handwriting. She also brought us a dictionary. I was a slow learner and Mama was teaching me to tell time. Since I would be home alone in the mornings, my job was to get up in the morning after our alarm clock rang. Mama would lay out my clothes on the bed at night. I was to get dressed, pick up my lunch money off the dresser, and be sure to close the apartment door. It locked when you closed it. Then I was to carefully cross 61st Street at the corner light. It was difficult to learn to tell time when I needed glasses. Mama had this analog clock, and my assignment was to tell Mama what time it was each time she changed it. Whenever I gave her the wrong time, she would hit my hand with a ruler. What she didn't know was that I never heard the alarm clock. We were close enough to the school for me to hear the school bell. I had to get dressed, eat my cereal, pick up my lunch money, which was on the dresser, and close the apartment door and make sure it was locked. I was careful crossing 61st Street. I ran ½ block farther, across the alley, then the rest of the way to the school and up the stairs to my classroom. I would run into my classroom; they placed my desk in the front of the room due to my poor eyesight.

I was late every day. I remember printing my name for the teacher. I learned to spell it Kattie Price and the teacher told me that I spelled my name incorrectly. The correct spelling was Katie. I told her that was the way my Mama told me, and the teacher insisted that it was incorrect. I checked my birth certificate, and it was differently listed there. So, I dropped that extra t. Mama agreed with the change. I never had time to play with the other girls on the school's playground because the children were already in class by the time, I got there.

One day as I stood to say the Pledge of Allegiance to the flag, I got as far as "I pledge," when a healthy wind blew up my skirt and I realized that I had forgotten to put on my panties. "Oh, my, I felt naked." I knew I would not be able to go home and retrieve my panties until Aunt Thelma came home. I would have to, as usual, wait for Aunt Thelma. She was usually the first to arrive. I waited outside for her. I was not old enough to have a key to the apartment. I was hopeful that I could get into my room and put on my panties before Aunt Thelma would notice that my panties were still on the bed. I knew if my Aunt saw those panties on the bed, I would not hear the end of it. When Aunt Thelma opened the door, I rushed into the apartment, went straight to our bedroom, and grabbed my panties. Then I sat on the floor on the other side of the bed and slid my panties on, and just as I finished pulling them up, Aunt Thelma came to the door, looked in, and asked me, "What are you doing?" I looked at her and said, "Nothing." I knew that if I were caught, I would have had not just the pain of that ruler. Well, I got caught the time I forgot my lunch money and went back to the apartment. As expected, no one was home. I sat on the door frame and cried. I was hungry. A man came by and asked me, "Why are you crying?" I told him I left my lunch money in the house, and I did not have any lunch and I was hungry. He reached into his pocket, and he gave me a dollar. Thank you! I ran over to the lunch counter and ordered me a burger.

When Mama came home and saw that money still on the dresser, she asked me if I had lunch today. I told her what happened, and she told me how important it was for me to not talk to strangers, that if I did what I was supposed to do every day, things like this would not happen. She said she needed me to do as I was told. She wanted me to be safe while she was not at home. She reminded me that not everyone is your friend and she depended on me to follow the families' instructions because they all loved me. I never had any of those problems again.

Colored Waiting Room

State of IL

BEFORE I SLEEP

Each night I spent time with my Mama. We would take a chair from the kitchen and place it in our room in front of the dresser's mirror. On the dresser was a 5x7 picture of Daddy. Mama would take down my hair and comb and brush my hair. Sometimes she would put some oil in the parts that she made. It was always a good feeling to have your hair combed and brushed. Most of the time we would share what happened in our day. Sometimes we would sing a gospel song. But all of the time we would look at the picture on the dresser of my Daddy. He was so handsome to me, and his charm seems to come right out of that picture. He was well dressed. He had on a suit and tie. The fabric of his suit was plaid. The suit was double breasted, but he left one side of the suit coat open. I thought the shirt was white and it was one of the wide collar shirts. His tie had a Windsor knot. Since the picture was in black and white, I had no idea what color it was. His front pocket was filled with a tri folded white handkerchief. Oh, the plaid in the suit was very low key with narrow stripes going one way and stripes going another way, very fashionable. He had two gold teeth on the left side of his mouth and a small mustache. I noticed a dimple in his cheek. His eyes appeared brown, and his hair had a small part on the right side of his head. He had a low haircut. He looked like he was in his 20s. That is what I saw looking back at the picture.

As a part of our ritual, Mama would look at the picture and say, "I Love That Man." I would add to the conversation: "I Love That Man Too." Then a big smile. Mama always brushed my hair upward. She would braid small braids in my hair, and they would connect to one another in a circle. It looked like a crown when she finished. I liked that style because it was different than the other girl's hair style, and since I did not have long hair, I thought the style was special. Before she tied my hair with a scarf, thinking it would stay that nice for the next morning, she looked at Daddy's picture and she said, "Your Daddy Ain't No Damn Good!" I was shocked. I looked up at her Image in the mirror and I said with pride, "Mama, he is as good as you!" She did not respond. She took the scarf and tied up my hair for the night, and she finally said, "Katie, say your prayers and go to bed." She took the chair and put it back in the kitchen. I squeezed between the two beds and got on my knees and said the prayer she taught me. "Now I lay me down to sleep. I pray the Lord my soul to keep. If I should die before I wake, I pray the Lord my soul to take. God bless Mama, Daddy, Aunt Thelma, Uncle John. Oh, God bless my brother James too. Good night, Mama." I lay in bed and covered my head because the light was still on. I never heard Mama say anything bad about Daddy before this night nor after that night. Until I was about 18 years old.

James Price

DADDY'S HOME

Late one night I thought the family was asleep, but only James and I were asleep. I heard Mama's voice talking with Aunt Thelma. They were greeting someone, I turned over and went back to sleep, Mama came into the room to wake up James and me. James made it into the living room before me. I saw his big smile into the face of the man who had his back to me. James said, Hi, Daddy and hugged his neck. I came around to the front of the man, and I saw the man that was in the picture Mama kept on the dresser. "That's my Daddy!" I screamed and jumped into his arms. He looked familiar but not exactly like the picture I looked at all those years while he was away. Oh, what a night! Daddy was home.

James and I were moved into the living room couch. After the first night James slept on the couch each night and I slept on the cot most nights It was different having another man in the house, for I was always sitting on Uncle John's lap whenever he was sitting down on the couch. He and I were drinking buddies. He made me a drink and he had one for himself. Mama was always working but my sitters, well, my Uncle always gave me what I wanted. If he had whiskey, I had some too. Then before long he would pick me up and carry me to my bed and then be free of me for the rest of the night.

My Grand Uncle John Black would come over with my Grand Aunt Almeda Stamps Smith. They would play a cardboard game with pennies. John Black gave me the biggest peppermint stick which ended up in my hair because they put me in the bed with it still in my hands. The next morning Mama had a tough time getting that sticky candy out of my hair. Daddy coming home spoiled my Uncle John's plans to talk Mama into letting him adopt James. He spent a lot of time teaching James how to work and how you work for what you want because nothing is going to be given to you. They bonded during their time together. Uncle John took him to work with him and kept James from running the streets. Mama told John that she appreciated all he had done to help her with James, but she was not going to give her son away. Mama had another offer from my sitter, who lived in our building. She and her husband wanted Mama to allow them to adopt me. They had even started calling me Mickey which I was not sure I liked. Mama said" Oh no, I can't give you my child." After that experience she stopped using her as a sitter.

Johnnie Ethel Stamps Williams, my Mama's older sister, had a daughter she named her after Aunt Thelma. Thelma Williams Wilson came to Chicago. Aunt Johnnie lived in St Louis, MO. We called her Little Thelma because it was confusing when both were in the house. Our little family had to move out of John and Thelma's place. Aunt Thelma and Uncle John were unhappy with something that Daddy was responsible for. It was serious enough for us to be told to move.

James and Mama were walking home from the grocery store with 2 shopping bags of groceries, and Mama starting walking bent over. She was having terrible cramps and could only walk with difficulty. James picked Mama up and carried her the rest of the way home, while still holding those 2 shopping bags. After getting home he called Daddy and then called for an ambulance for Mama, and off she went to the hospital. Daddy and Mama lost twin girls. I was so sad, how I wanted a sister. I did not realize the expense additional children would be on our little family.

James Price in hat

James Price

in the U.S., World War II Draft Cards Young Men, 1940-1947

Detail | Source

Name:	James Price
Gender:	Male
Race:	Negro (Black)
Age:	26
Relationship to Draftee:	Self (Head)
Birth Date:	1 Feb 1916
Birth Place:	Utica, Mississippi, USA
Residence Place:	Jackson, Hinds, Mississippi, USA
Registration Date:	16 Oct 1942
Registration Place:	Jackson Twp, Hinds, Mississippi, USA
Employer:	R H Bullocks
Height:	6 2
Weight:	154
Complexion:	Dark brown
Hair Color:	Black
Eye Color:	Brown
Next of Kin:	Fannie Thomas

Household Members	Relationship
James Price	Self (Head)

© 2021 Ancestry.com

James Price World War II Draft Card

39

ALONE WITH MY BROTHER

The apartment had an ice box, and when the ice man came around you would hear him yelling" Ice Man, Ice Man get your ice today!" My job was to tell him that we wanted a block of ice. They would have a pick in the Ice box that I was not supposed to touch. The man had a leather pad on his back and would bring the ice upstairs, holding it with an ice tong and it was the most exciting thing that happened that day.

Next thing that was interesting at our house was grocery day. The kitchen cabinets were tall and high. The most attractive thing about them was that the cabinet doors were glass. James's job was to get the step ladder and place the cans on the shelves with the picture in front with the same vegetables together, I really liked grocery day seeing all the wonderful stuff we had to eat. My job was to hand each can to my brother, and he would place it on the shelf, and then I was to give him another can, of the same kind. He was exceptionally good at his job. He would carefully stack them on top of each other. One day I made a game of my part of this project and as soon as he took one can from my hand, I had another one ready. My game was call express handling. He was not happy with me and my express handling so he decided to slow me down, and he pushed down on the next can that I handed him, and the can hit me on the nose. It was a painful lesson and today I still have that dent on the bridge of my nose. Of course, I told Mama.

One winter day while waiting for Christmas I could not contain myself. I was ready for Santa Claus to come to town. I had asked for a doll. I started singing" He knows when you are sleeping, He knows when you are wake." Since James and I were home alone he found me annoying. I started telling him that I was getting a doll for Christmas and Mama was going to make a sweet potato pie and I was going to leave it out for Santa because I thought he would like it better than those cookies everybody left for him. Then my brother broke my innocent heart. He said "Katie, there is no Santa Claus. He will not be coming here!" I responded, "Yes he Is! Mama said so." James got up from the chair and opened the hall closet door. It was dark and deep. He crawled in and brought out a box and showed me a blue-eyed yellow hair doll. That was not the doll I asked for. He told me, "See, Mama put that in there for you and she is going to put it under the tree on Christmas Eve. I still did not want to give up on Santa." He added, "See I told you. When have you have ever seen a white man in this neighborhood at night? You better not tell Mama that I showed you this doll!" Well, I pushed the conversation. "Who eats the sweet potato pie I leave out for him? Mama eats it, Katie!" I never remember seeing a Santa, just at school and talk about one on the radio.

I asked Mama why she always have nuts and fruit an apple or an orange with peppermint on top of my presents. Her response was, "That is what I received as a child, and all the children in the family would get one gift and nuts and an apple or an orange." I was unhappy that Santa was not real. I decided not to teach my children that there was a Santa Claus or a tooth fairy. Or an Easter bunny.

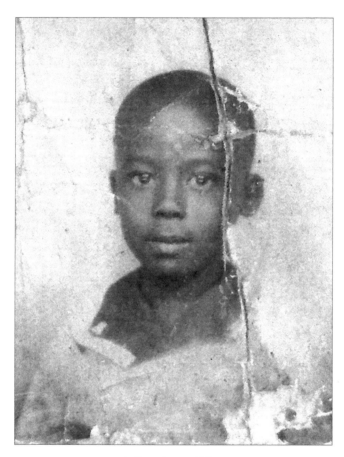

Jeffery James Price

DADDY DON'T YOU LOVE ME

After Mama and Daddy moved out of Aunt Thelma's apartment, we acquired a place of our own, Daddy, James, Mama, and me. It was nice for all of us being together. Our Daddy was home, and we enjoyed his being around. After he got a job, we ate better and had better things. I was going to Kindergarten, and I had my Daddy. Oh, how I loved him. We still had plenty of nothing, but Daddy was plenty for me. Daddy wanted to go out to meet people and have fun. Mama was truly into the taking care of her children, with no energy for what he wanted. She was not into wasting money partying.

There was one celebration at our apartment, and Daddy's friends and our relatives were over. Mama cooked and there were drinks. My brother was at the party, but I was in the bedroom and Daddy was doing his thing, too cozy with a woman from his job. Suddenly, a can of soda came flying toward Daddy and this woman. Mama's aim went astray, and the can hit the corner of a mirror we had. It. broke off a small piece of the frame. Daddy was upset and whenever they disagreed, he would leave, and he did. He met this woman at work, and they started going out together.

One day Mama and I came home, and he was packing his bags. She asked him, "Where are you going?" He told her, "I am leaving." Mama was shocked. "I thought you were going to help me take care of our kids." No response. "Why are you leaving? You promised if I took you back you would never leave me." He said nothing but pulled out a fist full of new $50 bills and asked Mama if she could give him this. She said, "No. I can't" "Well" he said, well, "I'm leaving." I was devastated. He walked out and never looked back.

A few months later Mama and I went to see Daddy's lawyer and as I stood next to her, she looked at the papers and you could see how sad she was; she signed the last page of the documents. I stood there and watched tears leak out of her eyes and mine. Soon Daddy married Sonora Wells, on 28th of January 1948. I was 8 years old. He was to give us $5 a week for child support. After prison, Mama, took a huge risk taking him back. He again failed to keep his promises. We had truly little financial support from him. He promised her while still in Mississippi that, if she took him back, he would never leave her. She took him back and he married the woman that gave him that money.

Before Daddy died, he told me, "I wish that I had stayed with your Mama!" I said nothing, I just looked at him to see if he was sincere. I did not tell him what my heart was saying: I am glad you left Daddy, you still would have been mean and unfaithful to Mama. She deserved better. There is a picture of Mama and Daddy at a night club. Sitting next to Daddy is Aunt Katie, and next to Katie is Uncle John, Aunt Thelma, Cousin Henry, and Aunt Estella. Henry was on leave from the Army. Mama and Daddy look so young in that photo.

I have always thought that this picture of them was taken after Daddy came to Chicago and our cousin Henry, who Mama and her sisters grew up with, was on leave. They always celebrated whenever Henry came to town. I had to take a note home from school asking Mama to come to school because I was so depressed that I was not doing the same quality of work. After Mama met with my teacher, she said, "Katie straighten out. I do not have time to take off work to come to school." After that meeting, she called Daddy and he started coming over on weekends to spend time with James and me. He also had his first car, a Plymouth. I do not remember the year of the car. I remember before he took us home, he would give the $5 to James which he had in one pocket, and he would show us a fist full of money he had in his other pocket. We were impressed then. As we got older, we realized we were bamboozled.

Family at Club

BUT HE'S MY BROTHER!

I was told as soon as I could understand was that my brother wanted a little sister, Mama said he just kept asking for a little sister. Six years after him I was born. Mama had a difficult time with my delivery she said how painful it was and I was turned the wrong way I came out feet first. The midwife was helping but nothing was working Mama asked the midwife for a knife so she could cut me out. She survived it and I am here. Hello World, my brother had a sister and I had a loving brother. I don't remember much of my childhood just the stories my family told me. We were born in Mississippi and Mama worked as a maid. We were poor during the Great Migration World War II had started money was scarce in Mississippi you could work all week for a quarter.

I was an infant and my cousin lived there with us she and Aunt Estella so they Ann and James was left alone in the apartment with me and they were playing and they sat me in the window as they were looking out, of course the window was open and I was sitting there and they ran away from me as I sat on the edge of the window, the bus passed and an acquaintance of Mama saw me sitting in the window all alone, he worked at the same place as Mama and he told her that he saw her baby sitting in an open window, and she ran home and it was a blessing that I did not move or I would have fell out of the window. Mama saved the day and James and Ann got whippings. All this was facing 61st street. This group of buildings formed a courtyard and there was plenty children around but we were not outside a lot.

Across the street on the corner was a Drug Store that had a Soda Fountain, when Mama would have money we would climb up on those stools and order a malt mine was vanilla and it included 2 small cookies, we would be so happy to have that big glass of ice cream and straws to slip it, slowly so it would last a long time. Oh, the memory of those moments are so precious. We also had the container where all of the malt did not fit in the glass, so we had a refill. James would order strawberry. Mama would hurry us up to finish, but I would take my time to really enjoy that ice cream. I learned that during Jim Crow in the south black people was never sold Vanilla ice cream because it was so good, and it was only allowed to be eaten by whites. There was a basketball hoop on the lawn of that drug store and the boys used to play there so it really did not have any grass anymore and the hoop was just an empty basket.

One day I was standing there watching my brother and his friends playing ball, getting excited when he made a basket and one of the boys must have said something about me, and my brother came over to me and threaten me, told me I had better leave there and go home and do it now! He went back to the game and I moved away a little from where I was standing until he hollered at me, "Go Home Katie" so I did. Angry that he would embarrassed me that way. Who did he think he is?

James was lucky with the girls they were always coming by the house he had one that was just beautiful she had long flowing hair and she was small in stature and she was so sweet. She would comb and braid my hair and wait for James to come home. Which ended up often that she was just visiting me. Nobody knew where James was or when he was coming home. Mama asked Uncle John to have a man to boy talk with him. Soon after the "talk" James started working with our Uncle after school. James and I never went to the same school, he had to take the bus to school. I had to wake up alone.

Jeffery James

OH NO

I attended Brown elementary school. where I performed in a play of" Hansel and Gretel." I was the witch. I thought I did an excellent job. After the performance Mama received a request for actors the agency sent a letter to come and bring me for an audition. The scout thought I had done an excellent job. Mama said," No, we do not have the money to get to California." They would pay our expenses after we got there. I was disappointed.

I was promoted to the fifth grade the teacher had a President and a Secretary in her class. the students nominated the officers and there was a vote to determine the winners. I was nominated for secretary and this cute boy was nominated for president. We won! I was so excited. Starting the next school day, we were to move to the seats assigned to the class officers. Those seats faced the class. We had special duties; not all of them had been discussed fully. But I could hardly contain my excitement. When I got home from school that day Mama was home. I was surprised to see her at home so early. I told her I had good news about school, but she said she wanted to talk to me first. So, I sat down on the bed and waited patiently for her to tell me her news. She said that Thelma and John bought an apartment building which had enough room for all of us to move into It was located on the west side. We were moving with them that weekend, no, I thought..

Mama, then asked me what my news from school was. I shared with her my good news about being elected as secretary of the class and about my moving to the desk in the front of the class where I sit facing the students. We would change our desks on Monday. Mama said, "Katie, you are not going back to that school. No, no, no, Mama I am not moving from here. You can move but I am staying here." That did not go over well with her. She explained again that we are moving with John and Thelma, and there was nothing I could do about it. "You cannot stay here alone. You are the child, and you do what I say."

I was going to miss Washington park; my brother would take me to the park, which was close to the school. there was a fountain called the Fountain of Time. The statues were eventually covered in mold and the water in the fountain was green with algae. the water was dark. This place had people who looked like they were in agony. As a youth I did not know the name of the fountain. it was not beautiful when I would visit it. There were so many people in the fountain that I never forgot it. Their faces were fascinating. I did not have any friends in the area, But I did not want to make this change since Mama said I would be going to a different school. This fountain was on the southeast portion of Washington Park. the sculpture was by Lorado Taft. this fountain was a historic place dedicated in 1922. A Chicago landmark that was to commemorate the hundredth anniversary of an 1814 Peace Treaty between America and Canada. There are a hundred human figures, babies, children, soldiers, and workers, and lovers, also the elderly. Father time stands alone facing them. It has been restored after Chicago weather affected it. No, no. I left with resentment. My favorite place was that park. They moved me to our new place. there were no parks nearby. I was stuck in the new apartment. The neighborhood was not welcoming. All the houses across the street were for sale (white flight) and Mama said to not go walking around, it might be dangerous.

Father Time

THE WEST SIDE OF CHICAGO

Moving day to the west side of Chicago, it was farther than I expected. The area was full of brick homes and Grenshaw was a residential street. The neighborhood was quiet. Where we were there was a bus route, and it was always busy. Where we moved to was just a block away from public transportation. The new place had a nice back yard,. But there was no fence. The alley was clean. Across the alley was a 6-story apartment building. All the way down Roosevelt Road were buildings. Some on Roosevelt Road were apartments with stores on the lower level. Thelma and John were happy now that they were owners and had renters moving in the same day.

Uncle Charlie and Aunt Estella and Ann moved into the first-floor apartment, and they had two bedrooms. The place had a nice sized back porch. John and Thelma settled on the second floor they had 3 bedrooms; that 3rd bedroom was extremely small. Each level had a bathroom with a bathtub but no plumbing for showers. There was a small linen closet in the bathroom on the second and third floor.

When I went into the lower level, the basement, there were two rooms with a bath and a long hallway that had a furnace, a big black furnace that used coal. During the winter that area was dark and scary. Whenever that furnace, started it made a horrible noise. Down the hall was a small kitchen with a stove and refrigerator. I thought the place was dark.

Mama and I had the same bed and James had a cot. We also had a chest to hold our clothes. We did not have that dresser with the mirror. Our living area had a small section of a couch and a couple of chairs. The kitchen had that small table from our first apartment. I thank God that we had a radio, to escape boredom. I was not allowed to go anywhere but the front porch. While I sat there on beautiful days, I noticed that the other side of the street were white owners, but we never saw any for sale signs, and we were experiencing white flight.

Soon I saw a different family in the houses across the street. It was like overnight. On the north side of Grenshaw and Homan was a tavern. White men would be standing outside drinking, and they did not want black people in that area. Sometimes you could see that they threw a can or bottle from where they were to the apartment building across from the tavern. So, I would not walk down to the corner without turning left to go down the alley and turn right to go up another alley and turn right and walk back to the basement grocery store. That grocery was on the corner across the street from that tavern. The elderly man in the grocery store was very friendly and nice. He was the only welcoming person I had met since moving in the area.

The school named A. O. Sexton, was located about 4 blocks from our house. I had to cross Roosevelt Road every day and the traffic was very heavy. Austin Oliver Sexton was a politician born and raised in Chicago and elected as a Democrat for the Illinois House of Representatives. The school closed due to having the lowest grades in the city in 2014. The area had a public pool. I never learned how to swim but my brother was a lifeguard there. He never had time to teach me how to swim. One time he showed me how to float. But we were interrupted because a girl called him. He let me sink.

After a while, my Uncle John built a tall fence in the back yard, because somebody stole his tools that were in his truck. After he built his fence, he bought a large red dog. They named him Red. The dog would spit every time he barked. There were times I had to feed him, and he would stay back until I put the food down. When I would step toward the gate, he would rush forward just as I closed the gate. He would stand up with his paws on the gate and he was taller than the gate, barking and spitting until I turned and left. I tried to never accept the job of feeding Red.

Uncle John put up a clothesline and that was wonderful because we washed our clothes in the tub. That line came from the second floor to the pole on that tall fence he built. My first day hanging the clothes I washed, my Mama got a complaint from a female neighbor because instead of hanging my panties straight down with one clothes pin, I hang them with two pins, one on each side of the panties. The woman said that we were trying to tempt her husband. I never heard such nonsense. Mama said she did not care if I had heard it or not, I was to use one clothespin on all panties. But Mama they dry faster, I said as she removed the two pins from the panties and just put a pin in the middle so they hung straight down, and you could not tell what they were.

Near to our house on Roosevelt Road was a movie theater On rare occasions we were given money to go to the movies,. James was in charge. We had popcorn and a drink that we shared. Whenever we went to the movies James would always go upstairs to the balcony. I said' James, why can't we stay downstairs.." The place was almost empty. I did not know at the time of the Jim Crow laws even if there were no signs. There are just too many stairs. James insists on going to the balcony. I enjoyed going to the movie with my big brother. He held and ate most all the popcorn. Now across Roosevelt Road on Homan Avenue was a hot dog stand the best hot dogs ever. A hot dog with relish, mustard and a dill pickle with French fries was so good. I remember the name of the stand was Dave's Hot dogs.

Behind the school was an activity center. You could play basketball, horseshoes baseball, and volleyball. They had a slide and swings. Across from the school there was a Boy's Club and they allowed girls to enter. I used to love to play pool there and when I was a winner, I held the table for a long while before I lost and had to give up the table. I only made friends with one family on my block. A daughter named Rose was my age. She did not attend A. O. Sexton. The playground put some of the girls together to play a game of baseball with some girls from an all-white team. We practiced one time before the game was scheduled. They had cute little uniforms. I was the pitcher, and we used a large baseball. I dropped a simple catch and my team groaned; their coach made it obvious to the next batter that I was the weak link. She told her to hit the ball straight at me. Oh, God, I thought. The score was tied, and I knew if I failed to catch the ball everybody was going to be upset with me. That batter hit that ball with accuracy, and it came right to me. If I didn't catch it, the ball would have hit me right in my stomach. I caught that ball and it hurt my hands, but I held on to it for dear life and I threw it to first base and then we were at bat. All of my team cheered for me because I was successful. Everybody there just knew I was going to drop that ball. We sent those white girls' home as losers! Of course, we lined up to shake hands with each other, but their hearts were not in it. Yeah, for Katie!

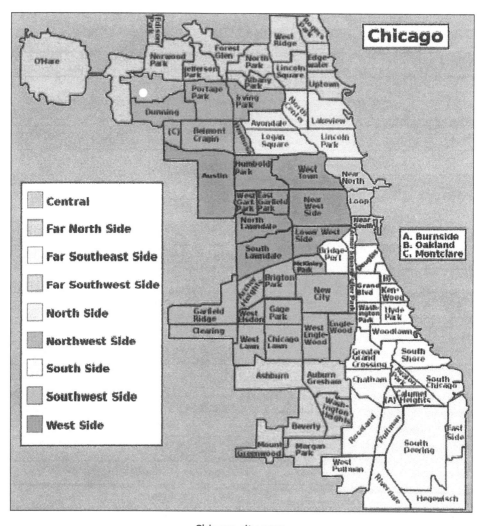

Chicago city map

Uncle John's Fence

TAKING YOUR CHILD
TO WORK DAY

This day there would be no one home to sit with me so Mama had to take me to work with her. No school. No sitter. I was excited because I had never ridden on public transportation. I had often seen the buses that ran down 61st Street full of passengers. We left early that morning. We rode the bus that stopped close to our apartment. then we transferred to another bus and then we transferred to a train. I was so happy. I had never ridden a bus nor a train. There was so much to see out of the windows.

Finally, we arrived in the north suburbs, where Mama worked. After walking a couple blocks, she said, "That is the house." I ran up the front stairs, but Mama said. "We are going in the back" We entered the back door. Their house was just beautiful. The lady there was friendly. She said, "Hello, Ida," and Mama said, "Hello Ms. Steinberg."

I saw more beautiful furnishings and glassware than the things my Aunt Thelma had. I met Ms. Steinberg's children, a boy, and a girl. They were very friendly, and they wanted me to see their rooms. Wow, I noted they had their own rooms. I played with them for a while; they seemed excited to have company, but they were too young for me to play with. Suddenly, their mother told them to get ready, for they were going out to lunch. They asked her if I could go with them, and she asked my Mama, who gave me permission to go. I said, "Come on, Mama." she said that she was not going. She had work to do and that she would bring me back

Another new thing for me was to ride in a car. I crawled in the back seat and the children rode in the front. We drove a short distance as I watched out the windows. There were no apartment buildings. there were all houses with beautiful lawns, and attractive houses in that area. Ms. Steinberg parked, and we all got out and entered the restaurant. It looked like a white wave. Everyone there wore white, and the only table left was right in front, just a few feet from the door. The girl sat next to her mother, and I sat next to the boy. The Server added the chair for me. I put one knee in it and my other foot was on the floor. The server gave us these giant menus that were laminated. I could not read yet, but I saw a picture of the hamburger, and the children ordered a hamburger, so I did too, but I did not use my in-house voice and suddenly you could have heard a gnat fart. I noticed it immediately, and I sat down correctly in my seat and was quiet after that.

The server came and asked each of us what we wanted, and I pointed to the picture of the hamburger and fries. She asked me what I wanted to drink, and I said a Coke. After all the ordering was done, we waited for the food. When it arrived, it was beautiful and hot, and the fries were consumed immediately, after we dumped ketchup on them. I do not remember if we said grace. I listened to their conversation, and, to myself, I wished my Mama were there. Of course, I was unable to eat all the food that I was served, so the server asked me if I wanted to take it home with me. I said yes, and she put it in a carryout for me. It was fun and so nice to be somewhere different, but I had never seen so many white people and they all had on white. Neither of the children wanted to take with them what they did not eat. We went back to the car, and I got back into the back seat with my treasure. Mama was almost finished when we got back to their house, so I did not have to wait long. The children asked their mother and asked my

Mama (I noticed that they called her Ida) if I could come back again. Our mothers said maybe. I said my goodbyes and we left, and I had a chance to ride public transportation again. All of that changing buses and train rides was exhausting. After my visit with them they started sending me treats, and silver dollars, candy, gum, little toys, and they sent me their pictures, which I still have. I also kept those silver dollars.

During my conversations with Mama, I would ask her about her day, and this is what happened with one of her weekly employers. Upon arriving to work, this lady asked Mama if she had taken her chicken that she had left on the counter when she was there last week. Mama said, "No, I did not take your chicken." Then she asked Mama if she was sure that she did not take her chicken. Mama again said that she did not take her chicken. She said she did not know where it could be, because she left the chicken on the counter to defrost, and she could not find it.

Mama started doing her weekly chores that the lady asked her to do when she was there. Mama got out the vacuum cleaner and started to vacuum the living room area, and when she went into the den to vacuum, hidden behind a chair were the bones of a chicken. Mama called the lady into the den and showed her the evidence of where her chicken was. The dog had taken the chicken off the counter and enjoyed their dinner. Mama and I laughed and laughed, and Mama said That lady needs to feed her dog better. She was so sure that Mama stole her defrosting chicken. I thought sure that since Mama did not steal her defrosting chicken she owed Mama an apology. Of course, she did not get one.

This is a different employer.: Mama was told to clean the blinds, so she had to get on a ladder. The woman's husband brought in the ladder and Mama started wiping down the blinds. Of course, she had to reach out to cover the large area, and the man was sitting in the room, so she cleaned the blinds and he watched her instead of reading the paper he had in his hands. When she stepped down, he got up to hold the ladder, and he lowered his voice and asked Mama if she would have sex with him. Mama thought for a moment and told him in a lowered voice, "If you get a letter from your wife that it is o.k. with her, I will have sex with you." The man scoffed and went back to his reading.

Mama stayed later than usual, and his wife usually took Mama to the bus stop so she would not miss her connection for the EL ride home. Since her husband had retired, she decided to ask him to take Mama to the bus stop. He pulled the car out, and Mama got in the front seat like she always did when his wife took her to the bus stop. He pulled off and after a block away from his house, he told Mama that he did not want to drive her to the bus stop. Mama said, "I did not ask you to take me to the bus stop; pull over and I will get out." He did and she did.

Chicago is cold in the winter. One of her employers asked her if she wanted this fur coat. It was a heavy brown beaver, with no collar and large lined sleeves. Mama said yes, she would like to have it, so she brought it home with her. When she got home, she showed the coat to me and told me that her employer was going to take money out of her pay for the coat, which would not give her enough money for the week, only just enough for transportation there and back. "Mama, you said she was giving you the coat. She is selling you this coat. Do you really need this coat? If I were you, I would take the coat back to her and tell her you could not afford this coat." Mama agreed and returned the coat to her, and she was angry, but she took it back. Mama did not work for her anymore after that. She should have given her that coat. It was beyond in style. She did not want it. I wonder what happened to the coat. She was bartering for services. She did not have a bartering agreement with Mama. She also never said how much she wanted for the coat.

Mama was serving at a luncheon, and she had just come from the kitchen to the dining room, which was full of ladies enjoying themselves, As she passed the front door, another guest arrived. The guest asked Mama to take her coat. Mama told her that she could not take her coat right then, because she had both of her hands full. The new guest was immediately upset and said loudly to the hostess, "You should fire your maid because she has refused to take my coat." The hostess said, "Just put it over there. Can't you see both of her hands are occupied with our meal?" The women threw her coat on the chair and sat down in an empty seat and continued to complain, "Your maid did not take my coat, and she should be fired." After the gathering was over, Mama said to the hostess that she was sorry that she could not take her guest's coat. The hostess said, "Oh, don't worry about that, Ida." She was just showing off. She wanted everyone to notice that she has a new fur coat.

Mama was interviewed over the phone by a potential employer, a couple who were referred to her by a previous employer. The couple agreed to meet her at the end of the bus line. She knew their names and the color of the car that was to pick her up. They lived too far for her to walk to their house; it also was an unfamiliar area. When she got in the car, their young girl was sitting in the front, and she seemed happy to see Mama. She was just chatting away. What surprised Mama was that the little girl asked Mama if she ever saw a penis. Mama said no, and the girl told Mama that she had seen her daddy's penis. Then she asked Mama if she wanted to see her daddy's penis, and that if she wanted to see it, her daddy would show it to her. Mama said, "No, Thank you." Mama tried to refrain from showing any emotions because the driver was watching her in the rear-view mirror. The woman said nothing, nor did the man. That ended just a one-day job. She told them it was too far from the bus stop for her to walk weekly, twice a day

She was working with another family the woman of the house had her mother living with them. The husband was upset because his mother-in-law was dropping food on the table and on the floor. So, the wife moved her mother from the dining room table and served her dinner in the den so that her husband would not have to watch her mother eat and thus would stop his complaining about her. The elder woman expressed her concern to Mama that she feared her daughter was going to send her to a nursing home. She did not want to be in a nursing home. she wanted to stay there with her daughter and to interact with her grandchildren. Mama expressed concern for her and told her that she would still be there when Mama returned. But the next week Mama went to their house and found that the lady's mother was not there. Mama asked, "Ms. B, where is your mother?" She said that her mother was now staying in a nursing home.

My Mama felt such sorrow for this woman, and she asked me to never put her in a nursing home. I told her, "Mama, you need money to go to a nursing home. Do not worry about it. We have no money. You will never go into a nursing home." I had to reassure her several times that I would not put her into a nursing home. She also told me that I should not take Daddy into my house while she lived with me. "O.K, Mama."

There was a young Jewish boy who insisted that his family invite Mama to his Bar mitzvah. Mama was excited. She got all dolled up and met them at their house. They planned for her to ride in the limousine to the banquet with them. She really enjoyed herself as she watched the young boy accept his religious responsibility at 13 years of age. Of course, she was the only one there of color. What an honor! She was invited to sit at the head table. The banquet was held at a beautiful hotel. She said that the food served was delicious. Some mornings when she came to work with his family, she found that she had to calm things down. This morning, he had kicked a hole in the bathroom door. She could talk with him, and he would become calm But, as some families experience, their father wanted his freedom from the marriage. He was an eye doctor, having an affair with the nurse in his office.

The family appreciated her. the Parents divorced; the boy's mother could not afford to keep Mama on full time. Since he was an eye doctor near my residence, I went to him for an eye exam. Mama insisted that I see him for my exam and glasses. While he was examining my eyes, he put his hand on my knee, asking me as he changed the lens, "Is it better now?" I tried to shake his hand off my knee, and he just let it stay there. I was prepared to hurt him if he had moved his hand any further. I knew he was unprofessional and had a roaming eye. He finally moved his hand from my knee. I paid him with a personal check since I had been working and had funds of my own. He took my check and showed it to the two white women who worked with him. He had seen my Mama's handwriting and had a negative expectation. I was embarrassed. After I picked up my glasses, I never used his services again. The last day she worked for them the boy drove her home. He also wanted to meet me. I was not home at the time, so he looked at all the pictures on the walls. He told Mama that he wished that I would come home while he was there, because he wanted to date me. They said their good-byes.

While I worked for I.R.S. I found out that Mama's employer was supposed to take withholding tax out of her pay, and she was to pay into the Social Security tax. I advised her of this and gave her pamphlets to show to her employers so she could acquire some quarters to collect Social Security when she was eligible. That was unacceptable. They did not want to do it. They were only willing to pay her, as said often, "under the table." After a checkup with our doctor, we found that Mama needed a pacemaker to help her heart. We had trouble getting her to agree to have the surgery, but she went ahead and had the surgery. Then we had to convince her to retire, because of all the traveling and walking, not even considering the work she did during the hours she was at a client's house. The doctor and I were successful. Mama finally retired. Mama endured racism, prejudice, sexual pressure, stereotyping, and micro aggressiveness. She kept our house clean, took care of our child, washed clothes, prepared meals, and kept the house orderly.

THE DINNER

Mama said we were invited to Aunt Thelma's for dinner today. Their Dad was coming to visit his daughters. Aunt Thelma was preparing a feast. Mama and I got ready to go to Aunt Thelma's. We walked together, not really talking to each other. I was very careful not, to step, on a crack so I would not break my mother's back. She seemed like she did not appreciate my thoughtfulness. she said, "Katie, stop hopping around." Aunt Thelma only lived a few blocks away. I was able to save her back because the sidewalk was not as cracked after we turned the corner toward Roosevelt road. So my hopping around was not as obvious.

We lived on Grenshaw with Aunt Estella in a house that Aunt Thelma owned. She moved out of the house we lived in and rented a store, on Roosevelt road near Kedzie avenue. Above the store was an apartment where they now lived. At the house we lived in, Aunt Estella lived on the first floor. We were able to move from the basement to the second floor after Aunt Thelma moved.` I remember living in the basement of 3331 west Grenshaw Chicago, Il. Mama, James, and I lived in 2 rooms with a bath and a long hallway where the furnace was. It was huge, black, coal burning thing that made a loud noise when it came on and went off. In the very back of the basement was an extremely small kitchen with a small stove, refrigerator, and a little table with just enough room for two. I hated walking from the front room to that kitchen because the furnace was really scary in the winter it would flare up and i would jump every time. There was a small mirror in the bathroom hooked onto a very small medicine cabinet. Pipes were exposed and painted black. The tub was deep and had cute little feet. It was dark and dreary in that basement. We slept in the same room. James slept on his cot, Mama, and I in a full-size bed. When the lights were turned off, it was graveyard dark. I hated it! I always bumped into James' bed on my way to the bathroom for late night relief. I finally convinced Mama to leave a small watt light on in the bathroom so I could find my way. Oh! What a relief that was. One night on my way to the bathroom I looked at my brother and his eyes were wide open, I ran and shook Mama saying Mama, Mama James is dead, she saw what I saw she placed her hands across his eyes and he closed his eyes. I was so happy that my brother was not dead. I never thought that people could see with their eyes open.

Kedzie Avenue was the best of all the streets. The street cars were on Roosevelt Road and was attached to the wires with long large poles. Buses ran along Kedzie Avenue. They carried a lot of people to this business district or they could transfer to continue their travels. All kinds of merchandise was sold on that street. You could rent furniture, buy stuff on lay-away. Beautiful jewelry was displayed in the windows of a jewelry store. Across the street was a retail store called the "Three Sisters." They had such beautifully dressed mannequins who were white with blonde hair and blue eyes, wearing clothes we could not afford.

I loved going to Aunt Thelma's store and looking at all the things she had for sale. She had such beautiful lingerie, both full an half-slip that had real nice lace hems. Leather handbags, scarfs, long and short gloves, delicately embroidered handkerchiefs, and silk stockings were displayed in the glass showcase. The stockings were my favorites. They were really silky and I loved running my hand through them, especially, the naughty black ones with the seams. She also sold tan, coffee, and nude. I loved the seams. When you wore them, the seams had to be straight up the back of your legs. I would quickly run my hand in each color very quickly because I was not allowed to for fear I would put a run in them. I was very careful because they were special and expensive.

One day I'm going to get me some of those silk stockings, especially the black ones. They would make me feel so grown up if I only had a pair. In the back of the shop, Aunt Thelma had a sewing area. It had 2 sewing machines, a singer model and the other was an industrial sewing machine. She was a seamstress, trained in Mississippi at the Utica Institute. She was the only child of 10 siblings who finished school and completed vocational training. She became good at her trade. Uncle John, her husband, made her a cutting table perfect for her height. She did not have to bend over when laying out and cutting patterns. I wanted so desperately to be like her, creating beautiful clothes. I wanted to look fine all the time. I never really liked my Aunt Thelma. She was so bossy but she was generous. I cut a picture of a dress out of "W," a designer newspaper. She designed the pattern and made the dress out of a beautiful yellow fabric. This dress was for me to wear to the prom. The dinner was a very special event. Aunt Thelma and her sisters, Mama, and Aunt Estella, were all in the kitchen, helping prepare the meal.

The table was beautifully set. A tablecloth matching China beautiful glasses napkins, and matching silverware, were all exquisitely laid out with a center piece. We had nothing like that at our house. Uncle John and Aunt Thelma had quite a few black and white pictures on their walls of ariel views of Chicago buildings. Uncle John must have gotten them from folks that did not want them anymore. He had given me a stack of post cards of all of the Chicago skyscrapers and sights, especially, the loop. I later used these post cards for a school project about Chicago and I got an A. I was so proud of that grade. I also wrote a slogan for a cleanup campaign and won 2nd place with my slogan "It

Is The I Will of Chicago Which Keeps Our City Clean." As an adult, I finally saw it on a billboard. Boy! My chest was puffed out that day.

The pictures in their apartment were in huge frames and they looked very impressive on the large walls of their apartment. They had a lot of windows. I found them fascinating. I carefully studied each picture and also gazed at each nick knack in the apartment. Where did she find all this beautiful stuff? I loved my Uncle John. He worked for a furniture company and he was a diligent worker. A small man in stature but he was so strong. I once saw him carry a refrigerator on his back by himself up to the second floor. He did not talk much. He was a father figure for me. I would sit in his lap every chance I got because he would give me a sip of his drink of alcohol until I went to sleep in his lap and then he would put me to bed. Mama was always working so I spent a lot of time with Thelma and John. James, my brother, was always gone too. John bought his own moving truck, going in business for himself like Aunt Thelma. I learned that a lot of the stuff in Aunt Thelma's house was what Uncle John brought home from businesses that disposed of their old furniture. The pictures were from a construction company that built some of those tall skyscrapers. Of course, they had also thrown away those post cards that I treasured. Their dishes, silver ware and tablecloths were given to John by some white folks who didn't want them anymore. While I was daydreaming and wandering around the apartment, Aunt Thelma called out to me, to tell Grandpa that dinner is ready and to come to the table. He was in the bedroom farthest from the kitchen. So I slowly made my way to the room. The door was open, so I stepped in. Grandpa was sitting in a chair with his head bent down. I did what I was told to do. I called out, "Grandpa, dinner is ready." I went back to my adventure of looking at all the things Uncle John and Aunt Thelma had on their tables and in their glass cabinets. Aunt Thelma screamed, "Didn't I tell you to tell your Grandpa that dinner was ready?" I meekly responded, "I did. I told him and he did not say a word." She then screamed, "Tell him again!" This time I skipped to his room, called his name, "Grandpa." I walked up to him, looked into his face. This was my first time ever seeing him.

Then I noticed he had his penis in his hands, playing with himself. It was scary. He seemed to be in a trance and not notice I was there because he still did not respond. I ran out of there to the kitchen. I simply told Aunt Thelma that he ignored me. This did not please my Mama and certainly not Aunt Thelma. She declared, "If you want something done, you have to do it yourself!" Aunt Thelma and Mama ganged up against me, scolding me for not doing as I was told. "but I did" I protested. Aunt Thelma went into the bedroom, when she saw what I saw, she just bent over him and put his penis back in his pants without saying a word. I saw her zip up his pants and she led him to the table. We all sat down to dinner. The sisters had made a delicious meal. My Grandfather never said a word, just gummed his food quietly. We didn't talk about what Grandpa was doing in the bedroom either. After dinner, while they were washing the dishes and cleaning up, I thought of what I saw. Grandpa's penis looked like a long stick. It was awful. It was really rigid and I thought to myself that Aunt Thelma must have touched it. She sure is bold, I concluded. I would have never put my hands on that thing. Later, they called out for me to bring them a couple of towels to them. Mama and Aunt Thelma was giving Grandpa a bath. Wow! Was he skinny. Luckily, his back was toward me. It was not long after that special dinner that my Grandpa died. My Mama was not sad about it. I told her I did not want to go to the funeral because I had a test that day and I wanted to go to school. She said I was not going to school. I was going to my Grandpa's funeral. She made me miss that test and I was one unhappy girl.

Many years later, as an adult, I learned how cruel my Grandpa had been to my Mama and her sisters. He touched them inappropriately. All the girls slept in the same bed. Thinking they were asleep, he'd fondle them.

They said they'd pretend to be asleep and would kick at him and turn over, hoping he would walk away. My Aunts, each one told how they had to run away from home to escape from being molested by him. Little wonder there wasn't any sadness at his funeral. Well, except for Uncle Lymon, who cried enough for everyone. He was inconsolable.

ALL I COULD DO WAS CRY

I had a two-wheel bike, and I was really having fun with my bike, but after learning how to ride, I was unhappy about the bumpy, uneven sidewalk that I had to ride on. I was a student in grammar school the bike was my birthday. present I left Grenshaw the street I lived on and went north past an apartment building I found a vacant parking lot that was recently black tarred. I was very happy, I rode and turned and went up and down the lot, it was smooth sailing. then I stopped to take a break, from riding as I stood there a car came up to me and told me to go back from, where I came, I think they must have thought I was a boy. I Image they saw me from behind. the car was full of white boys, and I was instantly afraid. I did not say anything, the white boy in the back of the car on the passenger's side told me to never come over there again, he then did something to me that I have never forgotten, "He spit on me." Tears formed in my eyes as I reached to wipe his filth off my face. the driver then stepped on the gas and sped off. I turned my bike around and raced home and went in the house and felt so bad, I wanted that boy to die, for what he did to me.

I grew up to learn, that sort of thing happens to black people all the time, I begin to not trust people who called themselves white. Why spit on me? They did not own that lot. When we moved to 3331 W Grenshaw the white people lived on the north side of the street, this area was close to Sears Roebuck and Company and many of the families worked at Sears, that store included the main office for Sears at that time, they had more than a retail store there. their administration office was there. I had a chance to watch white flight personally. You did not go across the street. Or on the north corner of Grenshaw and Homan Avenue there was a tall 5 story building white people was still living. Right there in that building on the west end side was a tavern, where the white men hung out, you stayed away from there, or took the long way and not go by that street corner, go one block down and go thru the alley and past that building then walk a block back to Grenshaw a L-shape walk we did this because we did not want to be yelled at by drunk young white men. Sometimes they threw bottles at people. The two-story building across from that tavern had a bullet hole in their glass front door.

One day my Mama came home and asked me to go into that building and do some housework for an elderly woman. I told her I did not want to, but she insisted that I do it, she said she did not have time, so she wanted me to do it, she said that I will be paid, and I will be able to keep the money for myself. So, I went, and I was afraid, when I reached the apartment, the woman open the door, she told me she was expecting my mother. I told her Mama said she did not have the time, so she sent me. O.K. the first thing she asked me to do was to wash the bathtub out. she gave me some kitchen cleaner and a rag, and we went into the bathroom and there was a lot of black rings around that tub, and I have never seen a tub that filthy. I sprinkled the kitchen cleaner on and around the tub and begin to scrub, you know those rings resisted ever effort I made to get rid of them, they were there to stay, I was able to make the real dark ones and little lighter, but they appeared to be a part of the tub. The cleaner was not doing the job and the woman of the house was furious with me and told me I was useless. I did not respond my Mama had told me to just do the job requested of me, she gave me the money and I left, the tub did look a little better, but she needed to clean the tub every time they got out of it. I profiled them that day I said no wonder they need a maid, they were lazy and nasty, and mean.

My Mama would be very angry if I left our bathroom in that condition. when I grow up, I will never ever be a maid. I do not know how Mama does that type of work. While in high school I talked with a counselor about my career goals I told her I wanted to be an accountant, she just laughed in my face and said all I could ever be was a waitress in a restaurant. That hurt! As I sat at her desk seeping with rage. I made a promise to myself that I would never ever work in a restaurant. I never have, I never had any problems with people who work in restaurants it's just that I did not want to do it. It is an art to serve people. that is not where I thought my creative talents lay.

AUNT MARY STAMPS BARTWELL AND UNCLE WALTER BARTWELL

A unt Mary was the oldest of Mama's sisters. She was born October 9th, 1900. She was the first child of Edna and Eugene Stamps. Her husband was Walter Bartwell; They married in 1944. Mama and I heard that Aunt Mary was extremely ill. Mama asked me if we could go south so she could see her sister Mary, so I told her we could go over a weekend. She fried chicken so we did not have to stop to eat, and we had fruit to eat and drinks. We had to stop only for gas and bathroom breaks. When we arrived at their house, there was a lot of tall grass. I am concerned about tall grass because of what could be hidden in it. They had a screened-in porch, so we ran into the house Uncle Walter saw us drive up, so we did not have to stand at the screen door.

I met my Aunt Mary. She resembled her sister Thelma. At the time she was confined to the bed. I kissed her on her cheek. She was very fragile. But she was so interesting. I asked her who was the woman in the picture on the wall, and she told me that was my Grandma Edna. None of the other sisters had a picture of Grandma Edna. It was attached to a round tin. I asked her if I could borrow it, and she said I could have it. I thought Uncle Walter was quite a handsome man. After being there for a few minutes I found out that they had an out-house. I was disappointed Oh, God, do I have to go out there! It did

75

not smell like the other one I have used. But they had corn cobs and Sears catalogs to use. Gross. There were lizards all over the screened porch. Mama was unhappy about them.

We spent the night sleeping together in a twin bed. I was exhausted. The house was small and clean. We ate the breakfast Mama prepared, and kissed and hugged Mary and Walter, and said our goodbyes after Uncle Walter gave me directions to get back on the highway. We left that afternoon. Mama was quiet on the way back; she was alert to make sure I did not fall asleep. After returning home Uncle Walter called a few days later. Again, the sisters decided that Mama should be the one to go and take care of her sister. So, they bought her a bus ticket to Mississippi she got off, at the wrong stop. Mama called me and I told her to call Uncle Walter, he asked his niece to go pick Mama up after determining where she was, I was so relieved, I felt so help-less to do anything about her situation.

Aunt Mary was quite a character, she told Mama and Uncle Walter to just throw her in the garbage. She was unhappy about her illness and Walter and Ida getting along too well. Aunt Mary died November 3rd, 1990, Mama was still visiting and helping Walter take care of Mary. After the funeral when it was time for Mama to come home. Uncle Walter tried to convince Mama to stay there with him, he gave her a fist full of money and when she returned, she gave most of it to me it smelled moldy. She wanted to send it back, but I wanted to keep the money. So, she did. I was annoyed that Uncle Walter wanted to marry Mama if she would come back and live with him. She gave it serious thought, but I was adamant that she needed to be here in Chicago with me. I told her he just wanted a nurse, Mama. So, she finally turned him down. His niece felt that he should not live alone, and we got a call advising us that Walter had moved to a nursing home. I had a chance to talk with him while he was there and when he came to the phone, he was praising God for feeling so much better, to be exact he had been extremely constipated. A few weeks later we received a call from his niece who told us Uncle Walter had died and was buried.

Aunt Mary

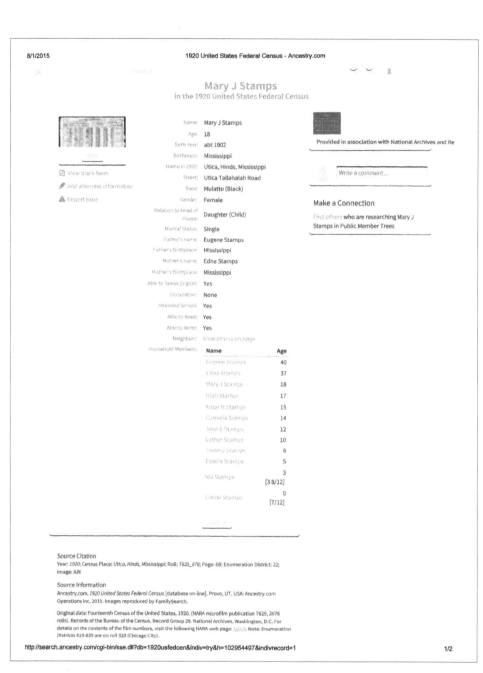

Mary J Stamps
in the 1920 United States Federal Census

Name:	Mary J Stamps
Age:	18
Birth Year:	abt 1902
Birthplace:	Mississippi
Home in 1920:	Utica, Hinds, Mississippi
Street:	Utica Tailahalah Road
Race:	Mulatto (Black)
Gender:	Female
Relation to Head of House:	Daughter (Child)
Marital Status:	Single
Father's name:	Eugene Stamps
Father's Birthplace:	Mississippi
Mother's name:	Edna Stamps
Mother's Birthplace:	Mississippi
Able to Speak English:	Yes
Occupation:	None
Attended School:	Yes
Able to Read:	Yes
Able to Write:	Yes
Neighbors:	View others on page

View blank form

Add alternate information

Report issue

Provided in association with National Archives and Re

Write a comment...

Make a Connection

Find others who are researching Mary J Stamps in Public Member Trees

Household Members:

Name	Age
Eugene Stamps	40
Edna Stamps	37
Mary J Stamps	18
Isiah Stamps	17
Katie M Stamps	15
Cunsella Stamps	14
John E Stamps	12
Luther Stamps	10
Thelma Stamps	8
Estella Stamps	5
Ida Stamps	3 [3 8/12]
Limon Stamps	0 [7/12]

Mary J Stamps in the 1920 U.S. Federal Census

Walter Bartwell

UNCLE HILLMAN

I have heard many stories about Uncle Hillman. He was the first son born to the family. Their second child, his nick name was Hillman; his legal name was Isiah Stamps. He was born in 1903. The census stated that he attended school and knew how to read and write. I heard of the argument that Hillman had with his father. They disagreed about money. Isiah worked and picked cotton with the others in his father's fields. He complained that he received nothing for his labors, except room and board. Isiah and Eugene's argument accelerated, and Isiah packed up his things and left his parents' house.

I wonder if Hillman was aware his daddy molested his sisters. Thelma was 9 years younger than Isiah she waited until she was about 90, while my Mama Ida was visiting, to share with Mama that Isiah their brother had raped her. Thelma was responsible for bringing water to the family that were working in the fields. She said that it happened on her way from delivering water to those in the fields He grabbed Thelma, pulled her into the bushes, and raped her. She said he also raped her another time.. I was not made aware of what age Thelma was when this happened. I am sure that Hillman was responsible for taking Thelma's innocence away. I also remember when I was younger, my brother and I were playing. He was tickling me. I was laughing, and he was playful and laughing too. Aunt Thelma saw us, and you would think that he was doing something awful to me. She scolded him for it and told him he should not play with me that way. He and I were puzzled about what she was saying. After that, my brother stopped playing with me. Neither one of us knew what she was implying.

I remember seeing Uncle Hillman's picture when I was visiting Aunt Thelma at the special dinner that she made to share with her sisters and their daddy, whom they had not seen in ages. Also, they knew that he was very ill. I asked my Aunt who was the man in the picture, and she said it was their brother Hillman.

Now that they both have made the transfer to another life, I wonder why she had his picture. He was well dressed in the picture, and he had almond -shaped brown eyes and full lips, the bottom lip pro-truding. His skin appeared to be dark. He had a pleasant face, but he did not smile in his picture. He had on a vest and tie. The suit was a light color. He had a flower in his lapel. He's wearing a hat. The 1920 census says he attended school and could read and write. After the agree-to-disagree departure, they did not hear or see their brother again until they heard that he died in a fight. He lost his life over a gambling debt that amounted to be 25 cents.

Isiah Stamps {Hillman}

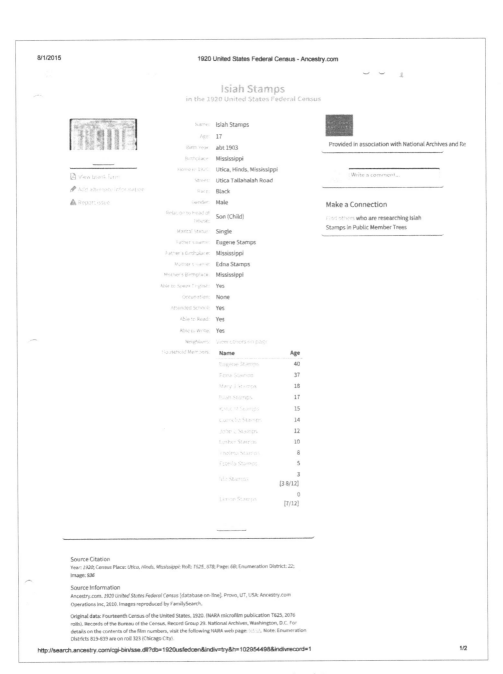

Isiah Stamps
in the 1920 United States Federal Census

Name:	Isiah Stamps
Age:	17
Birth Year:	abt 1903
Birthplace:	Mississippi
Home in 1920:	Utica, Hinds, Mississippi
Street:	Utica Tallahalah Road
Race:	Black
Gender:	Male
Relation to Head of House:	Son (Child)
Marital Status:	Single
Father's name:	Eugene Stamps
Father's Birthplace:	Mississippi
Mother's name:	Edna Stamps
Mother's Birthplace:	Mississippi
Able to Speak English:	Yes
Occupation:	None
Attended School:	Yes
Able to Read:	Yes
Able to Write:	Yes
Neighbors:	View others on page

Provided in association with National Archives and Re

Write a comment...

Make a Connection

Find others who are researching Isiah Stamps in Public Member Trees

Household Members:

Name	Age
Eugene Stamps	40
Edna Stamps	37
Mary J Stamps	18
Isiah Stamps	17
Kate M Stamps	15
Cornelia Stamps	14
John L Stamps	12
Luther Stamps	10
Thelma Stamps	8
Estella Stamps	5
Ide Stamps	3 [3 8/12]
Lenon Stamps	0 [7/12]

Source Citation
Year: 1920; Census Place: Utica, Hinds, Mississippi; Roll: T625_878; Page: 6B; Enumeration District: 22; Image: 936

Source Information
Ancestry.com. 1920 United States Federal Census [database on-line]. Provo, UT, USA: Ancestry.com Operations Inc, 2010. Images reproduced by FamilySearch.

Original data: Fourteenth Census of the United States, 1920. (NARA microfilm publication T625, 2076 rolls). Records of the Bureau of the Census, Record Group 29. National Archives, Washington, D.C. For details on the contents of the film numbers, visit the following NARA web page: NARA. Note: Enumeration Districts 819-839 are on roll 323 (Chicago City).

Isiah Stamps 1920 U. S. Federal Census

AUNT KATIE MAY
STAMPS BUSH

My dear Aunt Katie, she was a mystery to me. I asked Mama why she named me Katie, and she told me that her sister Katie was the first person to send me baby clothes when I was born. My Aunt Katie lived in Philadelphia. I asked Mama why she live so far away from everybody. Mama said that Katie was sent to Philadelphia after the family found out that she was pregnant. She was just a teenager who told her parents after they noted that she was pregnant, that she had been raped. In older days, it was not acceptable for a girl to be pregnant and not married. Usually, the families sent their pregnant teenagers away. So, the family found an employer in Philadelphia, Pennsylvania from information taken from an ad. A family was looking for a domestic. Katie applied and was hired. Katie left home at the age of 18 years old and boldly took a step with confidence to a place where she was a stranger. Her employers loved her, and she made friends outside of her workplace. She delivered a healthy boy on Thursday, February 22nd, 1923. She named him Henry Abron.

She returned to Mississippi to be able to work without having babysitters for Henry. She took Henry to stay with his grandfather and young aunts. She returned to Philadelphia and made Pennsylvania her home during the time of the Black Migration. Katie was able to send money home to her father to pay some of the family's expenses and to pay for Henry's care. So, Henry was raised with Mama and all the family that was still at home. Mama said that all the children slept in the same bed, and all in that bed tried their best not to sleep next to their nephew Henry because he always peed in the bed. Henry's skin color was lighter than the rest of them, He also said that his daddy was white. He also thought he knew who his daddy was, but I was unable to verify that information. While Henry was a teenager, he looked older than his actual age. He wanted to leave the Jim Crow South, so he lied about his age and joined the United States Army. He served as a cook in Germany.

When on leave, he would come to Chicago to see us. He looked dashing in his uniform and told us exciting stories. We would all sit at the kitchen table, and he would stand up. All eyes were on him, and he amazed us with German language expressions, including his escapades. He told us about his time in the service and the people in Germany throwing in some German language with the accent. It was exciting. The adults were drinking beer and smoking cigarettes. Laughing at Henry's adventures, when he started talking about his romantic adventures, which was when Mama made me, go to my bedroom and close the door." Aww, Mama I just want to be here with Henry." My bedroom was right next to the kitchen, and I did not close the door tightly, I left a crack in the door so I could still hear him, until I was reminded that I was to shut the door. I really was enjoying him. Before he left the house, Henry gave me his instruction book on how to speak German. I treasured that book for a long time. It had been Army issued.

Henry and his wife Jean had twins, David, and Johnnie Rose. Boy and girl. They looked like Henry with the same skin color and thick curly hair. I only met them when we all were adults. There was another son, Gus Abron. Henry spent his entire career in the army. He was a WWII veteran. Well, I told my brother that I wanted to go into the Army, he avoided being drafted since he was married and had a child when it came time for him to register for service to his country. My brother shut me down on that idea, he told me that only Lesbians were in the Army. I wanted to see the world like Henry, learn a trade, without paying for a college education. The idea of twins fascinated me also, since after me Mama lost a set of girl twins. I wanted a sister bad. But that wish was never fulfilled, When I planned my wedding and sent out invitations to my Aunt Katie, she came to our wedding, which caused friction in the family. Other nieces complained about why she came to my wedding and did not come to theirs. She told them that I was the only one who sent her an invitation. So, the other relatives upset over this did not come to my wedding. These were my Uncle Lyman's children. Well, my Mama was babysitting my son; she gave up her domestic jobs and came to our apartment every weekday babysitting our son while my husband and I worked. Not only did she watch Erik, but she also cooked and kept my house clean. Lamont wanted to be the one that paid her. Aunt Katie called Aunt Thelma and told her that she had to have major surgery. She wanted help. The three sisters got together and decided since they were married, and Mama was not married, she should go to Philadelphia to help her sister Katie before, during, and after her surgery. I was devastated, but how could I just tell my Mama, not to help her older sister? I needed her to keep Erik.

Well, she got on an airplane, which was her first time to fly. It was my first time ever being without her and not knowing when she would be back. When Thelma and Estella got together, Mama was always the one that had to go to the rescue. Well, my brother did not manage it well either. We put Mama on the plane and bought an insurance policy at the airport and we made jokes. She left, James went home, and the next thing I found out was he took his wife and kid to Philadelphia to see for himself that Mama got there safely. He could have driven her there. They only stayed overnight; then he drove back home to Chicago.

Aunt Katie had her own home and she also ended up owning the house next door to her. A friend left it to her in her will. I ran up our telephone bill by calling Philadelphia every day. Mama was doing fine. She met all her sister's friends and she cooked and helped her sister, who had a boyfriend. Then trouble started. After Katie's surgery she became upset over the laughter and kidding and attention Mama was getting from him. Katie and Ida really looked a lot alike. Of course, Mama was shapelier and younger. Mama was cooking for Katie and her boyfriend, and she knew how to present the food in an attractive way. Mama and Katie had words over an innocent incident. Mama had to reassure her that she had no interest in her boyfriend. I am not sure her boyfriend felt the same.

I have a picture of my Aunt Katie in her wedding dress. Her married name was Katie Bush. I also have a picture of Aunt Katie in Sunday attire with a man that was just as tall as her and they appeared to be in front of a church. I was made aware that he was her husband. We never met him. I found out on their marriage license that his name was Edward Bush and they were living in Syracuse, New York. When they married, he was thirty-two and he worked as a Porter. He was born in Newport News, VA. On her application they put her name as Katherine Stamps who was twenty-three at the time, her occupation was a maid, this was their first marriage. During this time, her residence was in New York where they applied for a marriage license. I have no idea what happened to the relationship between Katie and Edward. She never spoke of him to me or around me. The records say that he died February 22nd,1954. In Philadelphia Pennsylvania.

I was so happy to pick up my Mama from the airport. She was finally home. The babysitters I hired; kept my toddler in his play pen all day. After a few more birthdays Aunt Katie's health was at a place where she decided that she no longer wanted to live alone so she talked with her son. After his 25 years in the Army, he retired and was younger because of his age lie. He welcomed her and had a bedroom with a half bath for her to stay with him. She took the train back to Jackson, Mississippi to stay with her son, Henry. She sold her homes and brought cash on her person to Mississippi. I understand that Henry, had a substance abuse disorder and was mean to his mother. Once I visited them and he took me in his car and there was a crack in his front car windshield. I asked him about it, and he said that was your Aunt Katie's imprint. He laughed, I did not. I never saw him take a drink of alcohol. I thought he just drunk a lot of coffee. Well, he did not see me watch him pour whiskey into his coffee cup. A light bulb moment for me. When I got a chance, I sneaked into that cabinet and found his bottles. One thing I can say about Henry, while we were there, he fed us grandly, but I never saw him eat a thing. He always said he ate earlier, or he would say he was going to eat later. I could not get him and Aunt Katie, who was up in years now, to go to a restaurant and let me treat them to dinner. They stayed home or went to church. while I was in Mississippi, I saw the same restaurant franchises there. But I felt their fear. Being from the north I did not have that fear, never tasted it. At that time in my life. But I understood. While I was packing to leave, my Aunt knocked on the door and entered the room I was using, Henry's bedroom she said Henry sent her in to watch me pack to check to see if I was stealing something. I was very insulted; I do not steal I protested, but I did have a chance to just talk to my Aunt without Henry's comments. She never complained about him, but I heard stories that he was capable of elder abuse. Henry had issues because his mother did not raise him. Include Daddy issues and substance use disorder problems.

When Aunt Katie died, we went to her funeral and we stayed at Henry's daughter's house, Johnnie Rose's, and as we started unloading the car, she said that she had been raking the leaves out of the back yard. She told me as I was bringing in the luggage, that she raked up some leaves and there was a snake under them. She said that he just moved out of the way, but he scared her. I had just walked into the back-door screen, and I turned around and started putting my things back into the car. She said, "Katie what are you doing?" I said, "Johnnie you should have not mentioned snakes, no, you should not have mentioned snakes, I want to go home." They turned me back into the house, but I was uncomfortable.

Whenever I left her house to get in the car, I was uncomfortable until I was safe in the car or house. Aunt Katie looked so much like my Mama, who was sitting in the front row. We did not expect it, but the funeral director moved the casket forward to allow the family sitting in the front row to have their last view of Aunt Katie. My Mama jumped up and ran out of the funeral home. What to do? I thought. I was sitting at the end of the aisle on the second row right behind her. So, I got up to follow Mama. I looked for her and she was walking among the graves, and I found her with a woman, and they were walking and holding hands and laughing. I met this woman who was Mama's best friend when they were young. It was a Photo opportunity and again I did not have a camera. I started looking at all the graves that were at Institute M.B. Church Cemetery, Utica, Mississippi. Katie died in 1986; she was born in 1904. She was the third child of Edna and Eugene Stamps. Her obituary said her husband's name was Edward Bush. I watched a cousin bury my Aunt. It was not all the pomp that is done in Illinois. I saw several graves with the Stamps name my mother's family name, which was another Photo opportunity I lost. Now that information would have been helpful in building our family tree. I never knew her cause of death, but she was truly a lady.

I remember writing her a letter when I was in grammar school asking her for $20.00 and she sent it to me. In those days that was a lot of money. There was something in the store I wanted. Mama did not have it, so I reached out to Aunt Katie. I knew I had an advantage to hear from her.

After my wedding, she came over to our apartment and I was surprised that Aunt Katie opened the drawers in our bedroom dresser. She said that she wanted to see if my things were folded in an orderly fashion. She said that she could tell things about my character by looking at how I took care of my things. She also checked out the refrigerator. I passed her inspection. During the time my husband and I were separated, he went to Philadelphia and stayed a few days with her. He had a job interview there. I was furious that he lied to her about our relationship, pretending we were together. I also was jealous that I never took the opportunity to visit with her and learn her stories from her.

Until I met her, I was unhappy about my name. After meeting her I love that I was her namesake. I love and miss you Aunt Katie; I will hold you in my heart all my days. While we were preparing to leave Mississippi, my cousin Henry told me that we should not leave yet because he said we will just have to turn around and come back to his funeral. I did not know that he was diagnosed as having cancer of the throat. I was sitting in the car and my son was saying goodbye to Henry, offering him a handshake and Henry pulled him close, hugged him tightly, and cried. It seemed like that moment lasted forever. Erik was a teenager, and it took him by surprise, but he was gracious to his cousin. Sure, enough we had to return soon after to attend Henry's funeral. died August 13th, 1987. He had a military salute at his funeral.

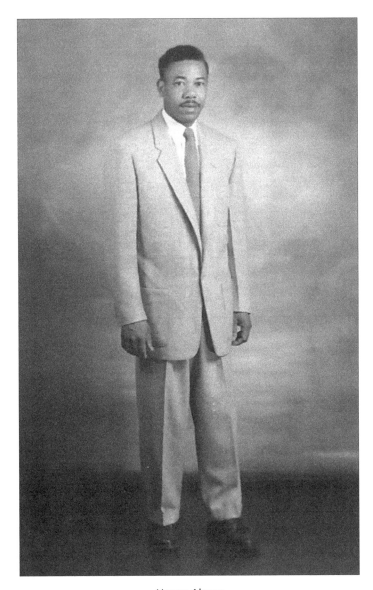

Henry Abron

Aunt Katie M Bush in Wedding Dress

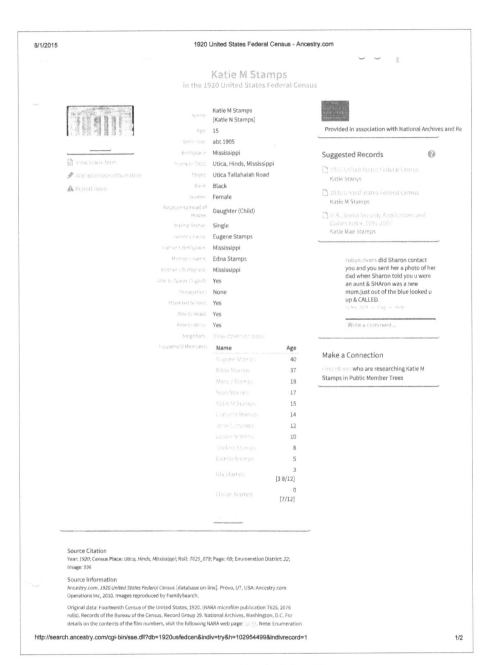

Katie M Stamps
in the 1920 United States Federal Census

Name:	Katie M Stamps [Katie N Stamps]
Age:	15
Birth Year:	abt 1905
Birthplace:	Mississippi
Home in 1920:	Utica, Hinds, Mississippi
Street:	Utica Tallahatah Road
Race:	Black
Gender:	Female
Relation to Head of House:	Daughter (Child)
Marital Status:	Single
Father's name:	Eugene Stamps
Father's Birthplace:	Mississippi
Mother's name:	Edna Stamps
Mother's Birthplace:	Mississippi
Able to Speak English:	Yes
Occupation:	None
Attended School:	Yes
Able to Read:	Yes
Able to Write:	Yes
Neighbors:	View others on page

Household Members:

Name	Age
Eugene Stamps	40
Edna Stamps	37
Mary J Stamps	18
Joan Stamps	17
Katie M Stamps	15
Cornelia Stamps	14
Jetie L Stamps	12
Luther Stamps	10
Thelma Stamps	8
Estella Stamps	5
Ida Stamps	3 [3 8/12]
Elmon Stamps	0 [7/12]

Provided in association with National Archives and Re

Suggested Records

1910 United States Federal Census
Katie Stanys

1930 United States Federal Census
Katie M Stamps

U.S., Social Security Applications and Claims Index, 1936-2007
Katie Mae Stamps

robyn rivers did Sharon contact you and you sent her a photo of her dad when Sharon told you u were an aunt & SHAron was a new mom.Just out of the blue looked u up & CALLED.

Write a comment...

Make a Connection

Find others who are researching Katie M Stamps in Public Member Trees

Source Citation
Year: 1920; Census Place: Utica, Hinds, Mississippi; Roll: T625_878; Page: 6B; Enumeration District: 22; Image: 936

Source Information
Ancestry.com. 1920 United States Federal Census [database on-line]. Provo, UT, USA: Ancestry.com Operations Inc, 2010. Images reproduced by FamilySearch.

Original data: Fourteenth Census of the United States, 1920. (NARA microfilm publication T625, 2076 rolls). Records of the Bureau of the Census, Record Group 29. National Archives, Washington, D.C. For details on the contents of the film numbers, visit the following NARA web page: NARA. Note: Enumeration

http://search.ancestry.com/cgi-bin/sse.dll?db=1920usfedcen&indiv=try&h=102954499&indivrecord=1   1/2

Katie M Stamps 1920 U.S. Federal Census

Katie M Bush & Edward Bush

Notice to Town and City Clerks. This form is to be used only by town and city clerks for making copies of marriage records to be filed with county clerks. It must not be given to applicants for marriage licenses or used by clergymen or magistrates for the certification of a marriage.

PLACE OF REGISTRY
STATE OF NEW YORK

County of......Onondaga......

Town or City of......Syracuse......

NEW YORK STATE DEPARTMENT OF HEALTH
Division of Vital Statistics

MARRIAGE LICENSE

Registered No...1751...

Know all Men by this Certificate, that any person authorized by law to perform marriage ceremonies within the State of New York to whom this may come, he, not knowing any lawful impediment thereto, is hereby authorized and empowered to solemnize the rites of matrimony beween..............................
......Edward Bush...................of......Syracuse......

in the county of......Onondaga......and state of New York and......
......Katherine Stamps......of......Syracuse......

in the county of......Onondaga......and state of New York and to certify the same to be said parties or either of them under his hand and seal in his ministerial or official capacity and thereupon he is required to return his certificate in the form hereto annexed. The statements endorsed hereon or annexed hereto, by me subscribed, contain a full and true abstract of all the facts concerning such parties disclosed by their affidavits or verified statements presented to me upon the application for this license.

In Testimony Whereof, I have hereunto set my hand and affixed the seal of said Town or City at ......syracuse...... this......First......day of......Dec-mber......
nineteen hundred and......twenty-seven......

Chas. L. Johnson

{ SEAL }

2nd assistant

Clerk

The following is a full and true abstract of all the facts disclosed by the above-named applicants in their verified statements presented to me upon their applications for the above license:

FROM THE GROOM	FROM THE BRIDE
Full name...Edward Bush......	Full name...Katherine Stamps......
Color......Colored......	Color......colored......
Place of residence...821 Almond St....... (street address) N.Y.	Place of residence...602 E. Adams St....... (street address) N.Y.
Syracuse (city, town or village) (state)	Syracuse (city, town or village) (state)
Age......32......	Age......23......
Occupation ...Porter......	Occupation ...Maid......
Place of birth...Newport News, Va.......	Place of birth......Itica, Miss.......
Name of father...Sylas......	Name of father......Eugene Stamps......
Country of birth...U.S.......	Country of birth......U.S.......
Maiden name of mother...Ann Jones......	Maiden name of mother......Edna Caston......
Country of birth...U.S.......	Country of birth......U.S.......
Number of marriage......1st......	Number of marriage......1st......
I have not to my knowledge been infected with any venereal disease, or if I have been so infected within five years I have had a laboratory test within that period which shows that I am now free from infection from any such disease.	I have not to my knowledge been infected with any venereal disease, or if I have been so infected within five years I have had a laboratory test within that period which shows that I am now free from infection from any such disease.
Former wife or wives ......no	Former husband or husbands ......no
living or dead......	living or dead......
Is applicant a divorced person......	Is applicant a divorced person......
If so, when and where, and against whom divorce	If so, when and where, and against whom divorce
or divorces were granted......	or divorces were granted......
I declare that no legal impediment exists as to my right to enter into the marriage state...I do......	I declare that no legal impediment exists as to my right to enter into the marriage state...I do......

(vertical text: COUNTY CLERK COPY)

☞ FUTURE ADDRESS (Enter here EXACT FUTURE ADDRESS after marriage if known)
......821 Almond St....... Syracuse N.Y.
(street address) (city, town or village) (state)

Marriage License December 1st 1927

95

Children (0)

Edward Bush   Parents
                                                     UNKNOWN
B: abt 1895 in North Carolina
D: 22 Feb 1954 in Philadelphia, Philadelphia, Pennsylvania, USA
                                                     UNKNOWN

Katie STAMPS Bush B: 10 Jul 1904 in Mississippi, USA

U.S., Social Security Death Index, 1935-2014

Does the Edward Bush in this record match the person in your tree? ⓘ

[Yes ✓] [No] [Maybe]   🖨 ⌁

No Image
Text-only collection

🛒 Request copy of original application

✎ Add alternate information

⚠ Report issue

Name: Edward Bush

SSN: ▬▬▬▬

BORN: 13 Oct 1895

Died: Feb 1954

State (Year) SSN issued: Pennsylvania (Before 1951)

Does the Edward Bush in this record match the person in your tree?

[Yes] [No] [Maybe]

Source Citation
Number: *167-16-4060*; Issue State: *Pennsylvania*; Issue Date: *Before 1951*

Source Information
Ancestry.com. *U.S., Social Security Death Index, 1935-2014* [database on-line]. Provo, UT, USA: Ancestry.com Operations Inc, 2011.

Original data: Social Security Administration. *Social Security Death Index, Master File*. Social Security Administration.

Description
The Social Security Administration Death Master File contains information on millions of deceased individuals with United States social security numbers whose deaths were reported to the Social Security Administration. Birth years for the individuals listed range from 1875 to last year. Information in these records includes name, birth date, death date, and last known residence. Learn more...

Edward Bush U.S. Social Security Death Index

Henry Abron
in the U.S., Social Security Death Index, 1935-2014

Name: **Henry Abron**

SSN: ▓▓▓▓▓▓▓

Last Residence: ▓▓▓▓▓▓▓▓, ▓▓▓▓▓, ▓▓▓▓▓▓▓▓, ▓▓▓

BORN: **27 Jan 1923**

Died: **Aug 1987**

State (Year) SSN issued: **Mississippi (Before 1951)**

Source Citation
Number: ▓▓▓▓▓▓ Issue State: *Mississippi*; Issue Date: *Before 1951*

Source Information
Ancestry.com. *U.S., Social Security Death Index, 1935-2014* [database on-line]. Provo, UT, USA: Ancestry.com Operations Inc, 2011.

Original data: Social Security Administration. *Social Security Death Index, Master File*. Social Security Administration.

Description
The Social Security Administration Death Master File contains information on millions of deceased individuals with United States social security numbers whose deaths were reported to the Social Security Administration. Birth years for the individuals listed range from 1875 to last year. Information in these records includes name, birth date, death date, and last known residence. Learn more...

Henry Abron U.S. Social Security Death Index

RACE AND REALITY

After Robert and I moved from Bolingbrook Il we chose Tuscaloosa. Robert did not want to be in the heavy traffic of Birmingham. We were both transferring from First Christian Church Maywood Il to First Christian Church Tuscaloosa. Our experience as Disciples of Christ was full involvement. I was not able to retain my status at this new congregation. I decided to look for a position at the Regional Level in Alabama Northwest Florida Region.

This was a voluntary position I was sitting on the Women's Ministry Board for District Two. Later I was voted into the position of Vice President and later President. The President of Women's Ministry was invited every January to a Leadership Conference. That was when I had an opportunity to travel to exciting places when I had no experience to travel around the states. It was informative and I met many wonderful ladies at the conferences I attended. I traveled to Florida, Carolina, Phoenix Indiana Los Vegas, and Atlanta.

In one of the workshops the Editor of Just Women magazine was looking for stories that could be shared in their magazine, so I submitted our family experience with racism in Mississippi. She and her board selected my story, and she said that they were interested in printing it. With a lot of help from her my submission was accepted for printing. I was beyond excited. I did not know that I would be paid.

When, I received a check. To me, that meant I was a writer I received a lot of help from the editor Kathy Mc Dowell. I also was invited to be Co-Chair to the Anti Racism Team. I felt it would not interfere with my Women's Ministries duties. Robert and I were both on the committee We went through train the trainer training and we presented the material to the ministers in our region. This was a wonderful project and encouraging. The Pastors openly shared with the group. I shared this to explain the cover of the magazine and the article I wrote about the racism and violence that our family endured.

Just Women Summer 2017 Magazine Cover

From tragedy to justice work by Katie Wallace-Davis

It was a beautiful morning in Chicago. I had the front door open. The screen door was locked. I wanted the fresh breezes to refresh our townhouse. This was unusual for me because I am always concerned about safety. That Monday my son and I were home together, singing along with the music. We were enjoying ourselves. It was a good day. No work for me; no school for him.

I turned the music down when the phone rang. It was my mother's nephew, Henry, calling from Jackson, MS. He asked to speak to Aunt Ida, my mother. I told him we were expecting her any moment. I offered to have her return his call. He paused, and then told me that he had called to let us know that Aunt Neal was dead. I repeated, "Aunt Neal is dead!" Aunt Neal and her granddaughters, Martha Ann and Alice Earl, died in a house fire, he explained. "What happened?" I asked. I got no response.

"Will you call and give us the funeral arrangements?" I asked. Henry said, "There is nothing to see. Do not come down here." He also stated that Neal and her granddaughters would be buried together. "Do not come down here," he repeated firmly. "I saw the badly burned bodies holding on to each other." He said goodbye, and before I could say anything else, he hung up the phone. The joy of the day was over.

When Mama arrived, I told her what Henry had said. She immediately got out her address book and called her nephew Henry. After getting off the phone, she started crying and shouting, "Oh God." Finally, she fell down in a seat. She told us Edna Lee, the mother of Martha Ann and Alice

Earl, was not at home when the fire started. Edna Lee walked up and saw her home completely engulfed in flames. There were white firemen standing around. One warned her not to say anything about what she had seen or something would happen to her. The fire had been arson.

Later we found out more. Martha Ann and her boyfriend fell in love. The passion they felt for one another went too far. When she told him that she was pregnant, he told her not to worry, assuring her of his love and his devotion to her and their baby. He wanted to marry her. They planned to raise the child together. They were excited about becoming a family. They decided to tell their parents.

The young man told his mother he loved Martha Ann and they were expecting a child. His mother told him that marriage with a "colored girl" was not in her plans for his life. They argued. It ended with him walking out of his mother's house. His mother knew it was not difficult to find out where Martha Ann lived. The shack where she lived only had one exit. The fire was set early on Sunday morning, the door barricaded from the outside, so they could not get out. Gasoline was poured around the house and the flames quickly consumed the dwelling.

This happened over 40 years ago, but it still comes to mind. I wonder what happened to the young white teenager who loved my cousin and his unborn child. How could his mother hate people of color so much that she could and would arrange the death of innocents? There was never anyone named as responsible for the fire.

I am like Martha Ann; I fell in love with someone of a different race.

When Robert and I became a couple, our families did not immediately share our happiness. We started our life together in Chicago in 1997, sharing our differences and our similarities, including working for social justice. Upon retirement, we made a major move to the Deep South. We wanted to continue doing justice work, and we were invited to join the Anti-racism Team of the Christian Church (Disciples of Christ) in Alabama-Northwest Florida. The first time I told this story about Martha Ann was with this group, sharing why I wanted to work to dismantle racism in our churches and communities. Both Robert and I stepped out in faith that our relationship with each other would be a strong bond and loving experience. Our lives demonstrate that the love of Jesus reconciles us all together as one. We pray that we can help others move forward in developing authentic relationships with persons who are different from themselves.

Katie M. Wallace-Davis, retired after 45 years of service with the IRS, is the current Disciples Women President in the Alabama-Northwest Florida Region and Co-Chair of the region's Anti-Racism Team.

Women in Mission article

Cornelia Stamps

Cornelia Stamps
in the 1920 United States Federal Census

Name:	Cornelia Stamps
Age:	14
Birth Year:	abt 1906
Birthplace:	Mississippi
Home in 1920:	Utica, Hinds, Mississippi
Street:	Utica Tallahalah Road
Race:	Black
Gender:	Female
Relation to Head of House:	Daughter (Child)
Marital Status:	Single
Father's name:	Eugene Stamps
Father's Birthplace:	Mississippi
Mother's name:	Edna Stamps
Mother's Birthplace:	Mississippi
Able to Speak English:	Yes
Occupation:	None
Attended School:	Yes
Able to Read:	Yes
Able to Write:	Yes
Neighbors:	View others on page

View blank form

Add alternate information

Report issue

Provided in association with National Archiv

Suggested Records

1930 United States Federal Census
Cornelius Stamps

Write a comment...

Make a Connection

Find others who are researching Cornelia Stamps in Public Member Trees

Household Members:

Name	Age
Eugene Stamps	40
Edna Stamps	37
Mary J Stamps	18
Isiah Stamps	17
Katie M Stamps	15
Cornelia Stamps	14
John E Stamps	12
Luther Stamps	10
Thelma Stamps	8
Estella Stamps	5
Ida Stamps	3 [3 8/12]
Union Stamps	0 [7/12]

Cornelia Stamps 1920 U.S. Federal Census

EDNA LEE

Edna Lee is the daughter of Neal her legal name Cornelia Stamps and Swanigan was her married name although she went back to her maiden name Stamps. Aunt Neal was one of the sisters that did not leave the South. Mama lived with her after running away from their Daddy. Mama also asked Aunt Neal to keep James when she moved to Chicago, just for a while until she could get a job. Aunt Neal was Mama older sister. Mama was the baby sister in the family.

Aunt Neal had a daughter's name Edna Lee, Lee was her married name. No one is left to clear it up for me if Lee is her married name or her maiden name. But these facts are correct that Edna had 3 children a son and later two daughters. They were all living with Aunt Neal. In the past when Ann Green was young Edna was in charge and she was chopping firewood for the stove she failed to make sure that Ann was not standing too close to her while she was chopping the wood, Ann was hit in the eye with a piece of wood, they took her to the doctors who was unequipped to save her eye. So she lost her eye, and everyone was disappointed with Edna. I do not know how older Edna was than Ann. As explained earlier, Edna lost her mother, her two daughters and everything she had that was in that house that was torched by the KKK. As the fire was engulfing the house, she was in walking distance to the house and noticed the fire and saw the fireman just sitting there. She addressed what she saw with the fireman, who asked her if she lived there, and she told him her mother and children were in that house. He told her she best not say anything to anybody about what she saw, or she would be next to die. It was a horrible way to die. They died holding onto each other, Henry said they were locked together so they were placed in a bag together. Henry heard about the fire because it was announced on the radio/tv that morning and he recognized the address as our Aunt's house. He rushed over there and saw the removal of his Aunt and cousin's bodies. He called our house the next afternoon.

Edna mentioned to someone that she did not understand why their relatives living in Chicago did not come to the funeral, She was told that we were instructed not to come down there by Henry, Not sure of the timing for this but her son killed himself in a motorcycle accident after finding out his grandmother and sisters were gone. The man she loved died and she was crying every day, she was living in a trailer There was a man that cared for her and when she fell, she seriously hurt herself he moved into the trailer and was her caretaker. She was inconsolable after all these tragedies in her life At a point in her health situation she was in the hospital and wanted to die. She felt none of the family loved her. I heard of her passing, and I hope she finally found peace with her loved ones.

Edna Lee

Women's Ministry Fall Retreat 2017

JOHNNIE ETHEL STAMPS WILLIAMS

My Aunt Johnnie Ethel Stamps was age 12 in the 1920 census. of Utica Mississippi. She was born in 1908. The census displayed her names as John E Stamps. Her legal name is Johnnie Ethel Stamps. Johnnie Ethel Stamps married McKinley Williams, they moved from Mississippi to St Louis Mo. I am not sure when she moved from the south.

Many who fled the south went to places like the Northeast, Midwest and West, Johnnie and McKinley chose St Louis to live and find work to support their family. I went to visit those in St Louis, but they did not share any history, but I enjoyed our visit. I never met her or heard anything about her. I knew her daughter Thelma Williams Wilson. My first cousin. we called her little Thelma she had three children Gwen, Evelyn, and Warren. Thelma was born September 4th, 1927, in Vicksburg Ms. she passed to a new life May 30, 2005. I have a picture of Johnnie's daughter Thelma Wilson. I wish I knew my Aunt Johnnie. Little Thelma attended my first wedding. Thelma Wilson's Obituary stated that Johnnie,McKinley, and her stepmother Jessie and her brother Donald, and her husband Sylvester proceeded her in death. She leaves Grandchildren and Great Grandchildren and Great Great Grandchildren to celebrate her life.

John E Stamps

in the 1920 United States Federal Census

📄 View blank form

✏️ Add alternate information

⚠️ Report issue

Name:	John E Stamps
Age:	12
Birth Year:	abt 1908
Birthplace:	Mississippi
Home in 1920:	Utica, Hinds, Mississippi
Street:	Utica Tallahalah Road
Race:	Black
Relation to Head of House:	Daughter (Child)
Marital Status:	Single
Father's name:	Eugene Stamps
Father's Birthplace:	Mississippi
Mother's name:	Edna Stamps
Mother's Birthplace:	Mississippi
Able to Speak English:	Yes
Occupation:	None
Attended School:	Yes
Able to Read:	Yes
Able to Write:	Yes
Neighbors:	View others on page

Provided in association with National Archive

Write a comment...

Make a Connection

Find others who are researching John E Stamps in Public Member Trees

Household Members:

Name	Age
Eugene Stamps	40
Edna Stamps	37
Mary J Stamps	18
Isiah Stamps	17
Katie M Stamps	15
Cornelia Stamps	14
John E Stamps	12
Luther Stamps	10
Thelma Stamps	8
Estella Stamps	5
Iola Stamps	3 [3 8/12]
Limon Stamps	0 [7/12]

John E Stamps 1920 U. S. Federal Census

Johnny E Stamps

in the U.S., Social Security Applications and Claims Index, 1936-2007

Detail	Source

Name: Johnny E Stamps

Gender: Female

Spouse: McKinley Williams

Child: Donald Clayton Williams

Johnny E Stamps U.S. Social Security Applications

Almeida Smith, Thelma Wilson, and Thelma Love

UNCLE LUTHER STAMPS AND AUNT ANNIE STAMPS

I met my Uncle when he came to Chicago for a visit. Mama asked him to visit us at our apartment. At that time we lived on the 17th floor in Lawless Gardens. The building had a beautiful view east and some of the windows view was south. The Chicago River was very interesting to view. I have spent many hours just watching the boats. I drove him in my little Volkswagen Bugg and brought him to our building he stepped inside the elevator and like a child was amazed at the speed of the elevator. We entered the apartment and he walked down the hallway and he could see the Chicago River out of the windows because we had no curtains, or drapes, or blinds covering them.. He took one long look at the vast area and insisted to be taken back to his sister's house. But, Uncle Luther, Mama prepared dinner for you. Uncle Luther said he wanted to go back now. So, I turned around and took him back to the ground floor and drove him back to the west side where I picked him up.

He seemed to enjoy looking out of the car window at this big city. When I went south I stopped at his house after calling and inviting myself and my son. We wanted to stop by and visit with him for a while, they welcomed us. I found out that he lived in a little shack like place. I was told by my cousin, that if I needed anything like food or water I should take it with me for they will not offer you anything. That was true. I saw the picture of me on the wall that I sent them. He had a pond that he kept fish, they were all catfish, which he sold to those that wanted to fish in his pond. I also heard but did not notice when I was there that Uncle Luther had carpentry skills, and all his sisters were talking about how Uncle Luther built his own casket and it was leaning against the front porch of the house. Their house was one room. My Uncle was experiencing dementia.

One Sunday Aunt Annie had a chance to go to church, their son picked her up for church. Luther stayed home and when she left him there she told him not to do any cooking and do not let the animals come into the house. While she was gone, Luther decided to do some cooking and he also let the goats come into the house. When Aunt Annie came back to the house. Luther had absentmindedly set the house on fire, when Annie returned from church and saw the house burned down, it was said that she told Luther Jr to take her with him, and they drove off and left Luther there, with the burned remains of the house. I have some pictures of Aunt Thelma's visit to see her brother, but I was unable to receive any information about his death or the death of his wife Annie. I was scolded when I returned from my visit with them, I was told that I should not have given Luther that $20 I folded up and slipped in his hand with a handshake. They told me I was supposed to give any money to Aunt Annie. She did not interact with us at all, and I told those that were concerned I made the money and I give it to whom I choose. They did not say what he did with it. Uncle Luther was 30 years old in the 1940 census his occupation was a farmer. His education was up to the 4th grade and he and Annie had a son and they named him Luther M Stamps Jr he was 2 years old in 1940. Aunt Annie was 34 and she had no formal education. Luther died on the 15th day of March 1996.

Luther M Stamps
in the 1940 United States Federal Census

Detail	Source

Name:	Luther M Stamps
Respondent:	Yes
Age:	30
Estimated Birth Year:	abt 1910
Gender:	Male
Race:	Negro (Black)
Birthplace:	Mississippi
Marital Status:	Married
Relation to Head of House:	Head
Home in 1940:	Hinds, Mississippi
Map of Home in 1940:	Hinds, Mississippi
Street:	Institute and Crystal Springs Road
Farm:	Yes
Inferred Residence in 1935:	Rural, Copiah, Mississippi
Residence in 1935:	Rural, Copiah, Mississippi
Sheet Number:	12B
Number of Household in Order of Visitation:	196
Occupation:	Farmer
House Owned or Rented:	Rented
Value of Home or Monthly Rental if Rented:	6
Attended School or College:	No
Highest Grade Completed:	Elementary school, 4th grade
Hours Worked Week Prior to Census:	60
Class of Worker:	Working on own account
Weeks Worked in 1939:	52
Income:	0
Income Other Sources:	Yes
Neighbors:	View others on page

Luther M. Stamps 1940 U. S. Federal Census

Household Members	Age	Relationship
Luther M Stamps	**30**	**Head**
Annie R Stamps	34	Wife
Luther M Stamps Jr	2	Son
Henry Simpson	73	Father-in-law

© 2022 Ancestry.com

Luther M. Stamps 1940 U. S. Federal Census

Annie Stamps and Katie Wallace and Luther Stamps

THELMA AND JOHN LOVE

In the year 1968 1 was working for the I.R.S. at their Kedzie office. In April that year Martin Luther King was assassinated. While I was at work the next day,. One of the managers said to me that I should leave for the day. I said no, I was not willing to leave. But she had a radio and was advising me to go home due to the riots going on in Chicago. I did not want to use any of my leave time so later, after she talked to the downtown office, she told me to go home for the day. Since I would not be using my leave time I left. On my way home there were no problems on the highways since my travel home was on the expressway. I lived southeast from the Dan Ryan expressway. There were no riots seen by me in my travels home.

But later I found out that my Aunt who lived on the west side of Chicago saw a lot of destruction. They were fearful. Nothing was done to their homes but just behind their homes was the business district and a lot of buildings were destroyed there. After the fire and destruction stopped, Chicago deemed that area as eminent domain. My Aunt had a 2-flat building. In exchange for her property, she was given a house on the southwest side, a small brick house with three bedrooms and a bath with a full-length of the house basement. with a nice size back yard. Whites previously owned this area. North of her was an area called Sportsman's Park Racetrack. Most of the people in my Aunt's neighborhood were given homes in that same area for exchange of the ones the city planned to destroy even though there was no riot damage to their homes. Creating another ghetto.

I was not made aware of the finances in that exchange, realizing that the value of that area was incredibly low. Uncle John had passed before the riot. He was home alone, and Aunt Estella his sister-in-law heard him screaming, so she went upstairs to check on him and called an ambulance for him. He spent two days in the hospital before he died. We lost him to a brain aneurysm. I had not been close to him since I met my Daddy, and the last time he and I spoke he was drunk and told me that I just left him and went to my "No good Daddy." I was visiting in their apartment, and he was outside in the back yard screaming at me. I was surprised that he felt that I had betrayed him, He should have realized that I was just a child. I had no maliciousness for him. Aunt Thelma asked me not to respond. I knew he cared about me, and I felt that he should know that I cared about him. He was correct when he labeled my Daddy. I just wished that he did not have a substance use disorder. I heard that he had gotten physical with my Aunt. He also felt that he had lost the closeness of his wife after they adopted a baby girl. He was one of those people who are quiet until they start drinking. I loved him and I still do. My Uncle made a better life for him and his wife, moving to Chicago. He did not have an opportunity to complete school and he accomplished so much although he did not have an equal opportunity as many whites had. He acquired his own business and purchased his own truck. He was a generous man and could fix anything, His drinking was a problem.

Aunt Thelma was someone that I wanted to be like. She read the newspaper and she was knowledgeable about current events. When I was an adult I discussed a lot of things with her, nonpersonal. I wanted to design patterns like she did. She was good in designing. Aunt Thelma's daughter put her in a nursing home and when Mama visited Thelma, she told her that their brother Hillman raped her twice. I was surprised that she kept his picture in a frame on her table. When I sat with her she talked about the trip she had the day before, going downtown to a fabric store. I knew that was not true, but I went along with her.

She also told Mama that the male nurse was changing her diaper or either washing her and he tried to do something with which made her uncomfortable. When she was home I would call to speak to her. Her grandson answered the phone he would call his mother to come to the phone and I would wait and wait and then someone would just hang up the phone. So,I sent the police over there for a wellness check, explaining to them that my cousin would not put my Aunt on the phone, they would just hang up. They would not let me talk with my Aunt. Of course, after the police came over, her grandson returned my call, wanting to know why I sent the police and I explained to him that you keep hanging up on me. He told me that his Grandma was not talking right. He said that Grandma told him that his mother was adopted by her. I told him that was correct, she was adopted. "Aunt Thelma adopted your mother when she was an infant." After I shared that, the distance between me and my cousin grew a bit larger. My cousin Ann was upset with me because she said I told that my cousin was adopted. I explained to her that I did not tell that she was adopted Aunt Thelma said that she was adopted I just verified that what she said was true. Part of the problem was my Aunt was using me as an example for her to follow. Once her daughter gave me a card that stated that she was glad that she did not have to be like me anymore.

Thelma previously asked my Mama if she would get me to come to be with her when she had her second cataract surgery, I asked Mama could I take her over their house and she could spend the night with them, Mama said no," Thelma wants you to be there." Her first operation ended with her being blind in that eye. Mama and I got up at 5 a.m. to go to meet them and follow them to the place where she was having the surgery. I stood with her until they took her in the operating room. The surgery was successful.

Aunt Thelma was born June 19, 1912, She passed 06/18/2003. Thank you, Aunt Thelma, for your love and care for Mama, James, and I.

We love you and remember how you and John helped us doing our growing up years.

Thelma Stamps Love

ancestry

Thelma Stamps
in the 1920 United States Federal Census

Name:	Thelma Stamps
Age:	8
Birth Year:	abt 1912
Birthplace:	Mississippi
Home in 1920:	Utica, Hinds, Mississippi
Street:	Utica Tallahalah Road
Race:	Black
Gender:	Female
Relation to Head of House:	Daughter (Child)
Marital Status:	Single
Father's name:	Eugene Stamps
Father's Birthplace:	Mississippi
Mother's name:	Edna Stamps
Mother's Birthplace:	Mississippi
Occupation:	None
Attended School:	Yes
Neighbors:	View others on page

Household Members:	Name	Age
	Eugene Stamps	40
	Edna Stamps	37
	Mary J Stamps	18
	Isiah Stamps	17
	Katie M Stamps	15
	Cornelia Stamps	14
	John E Stamps	12
	Luther Stamps	10

Thelma Stamps 1920 U.S. Federal Census page 1

118

Thelma Stamps	8
Estella Stamps	5
	3
Ida Stamps	[3 8/12]
	0
Limon Stamps	[7/12]

Source Citation

Year: *1920*; Census Place: *Utica, Hinds, Mississippi*; Roll: *T625_878*; Page: *6B*; Enumeration District: *22*; Image: *936*

Source Information

Ancestry.com. *1920 United States Federal Census* [database on-line]. Provo, UT, USA: Ancestry.com Operations Inc, 2010. Images reproduced by FamilySearch.

Original data: Fourteenth Census of the United States, 1920. (NARA microfilm publication T625, 2076 rolls). Records of the Bureau of the Census, Record Group 29. National Archives, Washington, D.C. For details on the contents of the film numbers, visit the following NARA web page: NARA. Note: Enumeration Districts 819-839 are on roll 323 (Chicago City).

Description

This database is an index to individuals enumerated in the 1920 United States Federal Census, the Fourteenth Census of the United States. It includes all states and territories, as well as Military and Naval Forces, the Virgin Islands, Puerto Rico, American Samoa, Guam, and the Panama Canal Zone. The census provides many details about individuals and families including: name, gender, age, birthplace, year of immigration, mother tongue, and parents' birthplaces. In addition, the names of those listed on the population schedule are linked to actual images of the 1920 Federal Census. Learn more...

© 2015, Ancestry.com

Thelma Stamps 1920 U.S. Federal Census page 2

119

John Love and his Truck

ME AND MRS JONES

Aunt Estella Jones was my favorite Aunt. She, Mama, and their older sister Thelma were a family unit who lived together when they came to Chicago. They worked and took care of each other's children, sharing the successes and failures of life. While in Mississippi living with their father, after their mother died, and their stepmother moved out. Estella told Mama that their father was touching her, and she did not want him to. So, Mama helped her run away, They tied her few clothes in a small blanket, and Mama watched out for Papa. While he was out of sight, Estella sneaked away She stayed connected with her sisters. For a while, she lived in New Orleans, where she married and had a daughter. They never talked around me about her life in New Orleans. I learned that her husband died at a young age.

After Aunt Thelma and Uncle John moved to Chicago on 61st Street, Estella, now a widow, with her daughter Ann came to live in Chicago in 1938, Mama came in 1940. We all lived in a one-bedroom apartment with their sister Thelma and John until they were able to be independent. Aunt Estella married Charlie Jones. I am not sure when they married but Estella and Ann moved when Thelma and John bought the two-story apartment building. They moved and took the first-floor apartment. Mama with James and me had the basement. Aunt Thelma and John had the largest space, on the second floor. Uncle Charlie, Estella's husband, was working at U S Steel, a large employer in Chicago. In those days, Charlie was not happy working for the steel mill. He decided to have his own business. He left the steel mill, drew down his pension funds, rented a small store, and opened a grocery store, located on 16th Street and Kedzie, Aunt Estella ran the store. It was a short ride on the trolley on Roosevelt Road then transfer to the bus on Kedzie to 16th street. In the middle of an apartment building was a store.

Now my Uncle had his own business, Jones Grocery. He was proud of his accomplishments. He asked me to help him write a check. I had never written, a check; I was still in grammar school. But as I was reading the blank check, all of a sudden he said, "Never mind. I am going to take a class in school."

Now here is where it takes a village to raise a child I admit I was attracted to this boy; I told my friend Cora about my feelings for him, and she told me that she could get me a date with him. She knew I could not be out after the streetlights came on, so she arranged things so I could have a chance to meet with this boy during the day. She told me that there would be a gathering at his apartment. She even walked me over to his place the day before the party, so I would know where he lived. He had his own place. I was in eighth grade and planning to attend summer school so I could graduate a little earlier than my classmates. Of course, he was older than us, but nothing was going to keep me from attending this party. When I got home that day, Aunt Estella was at home. I stepped into her apartment. (She always kept that inside door to her place open.) I said hello, and instead of doing what I normally do, which was to sit down in her living room and ask to turn on the television, I told her I was going downstairs. I changed my clothes. I put on a skirt and blouse; I usually wore dungarees. I slipped out of the back door and walked to his apartment.

For a small place, it was a nice size for one person. His room had a lot of windows and a small kitchen along one wall. In the middle of the room was a full-size bed. There was not a lot of room for a party.

We said hello and I asked, "Where is everybody?" He said, "They're coming." He offered me a seat, so I sat down in the chair. He obviously was checking me out while we had a polite conversation. Then we heard voices coming down the stairs to his apartment. He immediately crumpled up the bed linen. He said not to leave right away, but to remain in my seat. My thoughts: why is he messing up the bed? Making it look like we were in bed together! Cora and her friends came in, took one look at the bed, and started making jokes, very off-color jokes. I said nothing, just made a small smile. Cora made a remark and turned up the music. When I got a chance, I left. Since my friend knew I had an early curfew, no jokes were made about my leaving. I was very hurt. I was set-up. I ran all the way home. "That girl was not a friend to you, Katie!" That was a narrow escape. I rejoiced he did not take advantage of me. I slipped back into the house. I had not locked the back door since I did not have a backdoor key. I did not want to go through the front door, because my Aunt would hear me. I thought Aunt Estella would not know that I had left the apartment, but my luck started to go downhill fast. Aunt Estella called me to come upstairs. "Yes, Ma'am," I called out. I quickly changed clothes and put my regular clothes back on. When I went upstairs, she asked me where I had gone. I said I was downstairs. She then told me that she had called me, and when I did not answer, she was concerned about me, so she went downstairs and walked through the basement and realized that I was not at home. I could not think of a lie to tell her. I just could not believe Cora had told this boy that I wanted to have sex with him. I was not interested in giving up anything. I learned a lesson that day. I did not say anything to my Aunt. I just kept my eyes on the floor. She said I could go, and I went back to my room and hung up my skirt and blouse. Aunt Estella told Mama that I had left the house through the back door, and I would not tell her where I went nor explain my absence. Mama has never whipped me, so she called Daddy, who waited until that next weekend to come over.

Aunt Estella opened the door for him. I remained in the basement; he came downstairs. It was the only time I remember him coming into that basement. He did not know that he needed to duck his head and butted it against a low-hanging pipe. I laughed. He gave me a lecture and took off his belt, and he gave me a whipping that I have never forgotten. He hit me on my behind and legs. The tears flowed freely; I was so sorry. I wanted him to just stop! I knew I would not do that again. He was madder at me laughing when he bumped his head than me leaving the house. I never told them where I went or what happened to me that afternoon. If my folks had known what I had almost got myself into, they would have laughed at me for being so stupid. I never saw that group of so-called friends again. I went to summer school and graduated during the summer.

We all went to different high schools. I thought that I had been punished enough, without waiting a week for a whipping. It should have been timelier. What did my Daddy have to do with anything? He did not live here; he did not talk to me on a regular basis. Who did he think he was? I was glad he hurt his head. Had he ever come to visit, he would have known about that pipe. Mama was the one who whipped James. Why didn't she whip me? Why did she call him? What did he care? That was the one and only time my Daddy ever whipped me. I love my Aunt Estella. She was at home most of the time, and we spent a lot of time together until Uncle Charlie bought that store. She would ask me to write letters for her to send back home to her sister in Mississippi. I could earn a few dollars taking dictation. Problems came when she expected me to know how to spell names of the cities in Mississippi. One letter we wrote came back and she was angry with me. She said I was in school and should know how to spell. I could not meet the expectations she had. I thought, well, why didn't you tell me how to spell it? I did not know that she had not finished grammar school. I told her I did my best, and she calmed down. I tried to spell the town another way, and we sent the letter out again.

Aunt Estella and I would sometimes sing together, especially the song "Me and Mrs. Jones." When we lived on Grenshaw, she was a lot of fun. After Mama and I moved away, I did not have a chance to bond with my Aunt as an adult. When I was 36 years old, I had a partial hysterectomy. I had bought a house in Maywood, Illinois, and Mama and I were still living together. She said she could not take time off her job to care for me when I got out of the hospital. I promised the doctor that I would not walk up and down the stairs for another week. Now, Estella was then living in Southern Illinois, but she was visiting in Chicago, so she volunteered to come to Maywood every day for a week. She spent the day with me, preparing lunch and snacks for me. I did not have to walk so frequently down and up the stairs. We shared time and memories together. She had had a hysterectomy, and she showed me her scar, which had turned into a huge keloid. It started just below her breast, which was an old medical procedure. I showed her my bikini cut and she was amazed how small it was. She went back to Southern Illinois with her husband, and we heard that she was having stomach problems. Her doctor told her she needed surgery to remove the cancer. She came back to Chicago to have the surgery. The surgeon said that they had found the cancerous organs but did not get it all out. The women in our family would not say the word, they called it "C." I would like to know more about what they found, because it appeared to be medical malpractice. I felt that way because I was told that I had fourth stage cancer and there was no trace of any cancer in my organs that was removed according to the lab report.

We were all called to come to the hospital because she was terminal and would die that very day. Everyone showed up to be with Aunt Estella. Uncle Charlie had to keep leaving the room for he could not stop crying. She did not die that day or the next. They told Charlie that she needed to be in a nursing home, so they found one for her. They fed her, and the food would come out in a colostomy bag. She was in good spirits most of the time. When she had visitors, the nurses would come in often. Aunt Estella told us they did not come that often when she was alone During one of Mama's and my visits, I brought a book to read and after greetings, I kissed Estella on the forehead and sat down to get lost in reading this book. They were going down memory lane and I had no interest in their conversation. Mama noticed that I had my head in the book and she got upset with me. Estella said "Ida, let her be." I turned back into my reading. Mama walked out of the room to cry, and I closed my book and went to talk with my Aunt.

We shared some laughs. When Mama came back into the room all red-eyed, we decided to leave. It had been months since they gave Estella that death sentence. We came to visit again and found she was moved and was in a hospital bed now. I gave her a plant that had a beautiful white flower so she would have something to look at. She asked me to sing to her. I started to sing, and we were having a fun time. Mama had walked out, so Estella would not see her crying. After Mama left, Estella said "Katie, if the feeling that I have in my legs moved further up my body, would that be the time that I will die?" I was surprised, how could I know the answer to that question? "Aunt Estella, I don't know!" You could see she was not happy with me. She said, "You do know, you are just refusing to tell me!" She stopped talking and turned her face away from me. I started back singing "Amazing Grace" again. I regret that day, that I did not offer a prayer with her, hold her hand, and let her know I loved her. Mama came back into the room and we left, promising to come again soon. I never saw her alive again. Estella Jones passed February 26th, 1979. She was born July 17th,1914. Mama's brother Lymon Stamps died March 28th, 1979, born May 26th, 1918. We never told him his sister Estella had passed. Both gone but not forgotten. Whenever I hear that song, "Me and Mrs. Jones," I think of my Aunt Estella. She was a special lady. I love her.

Estella Stamps Jones

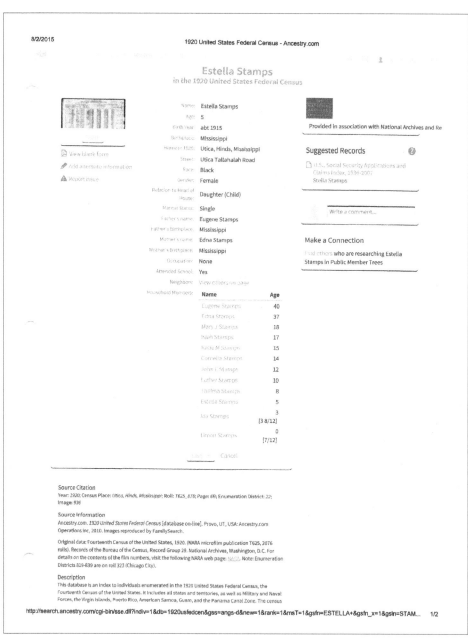

Estella Stamps
in the 1920 United States Federal Census

Name:	Estella Stamps
Age:	5
Birth Year:	abt 1915
Birthplace:	Mississippi
Home in 1920:	Utica, Hinds, Mississippi
Street:	Utica Tallahalah Road
Race:	Black
Gender:	Female
Relation to Head of House:	Daughter (Child)
Marital Status:	Single
Father's name:	Eugene Stamps
Father's Birthplace:	Mississippi
Mother's name:	Edna Stamps
Mother's Birthplace:	Mississippi
Occupation:	None
Attended School:	Yes
Neighbors:	View others on page

Provided in association with National Archives and Re

Suggested Records

U.S., Social Security Applications and Claims Index, 1936-2007
Stella Stamps

Write a comment...

Make a Connection

Find others who are researching Estella Stamps in Public Member Trees

Household Members:

Name	Age
Eugene Stamps	40
Edna Stamps	37
Mary J Stamps	18
Isiah Stamps	17
Nettie M Stamps	15
Cornelia Stamps	14
John L Stamps	12
Luther Stamps	10
Thelma Stamps	8
Estella Stamps	5
Ida Stamps	3 [3 8/12]
Linton Stamps	0 [7/12]

Save   Cancel

Source Citation
Year: *1920*; Census Place: *Utica, Hinds, Mississippi*; Roll: *T625_878*; Page: *6B*; Enumeration District: *22*; Image: *936*

Source Information
Ancestry.com. *1920 United States Federal Census* [database on-line]. Provo, UT, USA: Ancestry.com Operations Inc, 2010. Images reproduced by FamilySearch.

Original data: Fourteenth Census of the United States, 1920. (NARA microfilm publication T625, 2076 rolls). Records of the Bureau of the Census, Record Group 29. National Archives, Washington, D.C. For details on the contents of the film numbers, visit the following NARA web page: NARA. Note: Enumeration Districts 819-839 are on roll 323 (Chicago City).

Description
This database is an index to individuals enumerated in the 1920 United States Federal Census, the Fourteenth Census of the United States. It includes all states and territories, as well as Military and Naval Forces, the Virgin Islands, Puerto Rico, American Samoa, Guam, and the Panama Canal Zone. The census

http://search.ancestry.com/cgi-bin/sse.dll?indiv=1&db=1920usfedcen&gss=angs-d&new=1&rank=1&msT=1&gsfn=ESTELLA+&gsfn_x=1&gsln=STAM...   1/2

Estella Stamps 1920 U. S. Federal Census

UNCLE CHARLIE

I started watching television at my Aunt Estella apartment, well until her husband came home who would watch with me, but before long he would take off his shoes, and you really had to leave the room, you could not breathe. The aroma from his feet was intolerable. I would hope and pray that he would not take his shoes off until the show was over, but my prayers were not answered. I had to leave the room, not knowing what happened, but I could not hold my breath long enough to finish the program. My Uncle Charlie was dark as the night and he did not like white folks,. he said that they all were devils. He had a good job working at the steel mill, and he also was the one that opened a small grocery store. I got a chance to work for him, and Aunt Estella managed the store. It was fun for a while. I took the bus down Kedzie Avenue to 16th Street where his store was, it was interesting to see all of the people and the stores and houses as you traveled south. from Roosevelt 1200 south to walk and still work standing up.

He had no chairs for you to sit down. He wanted you to be working all of the time, if you are not putting up stock, then you should be dusting, or rearranging stock all of the time. I admired him for registering for school, to learn how to fill out a check. I told him I could show him how to do that, he said he would rather do it himself. Aunt Estella was robbed one night, and the robber made her lie down on the floor while he raided the cash register. I know she was afraid and soon after, Uncle Charlie started closing up early.

I was there one night to put up some stock and I could not open a box of cans. Uncle Charlie took a knife and was yelling at me for being so helpless, and he was not really paying attention to what he was doing and stuck the knife in the box. It went straight through the taped box and straight into his belly, boy, my eyes wide "Uncle Charlie, you stabbed yourself!" He looked down and saw the blood on his shirt. He told me to stay there until he came back, and to put up the cans. His friend drove him to the hospital. He told me to keep the store open and he left. It was dark outside, and I was not to go home alone, and I was not going to stay there in that store by myself, so I locked the front door, and found a crate to sit on. A man came to the door and saw me and found the door locked and wanted to get in. I shook my head and then he pretended to plead to be let in, I shook my head again. He was not getting in here.

When Uncle Charlie finally came back, I lied and said nobody came to the store. That I just locked it a few minutes ago. He had a big bandage on his stomach. nothing else was said about that night. Uncle Charlie gave me a cookbook when I got married. He also sent me $400.00 all brand new hundred-dollar bills, so I called him to thank him for his generosity then he told me that he had mistakenly enclosed all that money in the envelope and to send him back $200.00. Boy, did I regret calling him. He said he looked all over the house for that missing money, and I lost the smile on my face and returned the extra money to him. He presented me a cookbook when I had him over for lunch one Saturday afternoon. He ate what I had prepared but before he left, he complained that I did not offer him enough food. I felt bad about that. My Uncle was a big man. I guess I really needed to refer to that book he gave me. After all these years I still have that one; it is called the Family Circle Cookbook. Copy right in 1974. I also have quite a collection of cookbooks. that I have not prepared anything from them, but they have great pictures of food in them. Great reading. Mama was a great cook, but I was never really interested in cooking. I was more motivated to sew.

Aunt Estella Jones in their Store

Aunt Estella and Charlie Jones

WHEN IDA MET SAM

I found out that Daddy had married again. He said her name was Lois, I told Mama and she shared this information with her sisters, Estella, and Thelma. They talked to Mama and convinced her that she needed a man friend. She was the only one of the three that did not have a husband. James and I were still living with Mama. I was about 14 and James was about 19. At that time, we used one half of the biggest room in the basement for James's room. A small couch and regular chair was the living room area.

Since James was working, he rented furniture for his room, including a tv. He had a new bed and a dresser with a mirror. Mama and I had more room but just a full bed and the chest. The sisters decided Mama should meet someone, to show Daddy that she could get someone too. I was not happy about this. They dressed up. Aunt Estella and Mama looked great, and they walked down to the corner of Grenshaw and Homan to Buddy's Tavern. James and I were in the basement. I was reading since James did not want me to turn on his television, because he was sleeping. He was so selfish with that television, but since it was his, there was nothing Mama would do to help me. He also would cut it off when I was watching it, just as the Lone Ranger was about to catch the bad man in black off it would go.

It had only been about an hour and a half when I heard Aunt Estella come in. Since the basement door was open you could hear what was happening upstairs. Uncle Charlie started arguing with Aunt Estella and threatening her. Her daughter Ann was at home, and she was trying to stop the fight. Uncle Charlie got a knife to cut my Aunt. She and Ann came running down the stairs, making loud noises, and Uncle Charlie came running down right after them. I saw a big knife in his hand. I told James to help our Aunt he told me to leave him alone, they went out of the back door, and Uncle Charlie followed them. Mama was not home. She came home much later, and when she did, we found out that a man named Sam walked Aunt Estella home and waited for her to go into the house before he left. Uncle Charlie was looking out the window for his wife, and he was not aware of what the sisters and Mama had planned. He later found out that Aunt Estella agreed to go with Mama because she would never have gone alone. Sam was being a gentleman and making sure she got into the house safely. Since Mama was not with her, she explained to Charlie that she was waiting for Sam to come back to the Tavern so they could talk together longer. Sam, being a gentleman, did not let Aunt Estella walk back by herself. Of course, everything was okay. after Uncle Charlie learned what happened.

There was too much excitement that night. It was hard for me to sleep. But sleep came. After everything was cleared up, Mr. Sam came to our apartment often, and he and Mama would visit in the back of our place, which was that small kitchen, or she would go over to his place. I did not see Mama much without Mr. Sam. She would come to the house and bring Mr. Sam, who would give me a Dave's hot dog with everything and fries, but it was always bone cold. James and I did not like him at all. About that time, my Aunt Thelma rented the store with the apartment upstairs Thelma moved, Mama married Mr. Sam. James and I did not give Mama our blessings, and James said he would not go downtown to witness the marriage. So, I said I did not want to go either. This denial did not stop Mama from getting married. She thought that she would have someone to be with her and benefit the family. I never heard her say that she loved him. Also, her sisters had wanted her to show Daddy that she could have a life with a mate, since Daddy divorced Mama, his first wife. He was now on his third wife.

So, on Saturday, December 18th, 1954. Mama married Samuel B Buckingham in Cook County, Chicago, IL. Our cousin Ann was there. She gave me the attached picture. I was never positive what race he was, but he looked more white than mixed. He had straight hair. Now, we moved to the second floor, James and I finally had our own rooms, I had the bedroom across from the kitchen James had the middle room and Mama had a small room right off the living room area. Later James married Minnie and they were living with his Mother and Father in-law. When they tied the knot both Parents met downtown to witness the wedding, Daddy signed for James and Mrs. Hackett signed for Minnie. During the beginning of the ceremony, I was told to stand up and when I did, I forgot the camera was in my lap and it hit the floor and if looks could kill I would have died from my brothers stare on his wedding day. They spent their first night at Robert's Motel it was the most famous African American owned motel on the South Side of Chicago.

First, they lived with Minnie's parents and then after; Mama and Sam and I moved upstairs James convinced her to come and live with us, After a bit Minnie came to Mama crying that James did not want to move and she wanted a place of her own. So, Mama got James to get his wife a place of their own. My Mama had a miscarriage during her marriage to Sam. Sam was always drinking and smoking one cigarette after another. When I did my chores, dusting and running the vacuum, I threw out the cigarette butts; and cleaned his large brown ash tray. He complained to Mama that I threw away his butts, he wanted to keep them for when he ran out of cigarettes, he would smoke them. Mama asked me not to do that anymore, and I complained about the smell. She told me to take the butts out of the ashtray, wash the ashtray and put the butts back. I did it once and never again.

There was some laughter. He once cooked dinner for everyone, so all the sisters came to our place. A rare occasion Sam had prepared greens. One of Mama's sisters asked Sam about the greens and asked him where he had washed them, and he told us that he washed them in the bathtub. They were all surprised and did not eat any more of the greens. We were shocked and upset. I did not know why she asked that question, because they said that they were good.

I remember Mother's Day with Mama and Sam all dressed up to go to church. I have a picture that Sam took of Mama and me on Mother's Day. But it was not easy to live with someone who drinks a lot, and he also would try to get into the bathroom when you were in there. Once I did not have the door lock properly, and he pushed the door open. Since the door was right by the toilet, I immediately slammed the door shut. I scream" I am in here." Now, when I came out, I told him the bathroom was available. Do you think he went to the bathroom? No, he did not. I lost any respect for him. Sam had visitors from Canada that came to visit and were only going to stay a few days. His Uncle was a tall and handsome man with class, not like his nephew; his Aunt was white. I am not sure if he was related maternal or paternal. They wanted to go downtown to Marshall Fields, so I was volunteered to take them downtown to the famous Marshall Field's Company Store. 111 North State Street, Chicago, IL. The store opened in 1914. It sat on 3 acres and had 13 floors. The Walnut Room served excellent food. It was the second largest department store in the world, a Chicago landmark and tourist attraction. We rode the trolley on Roosevelt Road and then transferred to the bus on State Street and rode to 111 State Street and got off in front of Marshall Field's Company Store. I remember it being extremely crowded that day, but we had a good time. I decided that Sam must be the black sheep in his family.

Samuel Buckingham and Ida Buckingham

Samuel B. Buckingham
in the Cook County, Illinois Marriage Index, 1930-1960

Name:	Samuel B. Buckingham
Marriage Date:	18 Dec 1954
Spouse:	Ida Stamp
Marriage Location:	Cook County, IL
Marriage license:	{B46A2BE8-C7A7-4E40-9CEA-5A79934B846B}
File Number:	2340183
Archive Collection Name:	Cook County Genealogy Records (Marriages)
Archive repository location:	Chicago, IL
Archive repository name:	Cook County Clerk

Source Information

Ancestry.com. Cook County, Illinois Marriage Index, 1930-1960 [database on-line]. Provo, UT, USA: Ancestry.com Operations Inc, 2008.

Original data: Cook County Clerk, comp. Cook County Clerk Genealogy Records. Cook County Clerk's Oice, Chicago, IL: Cook County Clerk, 2008.

Cook County, Illinois

Description

This database contains an index to over 1.2 million marriages from 1930-1960 for Cook County, Illinois. Information listed in the index includes: name, spouse name, marriage date, file number, and marriage license ID. Learn more...

© 2017, Ancestry.com

Cook /County Illinois Marriage Index Samuel B Buckingham and Ida Stamps

Dave's Hot Dog

Katie Price as teenager

Katie and Ida

THE SUIT

I was sitting in my room when my stepfather, Mr. Sam,. came home and called me to come into the living room. It was his payday, and he wanted me to go to the store where he and Mama had a layaway. He wanted me to finish paying for the items we had purchased and to bring them home. There was also a payment on his account. I was excited; my Easter suit was in the layaway. I was disappointed that when I selected it, Mama said I could not take the suit home that day, that they were putting it in layaway. I did not have long to wait; Easter was just around the corner. Of course, I was willing to do his bidding. The store was near Kedzie Avenue on Roosevelt Road. The day was pleasant, and spring was in the air. My soon to have Easter suit was made of a wool tweed, black with pink specks in it. With long sleeves and black- and- pink- trimmed buttons. The jacket had a notched collar, and I planned to wear my pink blouse that would be tied in a bow at the neckline. It had a straight skirt with a double kick pleat in the front. The back was straight.

I sang songs all the way to the store, the" Easter Parade" song: "The photographers will snap at you, and you will find that you are on your way to romance." I reached the store that had women's clothes, men's clothes, jewelry, and washing machines, the ones with the squeeze rollers. We had one; Sam bought it from here. It made my washing a lot better. When I hung the clothes on the clothesline, they were not dripping wet. I loved that machine. I gave the cashier the money, and they gave me a receipt and that suit. It was not often that I got

anything new, mostly I got hand-me-downs. So, this was a special purchase. The suit was on a hanger, and I watched the salesclerk cover it
with a plastic covering. I was 15 years old. I went directly home. When
I got upstairs, I gave Mr. Sam his receipt and the suit was hanging
behind me. He asked me if I got the suit. "Yes, Mr. Sam." I immediately
turned in the direction of my room, and he said "Well, let me see it." I
noticed that he was drinking whiskey and smoking one cigarette after
another and saving the butt for later. Then I turned around and held
it up for him to see. He said, "Hold up the plastic, I can't see it." So, I
held up the plastic cover to show that gorgeous pink and black suit. I
said, after encouragement from him, "Thank you, Mr. Sam."

I turned and went toward the back of the apartment, to my bedroom.
I reached into the closet to make room for my new treasure. Before I
could turn around, Mr. Sam was in my room. This had never happened
before. Mama told me that Sam was never to be in my room. We were
at home alone. He was barefoot, so I did not hear him coming behind
me. He asked me for a kiss on the lips and said, "Your Mama doesn't
understand me." "Move; Mr. Sam. He did not move. I kept my head
down, it looked like he wanted a reward for the suit. Then I saw an
escape route. I quickly moved around him and thanked God the back
door was open. I went out, the screen door slammed hard when I left.
As I passed my bedroom window, I glanced at Mr. Sam still standing in
my room. I ran down the stairs. What to do? My Aunt Estella was not
at home, so I had to wait for Mama to come home.

I visited my neighbor Rose and told her what happened. She asked
her parents if I could stay with her family until Mama came home.
They said yes and invited me to dinner. I always enjoyed visiting Rose.
Her Dad would be in his favorite chair smoking his pipe and reading
the paper. I had visited often, but this was the first time I was invited
for dinner. We washed our hands. Rose's Dad gave the grace and her
Mama placed food on my plate. It smelled wonderful. I took a bite out

of the chicken and my tooth hit something hard. I pulled it out of my mouth, and it was a shell of some kind. Rose laughed and said that it was a bullet. I asked why they would kill a chicken with a gun, and they laughed again, Rose said it was rabbit I was eating. I never ate rabbit before, but it did taste like chicken. I left it on my plate and ate the vegetables they gave me. Interacting with another family was exciting to me, I enjoyed this experience. I knew I had to be home when the streetlights came on, so I thanked them for dinner and for letting me stay with them. As I approached my house, I remembered that I had not finished my chores. Seeing the lights on, I knew Mama was home. I went through the front door, walked up the stairs, and noticed Mr. Sam was in his usual spot on the couch, watching tv, smoking, and drinking whiskey. I went straight to the kitchen. Mama was washing the dishes that I was supposed to wash and put up. She did not look up when I came into the kitchen. "Hi, Mama." She said, "Where were you?" I knew she would be angry with me because I was late coming home. I told her all that happened to me, about picking up the suit and that Mr. Sam had come in my room and asked me to kiss him on the lips, emphasizing "Mr. Sam said you don't understand him, what does that mean Mama?" So, Mama I, moved around him because he would not move out of the way, Mama. I went out of the back door and stayed with Rose and her family until I knew you were at home. I cannot stay here Mama with him by myself." She never said a word, not even asked a question. Then, finally, not even looking up at me, she said, "Katie go in your room and close the door and do not come out no matter what you hear." I watched her still doing the dishes and went into my room and closed the door as instructed.

After a few moments, Mr. Sam came into the kitchen. I cracked open the door. I wanted to see and hear what was happening. I also checked out the stove, and thought to myself, if he touches her, I am going to hit him with that skillet full of grease. Without any explanation Mama told Sam, "You must leave the apartment." "Leave?" he said,

"Why?" She said, "Because I do not want you anymore!" He started talking loudly, and he picked up a fork and bent it in half to threaten her. She did not budge. "You have to go, Sam!" He yelled about all the things that he had done for this family! Mama told him that whatever he had bought he could have it back. He went into the front of the apartment and made some phone calls. When Mama finally finished the dishes, she walked up to the living room. Shortly, I heard her call me. I opened the door and she told me to bring the sewing machine into the living room. "Oh, God, why is he taking my sewing machine?" I was crushed. It was a portable Kenmore sewing machine. I put it down in the dining room and as I returned to my room, Mr. Sam said I could keep it. I picked it up and put it back in my room. I had wanted a sewing machine for so long, I just could not bear being without it.

The next day was school. I left for school and when I returned home evidence of Mr. Sam ever having lived there was gone. The washing machine, the television, his clothes, and my sewing machine, all gone. He lied when he said I could have it. I was angry. But still glad he was gone. I thought I will never get another sewing machine. "My suit!" I ran to look in the closet for my Easter suit, it was there. Mama said he took their marriage license and other important papers. For some reason, whenever I came home, before opening the apartment door I thought of a roaring lion. After he left, I felt safe in my own home. The lion was gone. Nothing else was said to me about that night. I was much older when I realized what a big deal that was that she believed me. I did not know at the time that my Mama suffered advances from her Father and that all my Aunts had the same experiences. It is so unfair and cruel that young children are subject to mental and physical abuse due to somebody's sick sexual desire. Other girls have suffered from abuse who, when they shared their experience with their mother they were not believed. I thanked God that Mr. Sam was not able to take my innocence from me.

Photo Mama in Suit

UNCLE LYMON AND AUNT ELSIE STAMPS

U ncle Lymon was born on May 26th, 1918, He-was the youngest child of Edna and Eugene Stamps. He attended school in Pocahontas MS. Uncle Lymon married Elsie Ross November 23, 1933. To the union they bore twelve children. Lymon was drafted and joined the. Navy in 1944. After the Navy Lymon followed his sisters and moved his family to Chicago in 1949. Part of his family lived in our old basement, and he also rented a place next door to his sister. To accommodate his large family. My Uncle was an excellent mechanic. With American automobiles I had a Volkswagen Bug that he was not able to help me with repairs I thought that my Uncle had a substance use disorder. When I heard that he was in the hospital, Mama and I went to see him, but I was not allowed to visit. Because I had on a pair of shorts and the guard told me that I could not see my Uncle in that outfit. I waited for Mama as she visited him alone.

He was a good person, but he and I did not have a chance to bond. He died in the hospital on March the 28th of 1979. His marriage lasted until death parted them. His sister Estella Jones was in a nursing home, the same time Lymon was in the hospital. The family never told him that she had died. Even after he asked about her. February 26th, 1979, His sister passed, and Uncle Lymon passed March 28th, 1979. Lymon and Elsie had 46 years as a married couple. Aunt Elsie became a social worker for the City of Chicago under the leadership of Richard J, Daley and he often awarded her recognition of outstanding work in the community. She had a passion for helping the destitute, finding emergency housing within 24 hours of their crisis. Aunt Elsie was born July 23, 1917 died July 11th, 1999. Leaving to cherish her memory her 12 children four of her children preceded her in death. Their family included 65 Grandchildren 87 Great Grandchildren 12 Great Great Grandchildren 4 surrogate children. A sister and brother and her mother survived her.

Uncle Lymon

Lyman Stamps
in the 1940 United States Federal Census

View

🅰 View blank form

✎ Add alternate information

⚠ Report issue

Name:	Lyman Stamps
Age:	22
Estimated Birth Year:	abt 1918
Gender:	Male
Race:	Negro (Black)
Birthplace:	Mississippi
Marital Status:	Married
Relation to Head of House:	Head
Home in 1940:	Hinds, Mississippi
Map of Home in 1940:	View Map
Farm:	Yes
Inferred Residence in 1935:	Sp, Hinds, Mississippi
Residence in 1935:	Same Place
Resident on farm in 1935:	Yes
Sheet Number:	1B
Number of Household in Order of Visitation:	18
Occupation:	Farmer
House Owned or Rented:	Rented
Value of Home or Monthly Rental if Rented:	3
Attended School or College:	No
Highest Grade Completed:	Elementary school, 5th grade
Hours Worked Week Prior to Census:	45
Class of Worker:	Working on own account
Weeks Worked in 1939:	40
Income:	0
Income Other Sources:	No
Neighbors:	View others on page
Household Members:	**Name** A
	Lyman Stamps
	L C Stamps

Lyman Stamps 1940 U. S. Federal Census

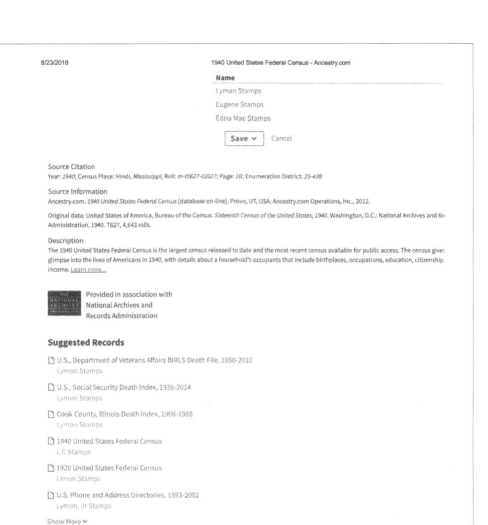

Name

Lyman Stamps

Eugene Stamps

Edna Mae Stamps

Save ⌄   Cancel

Source Citation
Year: *1940*; Census Place: *Hinds, Mississippi*; Roll: *m-t0627-02027*; Page: *1B*; Enumeration District: *25-43B*

Source Information
Ancestry.com. *1940 United States Federal Census* [database on-line]. Provo, UT, USA: Ancestry.com Operations, Inc., 2012.

Original data: United States of America, Bureau of the Census. *Sixteenth Census of the United States, 1940*. Washington, D.C.: National Archives and Records Administration, 1940. T627, 4,643 rolls.

Description
The 1940 United States Federal Census is the largest census released to date and the most recent census available for public access. The census gives glimpse into the lives of Americans in 1940, with details about a household's occupants that include birthplaces, occupations, education, citizenship, income. Learn more...

Provided in association with
National Archives and
Records Administration

Suggested Records

☐ U.S., Department of Veterans Affairs BIRLS Death File, 1850-2010
   Lymon Stamps

☐ U.S., Social Security Death Index, 1935-2014
   Lymon Stamps

☐ Cook County, Illinois Death Index, 1908-1988
   Lymon Stamps

☐ 1940 United States Federal Census
   L C Stamps

☐ 1920 United States Federal Census
   Limon Stamps

☐ U.S. Phone and Address Directories, 1993-2002
   Lymon, Jr Stamps

Show More ⌄

Write a comment.

Make a Connection

Find others who are researching Lyman Stamps in Public Member Trees

https://search.ancestry.com/cgi-bin/sse.dll?indiv=1&dbid=2442&h=119800776

Lyman Stamps 1940 U. S. Federal Census page 2

(L C Stamps) Elsie Ross Stamps Photo

SUNNY

My little cousin Sunny, he was such a beautiful baby. He was the first baby that I had a chance to hold and love. He was a beautiful boy, with a head full of unmanageable curly hair, so soft and easy to brush but you could not style it. He had light skin and a pair of beautiful brown eyes. I carried him everywhere he fitted perfectly on my left hip. I loved him. Sunny was his nickname. He often brought sunshine into my life when he would reach for me to pick him up. It was summer break, and I was told to babysit Sunny, at his house. They did not have anything but a radio, and they lived in an English basement apartment, which is partially below and partially above ground level It has its own entrance separate from the rest of the building. His mother would never come home at the time she said she would, and I absolutely hated to stay there. I wanted to go home and have a chance to play outside. Sunny would cry every time you bent to put him down, which was cute at first but later I began to hate it. If he were asleep on your shoulders, and you gently start to put him down, he would wake up and scream. Oh, what a monster we created.

While babysitting him I made a commitment that I was not going to have any children. Also I was to babysit without pay. Both of us did not see each other after he started school. I went on with my life and saw him less frequently. Mama and I had moved from the west side of Chicago to the south side. I remember he attended my wedding with his family. It was good to see him. Sometime after my wedding he as a teenager, called and invited my husband and me to come to a match at the pool in my old neighborhood. My brother and I both used that pool. I never learned to swim in the Fillmore pool. My brother was a lifeguard there. It was good to see my little cousin again who was now about 6 feet tall. Lamont and I went, and it was so much fun to cheer him on. He was happy to see us there. I don't think I had seen him since our wedding. I screamed "Go Sunny go!" Caught up in the excitement, after it was over, he raised that long arm of his and said hello to us. We left immediately after, didn't take time to talk with him.

The family mentioned that Sunny was having problems with gangs in the neighborhood. I do not know for sure if he belonged to a gang. We knew he was trying to get into the Army. He wanted to get away from what was going on around him. He applied and took some tests. He was 17 years old. He was waiting for a call from the recruiter. I received a call from his mother telling me that she had word that Sunny had died, and she was told to go to the Cook County Morgue to identify the body of her son. I jumped in the car and drove to her house; we drove to the morgue in silence.

When we arrived, we asked to identify Sunny, Eduardo Williams, and were told to take the elevator to the lower floor. We stepped into a small corridor which had windows all around and curtained. Slowly a curtain was raised and there was Sunny. They had him covered with a white sheet. They folded it down so we could see his face. He looked just like he was sleeping. His mother would not respond. I, his cousin said, "Yes that's Sunny." Someone in a white medical coat covered his face and closed the curtain. I pushed the button for the elevator, and the door opened immediately, as if it stayed there to wait for us. A sadness came over me, and when we stepped out of the elevator, his mother's grief took her to the floor. I stood over her for a moment and then I stooped down to talk to her and try to get her to stand up." Please stand up." Ann just didn't hear me and did not try to get up. Suddenly her husband showed up. He got down on the floor and whispered to her, consoling her. he put his arms around her. Now that he was there, I decided that I wanted to go home. This was too much. This boy I spent so many hours with, kissing his cheeks, carrying him around, feeding him and changing his diapers, was dead. I wished I had stayed connected with him and knew more about his life, and I could have helped him in some way. He was such a sweet and loving baby. Before the funeral we found out that Sunny and his friend were gambling, and Sunny owed money to this man and the man wanted the money and Sunny did not have it. The man embarrassed Sunny loud talking and bullying him. Sunny's friend steered him toward the exit of the hotel. This Hotel had pool tables in the lobby. The man was playing pool. Sunny and his friend were in the vestibule and Sunny decided to go back into the room and confront this man. His friend could not talk him out of it. Sunny went back in, and things got worse. The man, who they said was a boxer, hit Sunny one time and knocked him out cold. Then he did his worse. He took Sunny's life by putting a gun to his skull and pulling the trigger. Sunny died right on that floor. That very moment.

This was an older man and after killing Sunny, he left Chicago. The police took information, but they were unable to find him. There were many witnesses of the incident. The rumor was that he was in Mississippi. There was never any justice for Sunny's family. Another Chicago unsolved murder case. On Sunny's 18th birthday his party was a funeral. I was sitting in my Aunt's home waiting for her to finish dressing and the phone rang. the recruiter called to speak to Sunny. He told his grandmother that Sunny was accepted to join the Army. His grandmother told them they were too late. She said she was getting ready to go to Sunny's funeral. The recruiter offered his condolences. No one wants to bury their sons and daughters, life cut short! What a waste. It seems like the same things keep repeating.

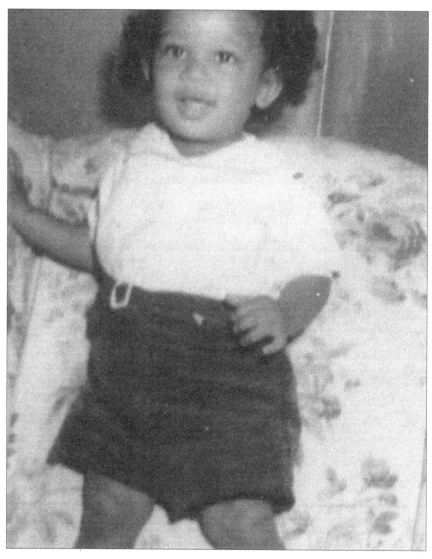

Sunny (Eduardo Williams)

ancestry

Annie Green
1930–2019
BIRTH 8 NOV 1930 • New Orleans LOUISIANA
DEATH 20 DEC 2019 • Cook County, Illinois, USA
maternal 1st cousin

New ①	Undecided ⓪	Ignored ①	Accepted ⓪

Family

◖◗ Ancestry Member Trees

Parents

From 1 other public Ancestry Member Trees

Estella STAMPS JONES
1915–

Name	Annie Green
Birth	8 Nov 1930
Death	20 Dec 2019

Spouse

Didn't find what you're looking for?

Discover more about Annie Green. Or you can view hints for others
in your tree.

Upgrade to All Access to search
≋ Fold3 and 𝐍 Newspapers.com

Search Ancestry

Annie Green Williams from Ancestry family tree

Annie M Green Williams

FANNIE MAY PRICE

M y Aunt Fannie is my Daddy's sister, {He was previously listed on a census report as Jean}, his name changed to James. Fannie's birthday April 30th, 1934. She was born in Copiah County Mississippi, her parents Will, and Mary L. Walford Price. I only met her once when she was in Chicago my Daddy stopped by our house. Daddy waited in the car she could only stay a few minutes, I opened the door and she walked in I called Mama to come to the door and Fannie May hugged Mama and remarked on how well she looked, and she wanted her to know that she was the only sister-in-law that she recognized. Mama was full of smiles. Mama introduced me to my Aunt and she hugged me, Then she said she was only in town for a short visit and she left. I found out that my Daddy was sending her a monthly assistance after their parents died. I also was told by Daddy's wife that she did not call his sister and tell her about her brother's death. I asked her why she did not tell Aunt Fannie and she said that she would have had to pay for her to come. Not a good reason to me. My Aunt Fannie had cataracts in both eyes. So as she aged, she went blind. That was one of the reasons Aunt Fannie was not here at Daddy's funeral. Aunt Fannie died August 31st,2020, She left 13 children 36 Grandchildren 46 Great Grandchildren and 4 Great Great Grandchildren I have enclosed a family Photo taken in Mississippi.

Fannie M Price and Family

Fannie M. Price
1940 Census Record

Gender: Female   Race: Negro

Age at Time of Census: 5   Estimated Birth Year: 1935

Birth Location: Mississippi Map

Enumeration District: 25-66

Residence: Beat 3, Hinds, MS Map

Language: English   Marital Status: Single

Relationship to Head: Daughter

Members in Household

Will Price	Mary Price	Charles Bartley
58 yrs, Male	49 yrs, Female	10 yrs, Male

Suggested Records for Fannie Price

Historic Newspapers - 18 mentions
Fannie Price located in MS

ARCHIVES

Search All Archives	Cemetery Listings	Newspapers
Vital Records	Census Records	Yearbooks
Military Records	Immigration & Passenger Lists	Obituaries
Living People Search		Surname Histories

Fannie M. Price 1940 Census Record

Fannie Mae Price

BIRTH 30 APRIL 1934 • Hinds, Mississippi, USA
DEATH 21 AUGUST 2020

Facts

Age 0 — **Birth**
30 April 1934 • Hinds, Mississippi, USA

Age 16 — **Birth of son Lawrence Crum Jr.** (1950–2014)
30 Apr 1950 • Utica, Hinds, Mississippi, USA

Age 64 — **Residence**
1998-2002 • Utica, Mississippi, USA

Age 79 — **Death of son Lawrence Crum Jr.** (1950–2014)
4 Feb 2014 • Lafayette, Allen, Indiana, USA

Age 86 — **Death**
21 August 2020

Burial
Utica, Hinds County, Mississippi, United States of America

Family

Parents

Spouse & Children

 Lawrence Crum
1921–

 Lawrence Crum Jr.
1950–2014

Sources

Ancestry Sources

 U.S. Phone and Address Directories, 1993-2002

U.S., Find A Grave Index, 1600s–Current

Fannie Mae Price Ancestry family tree person

Jean Price

1920 Census Record

Gender: Male   Race: Black   Age at Time of Census: 4

Estimated Birth Year: 1916

Birth Location: Mississippi Map

Residence: Copiah, MS Map   Father: William Price

Father's Birthplace: Mississippi   Mother: Lula Price

Mother's Birthplace: Mississippi   Marital Status: Single

Head of Household: William Price

Relationship to Head: Son

Members in Household

William Price
39 yrs, Father, Male

Lula Price
27 yrs, Mother, Female

Suggested Records for Jean Price

1930 Census - 1 record
Jean Price, born in MS, around 1916

1940 Census - 1 record
Jean Price, born in MS, around 1916

Historic Newspapers - 112 mentions
Jean Price located in MS

Jean Price 1920 Census Record

MY FIRST KISS

I met this guy from another neighborhood. He came around, and we had a chance to talk for a while, until I had to go into the house. He held the entry door open for me and opened the apartment door with my key. He handed me my key, and as I stepped in on the front landing, he stepped in too and went for it. My first kiss, from a boy a few years older than I. He kissed me long and hard, and I tried my best to get into it and kissed him back like I saw on the television. Then a problem started. He tried to lift my blouse. That was more than I wanted to do. I had so many talks about not getting pregnant before I was married and how my mother was going to throw me out in the streets, I did not know how far I could go without going all the way being forced or unable to resist. That hand of his started going down instead of up. I took my chance to break it up. He left, and I shut the door behind him. I joyfully went upstairs. I had my first kiss. Even if he took it farther then I wanted, he did stop! "I've been kissed. I've been kissed."

I did not hear from DeSoto again, but one day I was looking at the day's paper and was really surprised to see DeSoto's picture on the first page. The article said that he was captured after robbing the grocery store on the corner and shooting the elderly guy that owned it. I was mortified. The gentleman at the store was the only white owner that did not move away from the neighborhood when the homes were being sold due to white flight. He was an old, nice man. He always made me smile whenever I came into his store. I felt sad for him and his family. I was ashamed that I had let that criminal kiss me. I was happy that I would not have to see DeSoto again. The store at the corner of Homan and Grenshaw was the one we went to when you did not want to go across Roosevelt Road to the large chain grocery store, which was always crowded, and we had to cross a busy street. So, you had to walk all the way to the corner lights, on Homan Avenue walk down to the grocery store on Roosevelt Road, walk down Roosevelt Road to Jewels Grocery store. On the way back home, if quick and clever, they could run across Roosevelt Road if the traffic were sparse then run for your life across the street, walk through this opening that was a sort of alley that separated two buildings. Then cross another alley and enter the gate to our house. not really a safe way to travel, so I tried to get everything like small items from the nice guy at the corner grocery store. I was told not to go through that alley between those two buildings. It was full of Mexicans. Sometimes drunk men would be lying on the ground in that alley.

I really missed him, that sweet man that ran that store. I read his obituary. He had been at the store for many years. I kept the article about Desoto for many years just so I would not forget to make sure I knew as much as I could about the character, and morals of the person I get close to. According to the paper DeSoto was treated as an adult and he got 40 years in prison.

Well life moves on. There was another boy I liked. His sister, while just a teenager, had a child. He had joined the army to get away from the neighborhood. His sister was crazy in love with a guy from another school, who was the father of her baby. She became pregnant again, and the story was that if she got rid of this pregnancy, the guy would marry her. So, she and her girlfriend decided she would take laxatives and she also used a clothes hanger to try to get the baby out. She ended up in the hospital and what she did to herself shorten her life. She lost a lot of blood, and they could not save her, she died. She was not yet eighteen. I went to the funeral it was so sad. Her best friend complained that she could not breathe, so her friends took her out of the funeral home. She stuck her head out of a door and I left out of another door. I judged her and said to myself, "She is just faking. She should have tried to stop her friend." The girl that died had a brother to which I was attracted. He came home from the Army for the funeral. He came to my house to talk with me. He was so sad, I tried to comfort him. We just talked and then he left, and I never saw him again. I thought he would write to me. I wonder what he did with his life. He was very handsome, and he reminded me of my Uncle John. Since he joined the Army, he got away from the nonsense going on in our neighborhood.

SOME ENCHANTED EVENING

I was so excited it was time for the prom I will be leaving Marshall High our school song Marshall we are loyal to you, Marshall we will forever be true, pride for you will never oh, never die we are all for you Marshall High." Rah, Rah!, Not true! I was so glad to leave that place. 3250 Adams Chicago IL 60624. They said that the school was named after the fourth Chief Justice of the Supreme Court of the United States. He served from 1801until 1835.

When I enrolled, we were the first to integrate the school. I found out quickly that you could not walk home from school down Kedzie Avenue. Especially the boys of color. If you, did you should be prepared to fight, or be a good runner it would not be a fair fight. Girls, forget about it. Take the bus. That excitement when I first started was wonderful. Finding my way to different classes. Meeting new people. The seniors had a contest called Ms. Vogue, I was the captain of the girls' volleyball team, and I was a skillful player. I would select the girls that were not the popular girls, but they were talented players, our team won our game and then we played against the boys. At that time, you could hit the ball twice, set it up and hit it over the net or assist your teammate. We won against the tall basketball payers. My tall next-door neighbor was teased relentlessly after I spiked that ball right in front of him.

So, there were some fun times, but I was disappointed about the Ms. Vogue contest, I won against the popular girl her friends were working on the newspaper. They reported the winner correctly, but they put her picture next to the article. First real lesson on how we as women do not hold each other up. Years later I ran into her, we are going in different directions thru the underground walkway to catch a train. I asked her if she remembered me from Marshall High, she said yes, and then she pulled a zinger, she said she heard that I was dead. "Wow" I smiled and asked her" how did they say I died" she walked away. I laughed.

Now I want to tell you how much I wanted to go to the prom. I did not have a date, so I asked my brother to take me to the prom, he said no! I had nobody in mind from school that would ask me, so, I asked Uncle Charlie's nephew Willie Charles. He said maybe. Then he introduced me to his friend that agreed to take me to the prom, and he had a car. I told my friend at school that I had a cousin that may take her to the prom, and we could double date, since she wanted to go and did not have a date, so, Willie Charles agreed to take her. I was happy they were going since I did not know this young man that was my escort. When the prom was first advertised it was going to be at a country club in the northwest suburbs. Well, the country club did not accept persons of color to come to their club. The prom committee decided that the prom would be downtown Chicago at the Conrad Hilton on Michigan Avenue. I never thought they were segregating us, it was better and convenient it was a beautiful hotel, with the furniture and the chandlers and carpeting.

I found a dress in W magazine {a trade magazine} the dress that had a v neckline and sleeveless a fitted bodice with a full skirt, my Aunt Thelma, the modiste volunteered to design and make it for me. I found this beautiful fabric a Peau De Soie in my special color, a soft yellow. It fit perfectly; Daddy came over to see me off to the prom. Excitement was in the air. After we parked my date helped me out of the car and I held his arm to enter the Hinton. We walked to the elevator and walked down the hall to the room where the party. was to be held. When we got there and opened the door, I saw stacks of chairs it was a holding place or extra chairs, after we walked around this tiny room a young man came in with a record player and started setting it up. This crushed all my dreams of what a prom should be. I felt hoodwinked. Willie and my date talked among themselves and decided to leave.

So, we left, and I suggested we go to this club on Randolph. We entered and was sited, and my friend and I was told we could only order soft drinks. Then musicians started getting ready to start a show and there were no other couples there we had the place all to ourselves, and the greatest musician ever, started playing a set it was Duke Ellington and his orchestra. The photographer took a picture of our table and when it was returned in a folder, I asked Duke Ellington for his auto-graph. We had a wonderful time, we went home and a prom that I thought would be awful turned out to be an enchanted evening, with a stranger. I never heard from him again.

Now my prom was not the only one I got a chance to attend I went to the prom with Thomas His sisters asked me to go to the prom with him after I said yes. He called me and invited me to his prom. I was very happy. Out of his three sisters neither one of them wanted to be his date. I always wanted a strapless dress, so I got one I had white net fingerless gloves and I also wore a Tiara that sparkled like diamonds. Thomas bought me a wrist corsage we danced at the prom and had a great time. I met Thomas's friend Jerry Butler he was friendly his date was friendly but quiet. I thought she was a little old for him. I was invited out the next day to go to the movies. Jerry said his trade was to be a Chief. He also said he sang with a group He was more inter-esting than my date. While at the show Thomas got a little fresh and I let him know that I did not know want him to put his hand up my skirt. Hey Stop! I slapped his hand away.

Jerry Butler came to my rescue he grabbed Thomas by his coat collar and told him to stop. Thomas had a lot to drink before he picked me up for the movies Jerry my hero Thomas had octopus' arms and hands. I did not agree to be molested. Jerry made quite a few hits in his day; I enjoyed his records. Marshall High won State Champions in Basketball the year I graduated. Now that was exciting. About 5 years later when I was working at the west side office.

A man came into the office and asked the desk clerk for me when I walked closer to him, I remember he was one of the famous basketball players that this white girl who used to talk to me after class and finally said what she wanted from me, was for me to introduce her to this player, I thought to myself, why do white people think all black people know each other. We did not talk. So, to get rid of her, he passed by, and I called him to me and told him that Pat wanted to meet him, and I did the proper introduction, Pat this is J and J this is Pat and I walked away. No more conversation with her after class. Well, this time J had a brown bag, he asked me, "Do you want to buy a wig?" And partially pulled out a wig. Shocked, my mind was wondering what happen with his basketball career? "No thanks." I returned to my desk. He left.

YESTERDAY

I was sound asleep in the bedroom when loud music woke me. The voice of Ray Charles was singing a new favorite of my husband's, the words loomed loudly:

Yesterday all my troubles seemed so far away
Now it looks as though they're here to stay
Oh I believe in yesterday

Suddenly
I'm not half the man I used to be
There's a shadow hanging over me
Oh yesterday came suddenly

Why she had to go
I don't know she wouldn't say
I said something wrong
Now I long for yesterday

Yesterday
Love was such an easy game to play,
now I need a place to hide away.
Oh I believe in yesterday

Why she had to go
I don't know she wouldn't say
I said something wrong
Now I long for yesterday.

By the time I got out of bed and walked into the living room, I found my husband asleep on the couch. I took the needle off the 45 record and turned the player off. Before I could return to bed, he had turned the music back on. I turned around and advised him that the music was too loud and he was disturbing the neighbors. It was one or two in the morning. He did not seem to care. Many times, I have thought about that night and realized that there was a message in it for me. He would play only that record over and over.

One day before noon Lamont stated he was taking our son out to lunch. He changed Erik's shirt, and out the door they left. They were walking to the small mall west of the apartment and just across the street. I was straightening up the bedroom and I started sewing on my Singer machine. About an hour later, my son came back. His father used his key, opened the door, and closed the door behind our son, then left. My child entered the bedroom and came close to me. He looked into my eyes, looking serious for a little child. He said. "Mommy," "Yes, son," "Daddy said that he does not love you anymore! But he loves me." I replied, "Okay, son, I'm glad he loves you." When I think about that night when he first played that song over and over, my thoughts were, "What a coward." That was not something my son should be telling me. Then my mind goes to the conversation I had with my Mama, while I was sharing my marriage woes with her. She made this statement. "Katie, you have made your bed, now you have to lie in it."

I met Lamont when a friend invited me to her house. Her brother and his friend were going to be there. I met James Arthur Wallace. Our conversations were interesting and fun. I learned that my friend's brother was working toward being a professional football player. James and Tom were in school together. My friend Mary's mother made a lovely dinner. I enjoyed the visit. We all talked a while; it was getting late, and Mary warned me that the bus did not run all night. I left to catch the bus and go home. Mary called me the next day and asked me if it would be okay to give James my phone number, Of course, I replied. We did not talk long. We agreed to talk again some other time. I was excited that he wanted to be in contact with me. He did not call right away, but eventually, he started calling. He said he did not have a phone, and he lived with his cousin and her family. He asked me to call him Lamont, since my father and brother had the same name as he. I thought it was a promising idea.

I was working for the Christmas Seal Organization, a not-for-profit organization that supported Tuberculosis research, during the summer since I was 16, after graduation I started working there, as a clerk full time. making 0.90 an hour. Aunt Thelma and Uncle John decided they were going to let their lease expire on the store/apartment and they wanted to move back to their building. They suggested that we, Mama, and I, were welcome to return to live in the basement. If there was any way for me not to move back in that basement, I was not moving back into that basement! I took charge. Since, Mr. Sam was a veteran, even if he did not live with us anymore, I thought we could qualify for a place in the projects. A public housing constructed to house poor tenants. Mama was making poverty wages. I was right, we got an apartment, and all this happened before Aunt Thelma was ready to move back into her building. Uncle John was not available to help us move. I asked my brother to help us. Mama was excited she was paying her sister $25 a week and the projects only wanted $30.00 a month. I was walking on air,

With God, I made a good decision for both of us. I know she really did not want to leave her sister, especially after, they helped us tremendously. The apartment was on the 5th floor, facing west, lots of windows, nice size kitchen, electric stove, small refrigerator, one open closet and a closet in the bedroom with folding doors. It had a large bathroom with a shower in the tub. I was happy about the shower. I could only take baths at our old place; there the bathroom did not have shower plumbing. Here I could take showers every day. At Thelma's they always complained about the water bill. Mama insisted I could only take a wash up daily, until Friday or one weekend day

While I lived in the projects, I was attending college. after a few classes I did not have the money to stay in school. Daddy and Lois would not give me enough money to buy books. She also suggested that I re apply for a job at IRS. I had previously failed the typing test. This time I passed the test and the interview, and I secured a job at Internal Revenue Service as a clerk typist. The first time Lamont came to visit me was after I moved from 33 hundred West to 14 hundred East. Whenever he came over Mama would have prepared a meal and told him that I prepared the meal and then when he wasn't looking, she would wink at me. At the time I was not at all interested in cooking, We dated, talked a lot on the telephone, and went to movies I had to pay my own way. I thought that I loved him and thought that he loved me. We had fun together. I found out that the rental office wanted a copy of my tax return and W-2's the rent went up twice before I decided to move. When our new lease said to pay $100 dollars a month, I started looking for another place. I was surprised that my income affected our rent since I did not sign the lease, but the rent was determined by household income. I shared my problem looking for suggestions of where to live with the ladies at the office who suggested I check out Lake Meadows. I looked up the apartment complex and called to inquire about a one-bedroom apartment. The rental office set up an appointment. Mama and I got dressed up and took public transportation to the interview. It was located where both of us could easily get to the bus and El to get to our jobs. We had a good interview, and the interviewer was sure we could have the apartment after they verified my employment.

A few days later, I received a call at work and was told that we could rent the apartment since I was not 21 both Mama and I signed the lease. We got the apartment for 110.00 a month. I was thrilled. The apartment windows faced north, not a lot of sunshine but a wall of light with a view of green grass and a few small trees. The windows had white blinds and we are on the first floor. Coin operated washers and dryers were in the basement. We moved to 3420 South Cottage Grove Avenue, Chicago from Ida B Wells housing projects. where the housing authority begin to neglect the buildings. Lamont and I were an on and off relationship. He did not have a phone and I did not know how who to contact him, so I concentrated on my new job and the procedures,. Hopeful that I will establish a relationship with someone else. When I said the relationship was on and off, he would be around and then suddenly you did not hear from him. Lamont told me about his hitch in the service. He was honorably discharged from the Army. He was currently working as a lab technician. At Presbyterian St. Luke's Hospital. He served in Germany, and he had a chance to help a patient have her baby. It was all good, someone older than I and who had life experiences that impressed me. He attended college and was very personable, with an easy smile and not bad looking at all. He had a peak in his hair line, and he kept his hair short. He was not as tall as my dream man, but he was taller than me. I liked the fact that he was 6 years older than I. He came from a large family He had a half dozen sisters. He was the oldest. Wow, I thought he would know how to treat a lady, growing up with all that estrogen. He was raised by his mother and grandmother. he also mentioned that he did not know who his father was. His mother would not tell him his father's name or whereabouts. He and his siblings had different last names. I thought that was more normal than not. My Mama liked him, and my brother said he was a likable guy. but he said Lamont talked funny. Lamont told me he was helping his sister who was in college, and most of his money was sent home to his mother to help her. We started talking about getting married.

Ain't it funny I do not remember the one knee proposal if it happened! you would think I would remember that. He signed a contract for a set of rings, they were not what I wanted, when he brought them to me. He noticed that I really did not like them and of course they were too small. He said the jewelry store salesman said he could come in and exchange them. for size or style. We rode the bus to the outer edges of downtown Chicago where I would never shop. We returned the ring, and I must have looked at every set in the store at least three times. I did not see anything that I wanted. so, we told him that we did not want to get a ring there. The salesman was upset he mentioned he had a contract, Lamont said that you have the ring, and the contract is no longer any good. If you try to enforce that contract, we will sue you. We yelled back at him and left the store. I told the salesman that I would report him to the Better Business Bureau, for unfair practices. The jeweler kept the deposit. I went to the jewelry store across the street from Marshall Field's I went with a friend from work and looked at their rings and found the ring I wanted.

Lamont and I went together and purchased that ring the salesman measured my finger and Lamont told the salesman what he wanted engraved in it. He kept it a secret from me. We agreed on the wedding date, Saturday, September 07,1963 I selected and ordered the invitations. I gave him 50 and I had 50. The wedding will be located at Friendship Baptist Church. the church I was attending when I lived in the area. The minister wanted us to attend marriage counseling my fiancé refused. When I asked him about his invitations, he asked me to send one to his mother Charlie Lee. He quickly wrote down the address and left, so I sent her the invitation, addressed to Mr. and Mrs. Charlie Lee and family. Of course, it was addressed wrong but, he took the blame for the error. His mother's name was Charlie, and Mr. lee was deceased. I selected the 7th of September 1963 I would be finished with my period, but in the stress of the wedding planning I started my period on my wedding day morning. I called my groom and advised him. I previously ordered a photographer, who showed up at my apartment.

Oh, my dress was made by a friend at work. When I told her I was getting married she offered to make my dress free of charge. I selected the pattern and purchased the fabric and took all of this to her house and she took my measurements. She did a beautiful job with the Peau de soie and lace. it was a perfect fit. Daddy came over to pick me up and my 2 friends to take us to the church. his wife Lois brought a friend and went in another car. I had to wait in the apartment next door to the church. Lamont and the males in the wedding were late, I was beginning to think that he was leaving me at the altar. Finally, he arrived, and the wedding started. I was walking down this short aisle feeling scared. the photographer took a lot of time taking pictures that most of the guest left before we could gather and talk to our guest. The gifts were all opened, and I never saw a list of who gave me a gift.

My new husband's cousin prepared a party for us after the wedding on the northwest side. Lamont had borrowed a car and he put what he could in the trunk, but we filled up the trunk then he threw the rest in the back seat of the car and refused to take them to our apartment. He said he had to attend his reception. He parked the car in front of a tavern. His cousin lived above the tavern. While we were waiting for the food to be served, I got up to go to the restroom and I heard someone say" catch her." When I came around, I was lying on top of a bed they used smelling salts to arouse me. Lamont handed me some water I sat up and went searching for a washroom and someone was in there, the hostess said my mother-in-law was in there who then opened the door and asked me to join them we were all women and I said I wanted to be by myself then she wanted to know why, I said I wanted to change my sanitary napkin. She then asked me if Lamont knew I was on my period. I said of course, it started this morning and I called him this morning. She thought that her son married me because I was pregnant, but we married with more than just me in this marriage. There were others in our marriage, and it was doomed to fail.

Most of the men in the wedding was in one car and they were speeding when they were pulled over by the police the group thought that my groom was trying to get arrested. My flowers were a beautiful yellow which made the white dress stand out. the gifts were opened before we were finished with taking the pictures. Lamont has borrowed a friend's car, so we packed our gifts in it and we drove to his cousin's house I tried to get my new husband to take them to our apartment. He said it would take too long to get back to our reception.. The people at the church opened the presents but did not keep any record of what was in the boxes, I had no way to send a thank you Lamont got us a ride to our apartment with his friend Frank and Lamont was very drunk he put Lamont across the bed, and I was unable to move him so I could get under the covers. Frank was too drunk to drive back to his house so, he spent the night. Exhausted I fell asleep until the next day. then his friend Frank was at our house every evening to have dinner with us. Lyrics for Yesterday composers Lennon and McCartney.

Katie Price and James Wallace (Lamont)

James Price and Katie Price

Wallace, Price, Stamps and Lee Families

STOP LAMONT

We were invited to go with a co-worker from Lamont's job at the hospital on their boat to watch the fireworks from the lake. I was feeling o.k. Once on the boat I mentioned to Lamont that I was hungry, and the host offered me a sandwich and a drink that they had in a cooler. Which I enjoyed as we moved out from the shore. I ate the sandwich and drank a soda. I was concerned about being seasick, but all of a sudden, I was extremely sick, and I had to go to the bathroom. They directed me to the toilet with a sheet covering and I know I must have filled it up. I thought I would never stop Finally I was able to get off of the toilet at that point they was taking us back to the shore. But you had to climb a ladder and the exit it was not the way I got on that boat. Up the ladder I went Lamont was in the front and when I got to the last rim he started walking away. I did not receive any help from him He stayed as far away from me it did not look like he was even with me, We went home.

What had happen previously to me was his aggressiveness, one evening when he forced sex on me and would not let me use my birth control. I used a foam called Emko. He aggressively held me down. I was fighting him I hit him on the head and pounded him with my fists. He did not hit me, but he would not get off of me. I was screening so loud that his sister Shirley who was staying with us, came to our bedroom door knocked and asked if everything was all right. He said yes, I said nothing. Now I was not happy about us having sex without birth control, I was not happy in my marriage, and we had not planned to have a family. We had no savings. He was not a good husband, I thought, my premonition was that this marriage was not going to last. So, I did not want any children, to raise by myself. We were in our 13th month before pregnancy. I was happy whenever I was away from the apartment. I missed my period I made an appointment to see the doctor, and also Lamont asked me for urine sample, so I gave him the sample.

The doctor told me I had food poisoning. He advised me to come back in two weeks before the two weeks were up Lamont met me at work as I got out of the elevator, he was in the lobby waiting for me, something we used to do when we first got married.as we walked toward the train station he said he had to tell me that I was going to have a baby. No reaction from me. I was still pissed because of the way he treated me. I finally said isn't that what I should be telling you! He said the sample came back today. I said I was waiting for the doctor's advice. When I got the doctor's diagnosis, he gave me a due date of April 27th, 1965. The doctor eventually told me I was having a boy. After that I threw up a sip of water. I was so hungry, but my stomach kept growing I checked myself out in the mirror and cried crocodile tears, my 114-pound figure has gone away to stay. To stop me from throwing up everything I put in my mouth, the doctor prescribed the most wonderful white pill in the world. I could eat and drink and not throw up anymore. I gain over 50 lbs. I was praying not to have to go to church Easter Sunday, I managed to wish him out and I went into labor and was in the hospital the Saturday before Easter which was April 17th, 1965. They did not show me my baby until he was checked out by an infant heart specialist. She did not find anything wrong with his heart. They finally brought me my baby. I named him Erik Lamar Wallace. Proud Mommy and Daddy. When I came home, my sister-in-law was there and Lamont's friend Frank. Lamont took the baby from me and gave it to his sister on top of the book she was reading he laid him in her lap and walked away she made a face that was not welcoming so I picked up my baby from her, Lamont decided to take the baby from me and grabbed me by the elbow and took me inside the bedroom and grabbed my other elbow and started shaking me. I immediately was trapped against the furniture, and I started crying, I was afraid he was going to hurt me. We were leaning against the bookcase that held the phone and it rang, and he answered it and it was my Mama. He gave me the phone and I was still crying I answered the phone and Mama asked me what was wrong, and I was telling her Lamont grabbed me and was shaking me, she told me to give him the phone, I handed him the phone he had not moved from intimidating me. She talked with him for a few minutes, and he did not say anything to whatever she was saying, he handed me back the phone and immediately left the apartment and stayed away for three days.

I WAS WITH CHILD

After Lamont told me that he did not want to get married when he did, I no longer felt anything for him. I was just walking in a daze, thinking of my mistake in marrying him. After my groom told me that he did not want to be married, I no longer wanted a family with him. I had previously talked with my doctor, and he gave me a prescription for birth control pills which I happily took. but they would not stay down. up they would come. I took them with water, then with milk, then with food. my body rejected all of them I had problems eating. The pregnancy did not allow me to even drink a small amount of water--up it would come. I could not have anything to eat without it coming up too. I also was extremely constipated. I did not feel well every morning. I was only weighing 114 pounds. My doctor convinced me to stop working, stay home, relax, and take those wonderful white pills that kept me from throwing up. I loved them. I did not want to stop working, and the doctor said, "Do you want to keep this baby?" I said yes. He said, "Do not go back to work."

After I could eat and be regular, I lost weight. Then I had to go to the dentist. The baby was taking everything from me. I went to a dental college. I was about 7 months pregnant, and a student dentist was drilling on my tooth. My mouth was filled with cotton, and he was pressing against my belly, and I could not tell him that he was hurting me. But suddenly, my baby kicked him hard, and this guy turned beet red. It was so funny. After that the dentist made sure he did not press against my belly again. I wonder if he remembered his black pregnant patient. When discussing his dental patients. I shared it often because it was funny to me. He did an excellent job and he showed me his grade. He was so happy that he got an A for that tooth.

Lamont was still playing games, not coming home, saying he was taking a night college course, but had no books, no grades to show. I had to deal with his sister, who always showed her dislike for me. She had the nerve to tell me that I was not a good wife to her brother. I should have told her that he was no prize. But I just threatened her. I wanted her out of my house. I would find her in my bedroom in my things, without my permission. I decided to get her out.. After his sister moved out, I was happy staying at home with my beautiful red-dish-brown baby. I changed his clothes often; I had purchased nothing but the best for him. I did not ignore a sale for him. He was breast fed, so there were not a lot of bottles to take care of. He wore cloth diapers, so there was a lot of washing to do. Somebody gave us diaper service for a while. Paper diapers were only for taking our son out for the day.

I SURVIVED

Lamont and I had a discussion. It was a come to Jesus' moment. I told him if he was not at home when the baby came that I was not going to put his name on the birth certificate. I was just so tired of all the lies. Here I had to leave work and just sit at home with nothing to do. He was acting like a single man. One evening I was watching an old black and white cowboy picture, "The Rifle Man," and I started having pains. It was the 9th month at the last doctor visit the doctor said" I will see you next week". I did not want to hear see you next week; I wanted baby out now.

Finally, pain, baby daddy was home, and he did not believe me that the baby was coming but off to the hospital we went. He had some-body's car; we drove to the hospital. I had a ride in a wheelchair. Then the wait. Sometime early in the next morning the water broke. I thought I had urinated on myself. I apologized to the nurse, and she explained that it was my water breaking. I had forgotten about the water breaking thing. My doctor finally showed up and I asked for some medication. I actually said It hurts, it hurts! because it hurt more than this girl could stand. I was in and out of drowsiness. It seems like everybody in the hospital had to take a look in between my legs, and I could not do anything to stop this parade of people in green clothing. The pain was strong, and I heard the doctor who was standing out-side of my room talking with someone. I asked my husband would he call him for me, and he said no. I should have divorced him right then.

I screamed" Dr. Steptoe, Dr. Steptoe!," He told this person he was talking to that he had to go, because he was being paged by his patient. They laughed. It was not funny. When he came in the room of course, he looked at me and told the nurse to give me something for the pain, I remember being wheeled into another room. Another dressed in green person told me to push. I did and I felt the pain in my head. He told me "good" do it again. I faked a grunt and he tried to insult me. I did not care I was not pushing. It made the pain excruciating. I wanted the pain to just take me away. Then I do not remember if I was conscious. My next memory is of a woman washing my lower body, She was putting a pad on me. She asked me what did I have? I told her I did not know. She walked away and that guy in green came over to me and told me he saw where the doctor cut me and he had never seen that before. He said the doctor cut me sideways, not long way and he was really excited about it.

When the nurse rolled me to my room, I saw my husband sitting there and I asked him what I had? He told me that he was waiting for the doctor. He then said we had a boy, I asked him to have the nurse bring him in. Lamont said that They will not bring the baby in until the heart specialist examines him. I nodded off again. Finally a woman with a medicine bag came into the room and said that she did not see anything wrong with our son's heart. She said that he was healthy, and the nurse would be bringing him in the room soon. I was elated, there wasn't anything to worry about this child. God was going to bless me with a healthy child. When the nurse brought him in, and handed him to me, I thought he was the most beautiful baby I had ever seen. The nurse left the room, and I untied the blanket she had told me not to untie. I wanted to count his fingers and toes. He was perfect. But there was a small scar on his head. The nurse came back and saw I had untied him, and she had an attitude. Which I did not care about. He weighed 7 lbs. and fourteen ounces.

I survived. Lamont wanted to name our son Anthony and call him Tony and I wanted to name him Erik, I gave him a middle name I knew his father liked this name, I named him Erik Lamar Wallace. They told me that I could not take him home when the nurse and I were discussing when I could check out, I asked her why I had to leave him here? She said that the doctor had not circumcised him, which was on his file. They waited for the heart doctor and my doctor was not available to do the operation. I totally freaked out. I stated, "I am not leaving here without my baby." So, somebody called the doctor at home, and he gave consent for another physician to circumcise him. I heard my child scream when the doctor cut him because they were in the room across from me when they did it. The next day both of us went home They gave me a lot of baby gifts that I was glad to have, and they gave me suggestions on breast feeding Erik.

Mercy hospital was building a new hospital on the same land and the small one was to be torn down Since I had a semi-private room, and my windows faced the construction. The nurses would come into my room often and would stare out of the window checking the construction progress of their new hospital. When I visited the nursery I saw a lot of babies but did not know where the other mothers were, I walked in a different direction from my room and saw a great big room full of women in bed. I asked the nurse why was I separated from them and she said it was because I had asked for a semi-private room. All the time I was there all the babies in the nursery were white. Except Erik. My son Erik Lamar Wallace born April 17th, 1965. in Chicago Cook County Illinois.

Erik in 1965

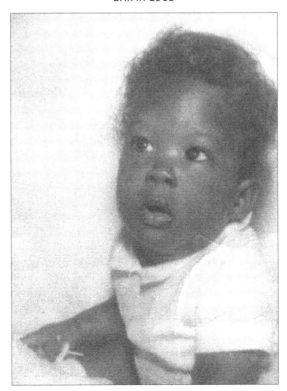

Erik

Erik and Katie

RAYFIELD CHANEY

After Erik was born. Lamont was very anxious to meet his Dad. His Grandmother told him his Daddy's name. His mother refused to tell him or his Daddy that he existed. His Grandmother told him that his Daddy lived in Chicago and his name was Rayfield Chaney. Lamont brought home a Chicago telephone book and started his search. There were a few Chaney's in the books he brought. After making a list of them, he started calling the numbers while at home in the evenings. Just that simple, he called and spoke to a Rayfield Chaney and asked him if he knew a Charlie Wallace from West Memphis, AR. Rayfield remembered her, and they chatted awhile. Then Lamont told him that he was his son. He stated that he found out recently that Rayfield was his Dad. They promised to talk again and Rayfield invited his son to come over to meet him and his family. We went to meet his Dad and his wife and stepdaughter. They lived further south, not too far from us. So, our son got to meet his Grandad on his father's side of the family.

Rayfield did not have any other children and he adored his newly discovered 2-year-old grandson. It was easier to relate with his grandchild then his adult son. I heard that he was run out of town by Charlie's brothers and at that time he was a musician. I do not remember what instrument he played. Lamont got to tell his Dad all about his life. Our son was very happy to know Rayfield. He always gave him something. Once he gave us a book of brand-new bills you could tear out one at a time. I wish we could have saved them. It was a unique gift. Erik had new one-dollar bills. He gave me a book of new five-dollar bills. Lamont got the same. His wife was very friendly. Her name was Lovie Chaney. She was open to this new family, including my Mama. When we invited them over to our house, they brought Lovie's mother with them. She was very friendly also.

I am including one of the pictures I have of one of our times together. I have received a call telling me that Rayfield had died at a job. He was installing something for a customer and had a heart attack in their back yard. I had to tell Lamont the news. He was so disappointed that he had lost his Dad so soon after meeting him. The funeral we drove to their house to ride in the funeral car, and Lovie refused to sit in the front with the driver. I was asked to sit there, and I did not want to sit there either. Our son sat in the back with his father. Lovie was very emotional. When we showed Erik his grandfather in the coffin, he said loudly," Grandad,get up from there and let's go home." Lovie burst into more tears and became very emotional again after settling down. I whispered in Erik's ear," Be quiet, Erik. He cannot go with us. Lamont tried to be with her during the funeral, but her daughter never accepted us. I asked her about bringing Lovie to my home and she told me that she does not drive far.I was glad Lamont found his Dad and had a chance to get to know him and bond with him. That was a blessing for both. I know he had always wanted to know him and appreciated the welcome he received from him. Everybody has a Dad, but everyone doesn't have a chance to get to know them. Being the oldest of twelve, he was the only one that carried his mother's birth name, Dads are an important place in a child's life. I wonder if Lamont ever had a conversation with his mother to find out why she never told him the story of how they met and why she felt that he did not need to know who his Dad was. Rayfield died 11/11/1969 in Cook County, Chicago IL. We miss him.

Rayfield Chaney

Children (1)
Erik Lamar   B: 1965
Wallace

 James Arthur Wallace

B: 16 May 1936 in Arkansas County,
Arkansas, USA
D: 06/21/2020 in West Memphis, Crittenden,
Arkansas, USA

Parents
👤 Rayfield Chaney
-1969

👤 Charlie Lee

👤 Katie M Wallace B: 5 Aug 1940 in Utica, Hinds,
Mississippi, USA

Rayfield Chaney
in the Cook County, Illinois Death Index, 1908-1988

Saved to: Chaney, Rayfield in tree "Katie Price Family Tree"   Remove
           Wallace, James Arthur in tree "Katie Price Family Tree"   Remove

No Image
Text-only collection

🛒 Purchase original record
from Cook County

✏ Add or update information

⚠ Report a problem

Name:	Rayfield Chaney
Death Date:	11 Nov 1969
Death Location:	Cook County, IL
File Number:	633222
Archive collection name:	Cook County Genealogy Records (Deaths)
Archive repository location:	Chicago, IL
Archive repository name:	Cook County Clerk

Save ∨   Cancel

Cook County, Il Death Index Rayfield Chaney

Rayfield and Lovie's family

THE SLEEP OVER

I was unhappy. Daddy was gone and I wanted to live with him and not Mama. She and I were not getting along. I was about 6 when I told her that, and she called Daddy and told him that I wanted to live with him and come and get me. I was excited to go live with Daddy, and I never thought that he had a new wife. Her name was Sonora. Mama pulled out this plaid suitcase and started packing my stuff. I was elated and passing her my things. My Aunt Estella and Aunt Thelma were upset that Mama was letting me go, and they were in the other room crying. For what are they crying? All they did was holler at me. I am so glad to be leaving. Daddy came and picked me up, carried my suitcase, and down the two flights of stairs we went. Bye, Mama

By the time we got to Daddy's apartment, it was bedtime, and I was given the couch to sleep on. Was I in for a shock. "I don't get to sleep with you, Daddy? I must sleep out here by myself." He made up the couch, gave me a pillow, and I said my prayer. "God bless Mama, God bless Daddy, God bless James." I lay down, it was dark. There were no lights anywhere, so I felt so alone. This had not gone well. I started crying, just whimpering at first. then I just let it all out. I cried loudly and was miserable. Daddy came out of his bedroom and asked me why I was crying, and I stammered" I'm scared of sleeping out here by myself. I want to be in the room with you." He said that I could not sleep in the room with him and Sonora.

I really cried after hearing that, so I said" I want to go home." He told me to get my coat on. We went back to my house in my pj's. Aunt Thelma and Aunt Estella were happy to see me. Mama said she knew I would be back, but she thought I would stay longer than I did. One thing I can say about Daddy. He always brought me my favorite soup. Campbell's Chicken Noodle Soup, and a Twinkie, my absolute favorites.

Today at my advanced age, many years later I still love to have some Campbell's Chicken Noodle soup, especially if I feel sick. My son and I had a similar experience. He was away visiting his Dad and he was about the same age, well, he was more like seven years old. His Dad wanted him to visit with him in Milwaukee for the weekend, so I let him go, not really wanting to for I was afraid for him, why? because I was always afraid that his Dad would take him and not bring him back. In several arguments he always said that he wanted to take Erik from me and that he could be a better parent than I was. Now Erik was there. He called me on the phone late one night and said that he was upset and wanted to come home. I asked him what the matter was. He said he went to sleep in his Daddy's bed, and he woke up and found that he was lying on the couch. I asked him, "Where is your Dad?" He said Dad was in the bed and that Alonzo was in the bed with him. I told him to get back on the couch and go to sleep It is late, and you should be sleeping. Everything will be alright in the morning, Erik. He asked me why his Dad moved him, and I said" I do not know."

After that I became very suspicious of my ex-husband. I began to question all the things that had happened in our marriage. I never said anything to his Dad about moving Erik or his questions to me since Erik didn't ask any more questions. In my heart I knew there would be more questions coming out about his Dad's relationships. With men.

I PROMISE

We all may make promises to one another that we sometimes are unable to keep. The marriage promise, to love, honor, and obey till death do us part. Oh, some of us took the obey part out of our marriage vows. Some say to love and to cherish. To love in sickness and health, rich or poor. Some of us stood in front of all our family and friends in beautiful attire with a reception following. Some stood in front of a Judge or a Justice of the Peace. Or in front of a Captain of a ship. A Minister or an Officiate. Even strangers have signed our certificate as witnesses of the marriage. Every state has different laws for securing documents to perform marriages. The most important part of a marriage is not the actual service, or the reception. The most critical issues are the vows that you pledge to each other. The promises that you made before God to your bride or groom and your family and friends who came as witnesses to share in your happiness.

I have compiled some of my family's history in marriage I want to share with you, my memories. I am not talking about any right or wrong or judgment on my part. I am just sharing what I know and sometimes I will share some conversation memories with my family, but some information I have not shared because I believe any more than this, they should share their own stories. Everyone has a story to share.

Abar married Sarah and she gave birth to a girl. Her name is Edna. I am willing to suggest that they may have Jumped the Broom, an African custom. Eugene Stamps and Edna Caston were found on the New York

County Marriages Index. Their third child Katherine Stamps was listed as their sibling. I was surprised to learn that they married in New York.

I have included some of the marriages in my family census record with some pictures. The examples that the parents could show to their children are examples as they grow. They could see how to make marriage arrangements work. Young boys often want to marry their mother and the young girls seem to want to marry their dads.

Our family had to convince my granddaughter that she could not marry her brother. She told several people that she was going to marry him. I explained that she will find someone else that she will want to marry when she is older, especially someone to whom she is not related.

Grandfather Eugene lived in Utica in Hines County Mississippi on Tallahalah Road. All their children were born in that area. Grandma Edna died after she had their youngest child,, Lymon. Eugene was a widower with ten children he needed a wife. Who else was going to take care of the children? I do not have a date when Grandma Edna died or the date that Grandpa Eugene married Flora Bell. We never even discussed a divorce after Flora left Eugene unless she stood at the front of the house and cried out," I divorce thee I divorce thee" three times.

Katie M. Stamps met Edward Bush. Edward was working as a porter. I am not sure how they met, but the marriage license shows that they lived at different addresses in New York both were experiencing their first marriage. When they married, Edward was thirty-two and Katie was twenty-three. They were joined in matrimony December 1st, 1927. She was my eponym. I visited her in Mississippi in her senior years. She came to Chicago for my wedding in 1963 and on other occasions. When her son was visiting in Chicago while he was in the Army, she visited the family then. Edward's life or death was never mentioned around me. Their marriage license states that he was born in Newport News Virginia.in 1895. His father was Sylas Bush and his mother's maiden name was Ann Jones. Edward B. Bush died February 22nd, 1954. He was about 59 years old. Katie M Bush died March 30,1986 at age 82

Ida Stamps and James Price, we were unable to determine when they married but we know that Mama did not marry before their pregnancy with my brother. He was born in 1934. We believe that Mama married Daddy while they both were 18 years old. I think that they did not have a good example of what a marriage should be like. From the stories I heard it was not all good. But there were good moments and some agreeing to disagree.

Will Price had a son with a different mother. Lula Price had a child with a different father. Fannie Mae Price. But they stayed together, there were some good moments. They stayed in the same household their entire married life. The next person I remembered that married and made those promises to love honor and obey was my cousin my Aunt Estella's daughter Annie M. Green Williams Johnson. She was older than my brother and her husband was a barber, J.C. Williams. I never knew what the J.C. stood for. He was handsome. I remember he took me out to the ballpark to watch a game with the Chicago Cubs. I was so happy. I got popcorn, hot dog, and a soda. I ate it all and then I announced that I wanted to go home. He said politely that the game had not started yet. I am sure there were some good moments in the game, but I had a full stomach, so I had a sunny nap. They had a beautiful son together we called him Sunny. Ann and J.C. terminated their marriage. Promises were not kept. They both moved on to another union.

Estella and Charlie Jones married July 28th,1949, and stayed together until Aunt Estella died. February 28th, 1979. I shared earlier some of the drama of their marriage. Back to Daddy and Mama. Daddy was incarcerated most of their marriage. They were too young to get married. Both were the same age. To me they did not have the maturity yet to be married. I shared earlier that Daddy's parent Grandma Lula was not ready for her son to marry anyone. Daddy wanted to simultaneously retain his cake and eat it too. The grass always seemed greener on the other side of the fence.

First divorce. Daddy made another promise to Sonora Wells and married her Wednesday 28th, January 1948. I do not know what happened in this marriage I know that Daddy had his first car a Plymouth, not sure of the year, he would pick us up and take us out and I was car sick for many of those drives, so I had to stick my head out of the window. We did not know the circumstances of Sonora Price's marriage but six years later, Daddy told me that he was married to someone else. I found in the Marriage Index Saturday August 14th, 1954, Daddy married Lois Ellis both marriages were in Cook County, Illinois. This marriage lasted until he died at age 94,.May 14th, 2010.

Daddy never changed, he still had girlfriends in his life. Faithfulness was not his strong point. He owned a Shell Gas Station and he loved playing golf. Mama was encouraged to date, and she met Mr. Sam and they married. Saturday the 18th of December 1954. I was fourteen the result of that marriage is in another chapter. No divorce was requested. After Sam moved out, Mama sent a Christmas Card to his Aunt and Uncle. His Aunt responded with the news that Sam had died from cirrhosis of the liver He had been dead for several days before he was discovered. I found out that he never divorced his other wife. The divorce information was requested by Social Security Administration when I tried to apply for benefits for Mama. They asked me to prove he was divorced. Of course, I could not. She asked me to get her maiden name back on her documents and I failed to get it done for her before she died.

Thelma Love married John Wesley Love no marriage data available Thelma was born June 19th, 1912. She died June 18th, 2003. They were special in our lives and their love was comforting. Also giving us shelter. They shared their lives with Mama, James and me and made privacy sacrifices. He became aggressive to Thelma in his older age. Verbal and physical. They stayed together until he died. James married just after graduation from high school. Minnie Barnes and Jeffery James Price married in Cook County Illinois I was there for this one. Thursday, January 20th,1955. I was excited I had a sister-in-law. They were happy and from this marriage they had two sweet girls. They were not able to keep their vows, so they divorced. James told us that he wanted a divorce.

We met Erma Jean Jones he told us after he married again. This marriage produce three boys. This marriage did not work for them, and James left that marriage and married again this time Mama and I was included in the wedding. Mama and I were not happy to see James leave his family, a wife and three boys. Nor his first marriage with Minnie and 2 girls. But this is what James wanted so we helped with the ceremony. He married Jeannie Evancho. I arranged for our minister to perform the wedding on June 1st, 1984. Mama made a wedding breakfast for them her new daughter in law had one female guest. Jeannie never thanked us for the work we did for her wedding or her breakfast. We did not become a Ruth and Naomi family. Of course, she did not tell her mother or brother since she knew they would not approve of her marrying a black man even in 1984. They stayed together until my brother died, Monday, January 3rd, 2022. Born on Thursday, October 25th, 1934.

Annie Green
1930–2019

BIRTH 8 NOV 1930 • New Orleans LOUISIANA
DEATH 20 DEC 2019 • Cook County, Illinois, USA

maternal 1st cousin

New ①	Undecided ⓪	Ignored ①	Accepted ⓪

Family

∙⟨ Ancestry Member Trees

From 1 other public Ancestry Member Trees

Parents

Name	Annie Green
Birth	8 Nov 1930
Death	20 Dec 2019

Estella STAMPS JONES
1915–

Spouse

Didn't find what you're looking for?

Discover more about Annie Green. Or you can view hints for others
in your tree.

Upgrade to All Access to search
≋ Fold3 and 𝐍 Newspapers.com

Search Ancestry

Annie Green

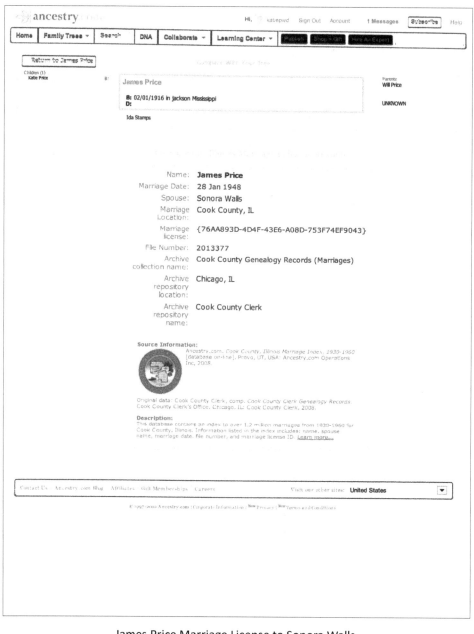

Return to James Price

Compare With Your Tree

Children (1)
Katie Price

B:

James Price

B: 02/01/1916 in Jackson Mississippi
D:

Parents
Will Price

UNKNOWN

Ida Stamps

Name:	**James Price**
Marriage Date:	28 Jan 1948
Spouse:	Sonora Walls
Marriage Location:	Cook County, IL
Marriage license:	{76AA893D-4D4F-43E6-A08D-753F74EF9043}
File Number:	2013377
Archive collection name:	Cook County Genealogy Records (Marriages)
Archive repository location:	Chicago, IL
Archive repository name:	Cook County Clerk

Source Information:

Ancestry.com. Cook County, Illinois Marriage Index, 1930-1960 [database on-line]. Provo, UT, USA: Ancestry.com Operations Inc, 2008.

Original data: Cook County Clerk, comp. Cook County Clerk Genealogy Records. Cook County Clerk's Office. Chicago, IL: Cook County Clerk, 2008.

Description:
This database contains an index to over 1.2 million marriages from 1930-1960 for Cook County, Illinois. Information listed in the index includes: name, spouse name, marriage date, file number, and marriage license ID. Learn more...

James Price Marriage License to Sonora Walls

ancestry

Cook County, Illinois Marriage Index, 1930-1960

Name:	**James Price**
Marriage Date:	14 Aug 1954
Spouse:	Lois Ellis
Marriage Location:	Cook County, IL
Marriage license:	{7B3EFF00-A355-4D64-8DE9-1CEAE80B84D1}
File Number:	2325281
Archive collection name:	Cook County Genealogy Records (Marriages)
Archive repository location:	Chicago, IL
Archive repository name:	Cook County Clerk

Source Information:

Ancestry.com. *Cook County, Illinois Marriage Index, 1930-1960* [database on-line]. Provo, UT, USA: Ancestry.com Operations Inc., 2008.

Original data: Cook County Clerk, comp. *Cook County Clerk Genealogy Records*. Cook County Clerk's Office, Chicago, IL: Cook County Clerk, 2008.

Description:
This database contains an index to over 1.2 million marriages from 1930-1960 for Cook County, Illinois. Information listed in the index includes: name, spouse name, marriage date, file number, and marriage license ID.

© 2012, The Generations Network, Inc.

James Price Marriage License to Lois Ellis

Lois Ellis Price and James Price

SAY WHAT

One cold Sunday in January 1986, my son and I were over my Daddy's house. His wife prepared Sunday dinner and left the house, which gave us a chance to talk she said she was going shopping. We enjoyed the day with Dad. The food was good and we told stories and laughed a lot. After we completed the meal, she returned and we carried the dishes to the kitchen. We thanked her for the meal, saying goodbye, and gave hugs to her and Daddy. Daddy put on his coat and stated he was going to walk us to our car, which was parked in the lot across the alley. You could view the lot from their kitchen window. After we got into the car and closed the door, Daddy asked me to roll the window down. I did, and that is when he told us with the biggest smile on his face that he had a son born on the 13th. He was clearly very happy. He put his arms in front of him and made a power gesture pumping them downward, several times. I was shocked, and I did that "Say What?" Facial expression. I noticed his wife watching us out of the window.

Daddy was 70 years old and next month he would be another year older. Here I am 46 years old with a baby brother a couple of days old. Too many secrets that I had to keep for daddy. I did not know what to say but he was proud, and he said he was there when the child was born. When we drove away, I watched him in the rear-view mirror still full of glee. My son and I laughed about it. I found it very uncomfortable. Now this has happened to me before when I was in grammar school. I was at piano lessons. When I left the teacher, it was dark outside so I was walking swiftly to get home. It was just a block and half away from my house so I always walked home by myself. There was a car that blew its horn. I looked at it and walked a little faster. But then the light came on inside the car, the window opened, and I heard my Daddy call my name. "Katie, it's me, Daddy." Wow, Daddy. I was glad to see him.

I let myself in the back seat of the car and there was a woman in the front passenger seat. Dad introduced me to the woman and then he told me that the little baby she was holding in her arms was my little brother. "Say What?" Aww, he is so cute. Daddy drove me the one and half blocks home and I said goodbye and he, his passenger, and the baby drove away. Of course, I told Mama. She didn't say much about it. I do not remember the name of the child, or his mother's name. Many years later, I asked him what happened to the child that you told me was my brother. Dad said" the child was with his mother who moved back to Mississippi." Then quietly he said the child was not his. Oh, "Say What" this new child was his. (what's going on daddy, you want a new chance with a son?) Well, I thought this child will go away like the last one. So, I was surprised to open the door to my house in Maywood and find my Daddy there with a woman and a baby. I usually know when he is coming over but this was not an ordinary visit. I welcomed them in. He introduced me to the woman and I offered them a seat and a soda. Each said no thank you. Then Daddy took the child from the woman and gave him to me to hold. I was uncomfortable again. I said Daddy he does not look like you! He told me the child's name and told me again that he was my brother. The mother's facial expression showed me she did not appreciate my remark, but I did not care. I was in my house; I was not trying to be rude. But I just did not approve of this situation. I took a few pictures of Dad holding the baby and me holding the baby, we visited for a while, my mother was home, but she did not come anywhere near us. I am sure she heard everything that was said.

Daddy gave me a picture of the 4 of them, Daddy, the woman, his son, and her daughter. Posed like a family. I never understood why he gave me that picture, but he said do not advertise this picture. He knew that I kept family pictures on my dining room wall. So, the picture ended up in my lingerie dresser hidden under some clothes. I run across it occasionally. I look at it and cover it up again. One day I received a call from Daddy and he asked me if I would go to the zoo with him. Of course I said yes. I asked my Grandson's Parents if I could take my Grandson to the Zoo with me. They said yes and brought him over. When Daddy arrived, his son sitting quietly in the back of the car. He was tossing a football back and forth in his hands. My Grandson joined him in the back seat. My Daddy and I exchanged pleasantries. Soon my Grandson asked the boy "Who are you?" The boy did not say anything and I did not say anything and Daddy did not say anything. So, we went to the Brookfield Zoo. When my Grandson and I were alone, he asked me "Grandma Katie, who is that boy?" I told him that I did not know; maybe he was just a friend of my Daddy's. Secrets had to be kept.

I told my Daddy that Mama was in the hospital, she had some heart issues. He usually came to the hospital to visit her. She would always say after his visit that she would feel so much better, and we would share a laugh. But this time he brought his son with him. Mother did not have that glow after he left this time. She was upset that he brought the boy to the hospital to see her. She told me to tell him if he brought him around again, she would call his wife and tell her all about the child. So, the next time I talked to Daddy, I told him what she said. He did not come around without invitation anymore. We had several dinners and we celebrated his birthday at our home. His wife came over our house in Maywood, once. She came over once in my new place in Bolingbrook, il all other times Daddy came alone or with my brother. And a couple times his girlfriends. The wedding breakfast for my brother and his new wife, I planned Pancake Wedding cake breakfast. His polish wife and her friend attended the celebration. James reimbursed me for the cake. Dad came with his girlfriend. She seemed nice. We enjoyed the time we spent and the woman was very comfortable with us, laughing and talking. Mama made the pancakes and pretty much stayed in the kitchen. But was happy to cook the food and enjoy this celebration. This was my brother's third marriage and we were not at number 2's wedding but we were at number 1. This time instead of just telling us that he got married the other day, we knew about his intentions of marrying again. He wanted us to be a part of it. We always thought that he married too soon after a divorce. But we wanted him to be happy and we wanted to support his decision. I confess that I did not want him to leave another wife. He had 3 boys by his second wife and 2 girls by his first wife. His youngest daughter showed up at his third wedding just as it was over, which was sad, but it was good to see that she wanted a relationship with him.

Well, back to Daddy I received a call from him telling me that my Grandfather Will Price died who lived in Mississippi. I wanted to come with him to the funeral and he basically said no. I insisted and he still refused me giving me excuses about my taking off work. But I almost wanted to go by myself just to see the people on my father's side of the family that remained in Mississippi. I do not remember my Grandfather at all, nor my Grandmother on my father's side of the family. Those that remained in Mississippi and did not migrate north were sort of left behind and did not come up to visit although they were visited occasionally. After the funeral, my brother told me that Daddy took his girlfriend. His wife never wanted to go south with him. I was really pissed about it because I was not allowed to go to my own Grandfather's funeral.

Well, one day I received a call from Daddy that he wanted me to help my young brother, who needed transportation to an interview at Lowe's in Bolingbrook. He wanted me to provide transportation for him, so I said o.k. Well, when I saw him, he did look more like Daddy. He was a tall kid and looked very fashionable. When he arrived, he asked if he could use my computer. I allowed him to use it. He appeared to be full of energy with dreams of making a living. He would be working in his neighborhood but the training was in the Bolingbrook store. There was no public transportation to get there. After taking him to the store and receiving a call after his interview to pick him up I returned him to the train station to get home. There were no other requests from him. I wonder how was it to be a child of a man who had several adult children that were not involved with him. My brother James and I were close. I did not even know this brother. After I moved from Bolingbrook, Il; and came to live as a Chicago girl living in an Alabama world. My Daddy was not doing well. He said he had told his wife about the child. He said that she was so upset that she stopped talking to him for about two weeks but she still cooked his food, then one day she just started back talking to him. He asked my brother to send me a letter that his son had written to him. Daddy never told me that his child was in prison, but he wanted me to write to him and if I had money would I send him something. So, I received the letter and started writing to him. He was in prison for a "white collar crime" he was living in California and going to school taking fashion design. But he started doing something with his credit card and his phone that resulted in a huge bill. He was caught and sentenced to 5 years in federal prison, (like father, like son), he told me the same day he was arrested, he found out that he was HIV positive.

Also, there were letters sent to him at our father's address. He told me that all this was due to his identity being stolen. The amount that he was charged with was in the 6 figures. "Say What" this situation happened when I was in Maywood, my Mama needed to stop working so I applied for social security benefits. Marriage to Samuel Buckingham and also marriage to Daddy should help get her some benefits. I had found that her employers did not pay household taxes for her services, which was just insane to me. Dad refused to give me his social security number and they could not find his records. Also, I found out that Mama could not get benefits from Sam either because there was no evidence that Sam had divorced his other wife.

So now we know why he took that marriage license. Well, I received a call from the mother of my young brother asking me to have my Dad call her. I asked her why she did not call him herself; I did not want to be a go between for them. She finally told me that her son's social security check had been decreased and she wanted to know why. I found out that Dad's wife had applied for benefits, which decreased their check. I thought what she got she should be glad. We got $5.00 a week. Sometimes I got 2 cans of chicken noodle soup and I pack twinkles. They were my favorites but not what I thought was real child support. My brother had moved out and was living on his own with his wife. If I were sick and called Daddy, he would bring me some soup and twinkles. I was upset that Daddy would give him benefits. When my brother and I got such little chance to have what we needed. Everything like food and care came from my Mama who worked so hard and long hours for us to have just the basics. Since he was elderly, it took care of his child support. I asked my young brother for a copy of his birth certificate and he sent it to me. Sure enough I found Daddy's signature of the birth certificate. Daddy was not cheap in his later years; he owned a gas station and he helped me a lot. It did not matter what he gave me, I loved him whatever he did. I kept his secrets from his wife, I felt dirty because of it. I know she knew I knew what Daddy did; I thought that she felt I betrayed her. Not that we were friends,or anything, but I was always respectful to her; you know that woman helping woman thing. But I did not want her and Daddy to break up. They had been together for many years.

Daddy once asked me what I thought of him marrying this younger woman with whom he was involved. I told him from my heart. "Daddy, when you run out of money, she will leave you, but if you stay with L, she will take care of you for the rest of your life." I do not know if my answer helped him with his decision. But when he said" would you like (her name) for a mother?" I kind of died inside. "Say What?" He stayed with his wife and moved on to older women. In 2010 Daddy died from stage four Kidney failure at the age of 94. Born February 1st, 1914–May 14th, 2010. I miss him he would call me just to say I love you.

Daddy in his gas station

Daddy's gas station

Daddy and Rose

James and Minnie Price

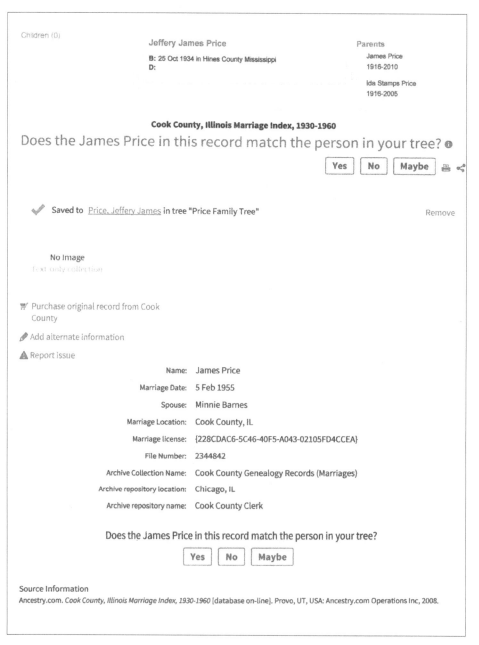

Children (0)

Jeffery James Price

B: 25 Oct 1934 in Hines County Mississippi
D:

Parents

James Price
1916-2010

Ida Stamps Price
1916-2005

Cook County, Illinois Marriage Index, 1930-1960

Does the James Price in this record match the person in your tree? ⓘ

[Yes]   [No]   [Maybe]   🖶 ⤴

✔ Saved to Price, Jeffery James in tree "Price Family Tree"   Remove

No Image
Text only collection

🛒 Purchase original record from Cook
County

✎ Add alternate information

⚠ Report issue

Name:	James Price
Marriage Date:	5 Feb 1955
Spouse:	Minnie Barnes
Marriage Location:	Cook County, IL
Marriage license:	{228CDAC6-5C46-40F5-A043-02105FD4CCEA}
File Number:	2344842
Archive Collection Name:	Cook County Genealogy Records (Marriages)
Archive repository location:	Chicago, IL
Archive repository name:	Cook County Clerk

Does the James Price in this record match the person in your tree?

[Yes]   [No]   [Maybe]

Source Information
Ancestry.com. *Cook County, Illinois Marriage Index, 1930-1960* [database on-line]. Provo, UT, USA: Ancestry.com Operations Inc, 2008.

Jeffery James Price and Minnie Barnes Marriage record

James and Erma Price after wedding

James and Jeannie Price Erik and Daddy

Jeannie and James Price

Alycea and her Dad Erik Wallace

Renee and Erik's wedding day with family

Renee and Erik Reception

OLIVIA NANETTE
COSEY WALLACE

Olivia was born December 18th, 1966. Her parents are George & Olive Cosey. She was born and raised in Chicago. She pursued her Accounting Degree at Hampton and Roosevelt University. Erik and Olivia met in their high school years. He was her escort to her prom.

September 28, 2002, Erik, and Olivia married. From their union they have two children, Tyler George Wallace, and Taylor Olivia Wallace they have guardianship of her niece Gene Nicole Woodland. Also, she shared her life as stepmother to Alycea, Erik, and Devon Wallace.

On Friday April 16th, 2004, she made her transition to God. He had often spoke excitingly of their friendship and they spent a lot of time together. Even flying out to visit her in college. `Many years later he told me that they wanted to marry Olivia and Erik invited me to come to where he worked and have lunch with Olivia and her mother. "Sure," I said, What time? He was working at a fast-food restaurant, so we met Olivia and her mother there. We sat in a booth and Olivia introduced me to her mother. My Mama knew Olivia better than I. I only remembered Olivia as someone that my son talked about or tied up the phone talking with her. I never had the impression that her mother agreed with her getting married. But they were with child. A wedding date was set. September 28, 2002. They chose to raise their child together. I hoped for a girl. Mama and I planned to have an engagement luncheon for Olivia a joining of families It was fun to plan. I selected the menu, and Mama prepared the meal for five people.

Olivia's mother and Erik, they were who we prepared for. Our guests were an hour late and their whole family walked in the door. I was shocked because I only invited Olivia and her mother one of my uninvited guests complained that the food was cold. My Mama quickly responded that it was warm at the time that we expected them. It did not go well. Mama and I did not eat in order to have enough to serve everyone, but we took several group pictures to remember being together.

Before their wedding, I invited Olivia to a show that I often attended. It was Dance Africa Dance, a powerful dance group from Africa that was amazing to watch, all of us had a great time Olivia drove to my house in Bolingbrook and my cousin Ann met us in front of Chicago Theatre located on North State Street in the Loop area. It was built in 1921. It was added to the National Register of Historic Places on June 06, 1979. I drove us from Bolingbrook and Ann's son picked her up after it was over to avoid the group from taking her home to the west side of Chicago. Since Olivia parked in front of the house, she still had to drive quite a distance to get home after we reached my house. We were living in the suburbs, and they lived in Chicago I had a great time with Olivia we had a chance to bond.

They asked Robert to officiate the wedding, he agreed, and his daughter Cindy joined us at her new brother's wedding. It was outside in Olivia's mother's backyard, and it was a sunny day. We all had fun. My niece Mitzi sang at their wedding. My Daddy quickly visited to congratulate the couple. Olivia had given me a blue kufi that I wore to the wedding. I walked in their house and one of them was making fun of me. I also heard Olivia say to them that she purchased that kufi as a gift for me, and she thought it was special that I chose to wear it to her wedding.

Erik and Olivia seem happy and compatible I thought finally my son has found his soul mate.

She left us to care for her two children Tyler George Wallace, born 03/01/2003, and Taylor Olivia Wallace, born 04/15/2004. I loved the fact that Olivia called me Mom. She has truly been missed.

Chicago theatre

Erik and Olivia's wedding

Wallace children

All 5 of Erik's children

Erik and Jessica marriage

Erik and Jessica's Wallace's Family

KATIE MET ROBERT

It was Sunday. I was recently elected as Chair of the Elders, First Christian Church in Maywood Il. So, part of my responsibilities were to schedule monthly who would be assisting on serving the communion each Sunday. I needed 4 Elders. One prays for bread, then the other prays for the wine. The other two uncover the elements and serve the Deacons. Each Deacon would have a tray of Bread representing the body of Christ and a tray of the Wine representing the blood of Christ. Sometimes the assigned Elder would forget that it was their Sunday to serve, or they would not show up for Church and did not get their own substitute. I was standing in the lobby waiting for the Elders to come into the Church.

Each Sunday I had to be sure that the positions for Communion were covered. There was a gentleman at church early. I had never met him. He approached the minister's office while two young girls were hanging on his arms, One on the right arm and the other one on the left. He had a lot of patience with them. Our minister walked into the lobby and invited me to meet this new person. I was standing near the office in front of the library where the Elders meet to gather and pray before church starts. His name was Robert Davis. Our minister said that our Church was going to sponsor his ordination. He introduced me as the Chair of the Elders and we shook hands. Since I was Chair it would be my assignment to work with him and help plan his ordination, with the other Elders. The when, how, and what. I had no idea of either. We did not get a chance to discuss anything that Sunday, but we made plans to get together and start discussing his ordination. His girls had returned home to Nebraska. He extended an invitation to me to have lunch with him After Church we decided to meet at Baker's Square, a place well known for their pies, located in Melrose Park, a suburb north of Chicago near to where our church was in Maywood.

We drove in separate cars, talked, and ordered our meal, and exchanged information, you know, getting to know each other. He had six girls 4 lived in Nebraska and 2 lived here in Illinois. He worked as the Executive Director of Love Christian Clearing House in Westmont Il,. His mother was deceased. He was born in Butte Montana 10/18/1951. He has lived in California, Nebraska, and Westmont, IL. He studied at Judson College, Elgin IL, and Northern Baptist Theological Seminary in Lombard, IL.I shared that I have a son and I am currently working for I.R.S.as a Tax Collector in Schaumburg, IL. I said my Mama and Daddy were alive but not together He and I were both divorced. After sharing our horror stories, we moved on to the conversation of planning an ordination, discussing dates on the Church's calendar, people who would install him and those that would be speaking in his behalf. The music and who from other Disciple of Christ congregations and family and friends to be invited. Of course, what to serve for lunch? The weather was good for soup and a sandwich. As Chair of the Elders, it required me to sign his certificate of ordination. We became friends and spent a lot of time together and on the phone. He invited me to go with him and his children, who were in town and planning to spend the entire day at the Brookfield Zoo. All 4 of them would be with him. But I had a date that day with my Daddy we were celebrating my birthday at the Medial Times in Schaumburg, Il. I enjoyed myself not sure if Daddy did.

Robert and I spent a lot of time together and became close. We started talking about marriage although we had not known each other for a year. We told his oldest daughter that we were going to get married and she tried to talk us into living together first for a while before marriage. We both said we did not want to just live together; it was against our principles. So, we set the date for May 17th,1997. We had looked at some rings, and one evening he gave me this little shopping bag with a white teddy bear in it and the ring, He got on one knee and asked me if I would marry him. I said, "Yes!" His second to the oldest got married in April of that year and all the sisters came in town for the wedding. In May we married, and his oldest daughter was his best female, and my son was my man of honor. We even included jumping the broom in the ceremony. His second oldest read a poem from the Prophet Kahlil Gibran His first wife attended and her husband volunteered to take pictures at the wedding. Erik and Devon were our candle lighters and they looked so handsome in their tuxedos. My son and his wife purchased the wedding cake as a gift to us. It was beautiful and delicious. I have not mentioned all the people, from friends and others from Church, which helped us plan an excellent program and delicious food. I prepared wings and Mr. Jackson prepared ribs. His wife Shirley also took some videos with a new camera that she was learning how to use. There was a couple that sang at the wedding, a song that they wrote for us. Also the song "In this very Room", was sung by an Opera singer, as a gift, and it was beautifully done. There was a Chinese friend that played the piano for us as a gift. What a blessing they all were. There was a neighborhood paper reporter that attended who authored an article in her paper of her experience in attending our wedding. I made my dress. Robert rented a tuxedo. The most exciting thing was that we walked down the aisle together, holding hands. Oh, I don't want to forget that we attended 3-pre marriage classes. One was a remarried class and all of them was extremely helpful. Since I had accomplished a lot on my own and I needed assurance that what was mine would stay mine if this marriage fell apart, I had a female lawyer write up a pre marriage agreement, which he signed. I had bought a house for Mama, Erik, and me to live in and I was really close to paying it off. Getting to know his children was special and I can understand what my father's wife went through. My child and his oldest child were waiting in the hall for the wedding to start, betting on the length of our marriage. They will not admit who had the highest number of days, months, or years. We are currently on 25 years together. We married May 17, 1997.

Katie Wallace and Robert Davis

✥|ancestry·

Robert Keith Davis
1951–

BIRTH 18 OCT 1951 • Montana, USA
DEATH Living

| New ① | Undecided ⓪ | Ignored ⓪ | Accepted ⓪ | **Family** |

📄 **Montana, U.S., Birth Records, 1897-1988** Source info
Birth, Marriage & Death

Parents
Spouse

Quick compare

In this record	In your tree
Name	
Robert Reith Davis	Robert Keith Davis
Birth	
18 Oct 1951 **Butte, Silver Bow, Montana, USA**	18 Oct 1951 Montana, USA
Father	
Elmer Burt Davis	-
Mother	
Bonnie Marie Davis	-

Didn't find what you're looking for?

Discover more about Robert Keith Davis. Or you can view hints for others in your tree.

Upgrade to All Access to search
≋ Fold3 and 𝐍 Newspapers.com

⁂ Search Ancestry

Robert Keith Davis Ancestry person

Katie and Robert's wedding picture

WEDNESDAY
Surprising 60s

*Bride and groom share hope in their own future,
in the country's ability to deal with racial issues*

Wedding shares happiness and opens our eyes

Robert and Katie got married in May. Just an ordinary middle-aged couple walking down the aisle to start a new life together. Or two extraordinary people taking a leap of faith. You decide.

They met last summer when he started attending the church where she was chairman of the elders. He had met the church's pastor at a Disciples Justice Action Network conference in Chicago.

"We got to know each other and found out we were both single," Robert said. "We were just friends at first, went out to plays and different things." They decided to get married three months before the wedding, which they thought was plenty of time for planning. "Little did we know," Robert said.

His oldest daughter stood up with Robert; Katie's son served as her attendant. Katie's grandsons lit the candles, friends sang; family members and friends participated in the readings. The beaming couple walked down the aisle hand in hand. Nothing that different from countless other weddings, you say. But wait.

I've attended many weddings in my life. Yet this was a new experience for me, and probably for many of the guests. What was unusual? The bride was black; the groom was white. She had been alone for 26 years; he, for

four. And they were both ready to try again.

When I asked Robert about the issue of race, he said, "Of course, we had to deal with that." But deal they have, at least so far. They went to a seminar at Christ Church of Oak Brook for remarrying couples. They counseled with their pastor, who explored interracial marriage. "We found out that we work very well together on issues," Robert said. "What we have to deal with is other persons' racism. And maybe we won't be accepted at churches. It may be an issue if I seek a church (as a pastor)."

Robert, who has long been interested in issues of race and justice, has graduated from seminary and is looking toward ordination in the future. It surprised me, but perhaps it shouldn't, that he is concerned about being accepted in a church. Even in Katie's multicultural church where they were married, the issue of racism from both sides "has not been completely dealt with," Robert said. "I belong to the race of privilege."

That statement brought me up short. Who among us likes to categorize our-

ANN HAMMAN

selves in those terms? But to African-Americans, that's how it is. How do we all deal with these ongoing problems in our society?

Robert wants us to acknowledge that we do have prejudices. "We have to be honest enough to express them. The basis of reconciliation is to develop attitudes of appreciation for those who are different from us," he said.

We need to provide opportunities for all of us to develop this appreciation for one another, he said. Institutions from government to churches should be in the forefront of bringing us together so that we get to know each other better, to discover that our differences need not keep us apart and that we are more similar than we realize.

In the congenial setting of the wedding and reception, the opportunity presented itself for blacks and whites to mix and get to know one another, at least for an evening. Did it happen? Only to a limited extent. We, myself included, sat at tables with our friends. We had the chance, but we didn't take

it. Why not? Is it so ingrained in us to stay with those we know and not reach out? At least we were together for the occasion and we share this memory.

Robert admitted that some of his family is having a hard time dealing with his marriage. His father is friendly but not "ecstatic," by a long shot, he said. His oldest daughter is struggling with it, and his sons-in-law did not come to the wedding. Katie's son is married to a white woman and Katie's mother is "very accepting," Robert said.

This couple got married because they love each other, not for the purpose of furthering good race relations. Their witness and presence in different settings may or may not have that effect.

In a guest commentary in the June 26 Chicago Tribune, M. Cherif Bassiouni, a law professor at DePaul University in Chicago, writes that the real strength of our country rests in its people.

"With all their flaws and limitations, Americans remain the best expression of tolerance and diversity, even though discrimination, racism and poverty still exist in our midst."

So it is with hope in the future that the bride and groom walked down the aisle. And it is with hope in the future that our country continues to try to come to terms with our legacy of racism.

Ann Hamman Article

Katie and Robert in Los Vegas family reunion

Robert and Mary Davis Wedding photo

Robert and Debbie Davis family photo

Robert's extended family

Robert's sibling family

SOMEDAY WE WILL BE TOGETHER

One year I had this great idea, to have a party and ask each guest to prepare something to entertain everyone. So, after eating, we began asking my relatives to perform something, and we were getting a "no" from everyone until I asked my little niece Mitzi. She said, "O.K." and began to search our 45s for music. She found some music and put it on the record player. She had the music low; she began to sing with the record, and she sang "Someday we will be Together", Mitzi girl has a great voice. We all were amazed, and we really enjoyed the song performed by my niece, my brother's daughter. I knew then that she would go somewhere with that voice of hers. After she stopped singing, we gave her great praise, clapping and we were feeling good inside my Mama left the room and I followed her.

She was crying, and it took me quite a while to get her to tell me why she was crying when we were having so much fun together. She remembered someone she had promised to come back for. When Mitzi sang the phrase "I made a mistake when I said goodbye." She had a flashback to the day she left her father's house and someone living there wanted to go with her. She told her she was too young to go with her, but the child persisted. Mama said that she would come back for her. Her regret was that she never went back, never did she ever go back. She was so sad that she did not keep her word. She did not help this relative and if her Dad had not changed, he surely molested her too. All the sisters that stayed together were there at the party. They were together that day and someday they would be together in heaven. If there were hard feelings maybe while they were together, they embrace each other with sisterly Christian love they have for each other.

Any neglect and bad feelings for failed promises will be forgiven and forgotten. I really have missed you, Mama, since God called you home. We often laughed together and sang songs together. It was all so much fun. Growing old, it is amazing! I wish you were here to tell me about what these body changes mean.. Something goes wrong every day. I wish I were more like you when it comes to aches and pains. You never complained. I know that you were suffering, and you did it in silence. I believe that someday we will all be together, and what a glorious day that will be! Current information about my niece Mitzi who is not so little anymore she has put together a cd called "I have come to Worship" 12 wonderful songs, one was written and arranged by Mitzi EkekHor, titled *This I Know*. It is an amazing album she has really developed her voice I am so proud of her voice; it is a gift.

Mitzi Ekekhor

MAMA, ARE YOU WHITE?

My son and I were sitting on the couch, and I had on shorts. He laid his little arm on my leg and looked at the differences in our skin color. He said, "Mommie are you white?" I smiled at him and looked directly in his little 4-year-old face and said, "No son, I am not white." What makes you think that I am white? "He noted that our skin color was so different and since his skin was very dark compared to mine, he thought that I was white. No, Erik, I am the color of my Mama and Daddy combined. "You are the color of your Daddy and me. Some people call us black, but we come in all different colors. Some of us are absent of any color and they are called white. There are some of us are very dark. But we are the same inside."

But Mommie, there is a boy in my class that has real curly hair and is light skinned and all the teachers really like him. They are always smiling at him and putting their hands in his hair. They never do that to me. Well Erik, you are right, they should treat every child the same. You are not responsible for the way you look. God made you and you have the type of hair of your Daddy and me. When you were born you had curly hair, and when I would comb it, or brush it would always curl back up. You are loved by me and your Daddy and everyone who knows you, Do not expect to get attention on looks alone. We think you are a very handsome boy.

The things that come up once your child leaves the nest and starts noticing other people, seeing the differences that we create ourselves.

By making one child more special than the others. We have been treated that way all our lives. You would think that persons of color would not be so racist, to make little children feed badly about themselves. Now, the first week of his pre-school experience. He came home very boldly that I have told him wrong. I thought that phrase was very interesting. He said Mommie you told me wrong my eyebrows lifted. "Well, Erik, what have I told you, that was wrong?" He said, "Mommie" and he pointed to his private place and said, "You told me that this was a penis, I found out that this is not a penis. It is a dick!" I wanted to roar with laughter, but I also felt betrayed that he would believe what he learned in school from some child rather than believe in me. So, I carefully explained to him that what I taught him was the correct name of his body, and what he has heard was a name that someone has made up to call their penis. So, the next day at work I decided to tell the women what my son said to me, and we all had a good laugh, but then several women admitted that they told their sons different names for that body part, we had a good laugh when they confessed to us the names they gave their boys male part of their body.

 **ancestry**

Ethnicity Estimate

Your DNA looks most like DNA from these 10 world regions

We compare your DNA against a worldwide reference panel to see which populations your DNA looks most like.

How do we calculate this?

Nigeria	47% >
Cameroon, Congo & Western Bantu Peoples	22% >
Benin & Togo	16% >
England & Northwestern Europe	4% >
Ireland	4% >
Senegal	2% >
Mali	2% >
Wales	1% >
Sweden & Denmark	1% >
Basque	1% >

© Mapbox © OpenStreetMap

I OUGHTA BE IN PICTURES

I have always loved fashion. As a pre-teen, I modeled for my Mama and Mr. Sam while they were watching television. I would tear out pictures of outfits in" Vogue" and "Glamour" magazines. And cover my bedroom walls with the outfits that, if I had the money, I would wear to school. Now I really wanted to be like my Aunt Thelma. She was a skilled in her trade a professional seamstress. If only I could learn how to sew. In high school I tried my best to be fashionable, but there was no money for my dreams, and I wore quite a few hand-me downs. One morning I stole my brother's wife's poodle skirt, well I just borrowed it. I had to put a big pin in both sides of the waistband for she was larger than me, but I looked great in it. My sweater covered the pins in it. I was a hit with my friends, like when and where did you get that! All of the girls wanted one. I did not tell them I took it without permission. Of course, I was caught, I returned it before she got home, but I forgot to take the pins out of it. Caught red-handed, I thought she would never stop complaining. Then my brother had something to say. After him, my Mama preached to me about honesty. Never again did I wear something of hers. Also, I never got my own poodle skirt.

In high school, I was popular with the girls, because I was a good volleyball player, and I was always selected team captain. I would try to look fashionable, every day. The graduation class had a "Miss Vogue" contest. I ran with the encouragement of my friends amazingly I won!. I think I won because the girls did not like the other candidate she was one of the "in crowd." I was not. But I was the captain of the volleyball team and I picked the girls that the other snobs did not want. We were good together. The "in crowd" put their candidate's picture in the paper and reported that I had won, making it look like she won, what a slap to the face. I was furious but happy that they reported my name. The correct winner. I ran across my competitor in the subway tunnel one year and stopped her, and said hello, she was still bitter, and after she realized who I was, she said, "I heard that you were dead." Now that surprised me a lot so I smiled and asked her did she know how I died. She had no answer to that, so I walked off, amused, wondering when do people from high school really grow up. While working for internal Revenue Service downtown Chicago I noticed a sign that stated John Robert Powers Modeling agency was opening up right across the street from work, so I dressed up and went in and asked to attend the school.. I was interviewed and accepted into John Roberts finishing school, where I was exposed to a lot of exciting things, such as table settings, fencing, runway walking, make up, face shape, body shape best colors for your skin tone, and social requirements. Such as thank you cards. When we completed the training. I was the only person of color at the school at that time. It was all very exciting for me. Expensive but I paid for it and I became more aware of fashion and make-up. I got my Daddy to come see me in a number of fashion shows, most of the clothes I wore were mine. Finally I read up on how to get your pictures out there so I could get some fashion work. I had a composite made and changed my name to "Katina." Then I went to work and mailed my composite to all the photographers downtown and on the north side of downtown Chicago. One fine snowy day I received a call to come to a photographers office for a shoot, it was almost impossible to get out of the parking lot I drove a Volkswagen bug and I was stuck, I called them and explained why I was having problems getting there, he told me to come when I can, that they will wait for me. So I got busy and got out of the snowbank and found that the main roads were clear.

I brought casual clothes which the photographer selected which one he wanted me to wear. They started to work as soon as I arrived and I leaned against the dryer and the photographer said, "Oh, no! You are going to hold up one of those signs." They were on the floor face down so I just picked up one, but he told me he had a special sign for me. All the other models just picked up a sign, and the one he had for me smelled of racism my sign said, "We love Kelvinator." I was a representative of the entire brown and black people. But I thought, I'm getting paid. $75.00 an hour. After the shoot I looked at all the pictures he made and was very excited at how well they looked. So I had read all about the modeling stuff that was available, so I asked for any reject pictures, he seemed to be surprised but he gave me 2 reject photos, wow, I left with pictures that I will treasure all my life. I got another call for a Photo shoot and was told to bring simple party type clothes; this was a near north photographer so off I went. They took black and white pictures of me and two young men of color and we were holding 7up drinks, one at a piano, one was pouring 7up in some ice cream I had a glass and the other guy was drinking his. One of the men was an actor and the other one said he was a musician. They had piped in music,we laughed and danced to the music, it was such fun I never saw the billboard but I was a professional model because I was paid well. Two jobs don't make me well known, but it was a dream that came true for me. My third offer for a job they wanted a person with long natural hair for a product shoot. They also wanted to wash my hair with their products. I was not able to get any other shoots without getting a new picture or an agent.

Katina model composite 1

Katina model composite 2

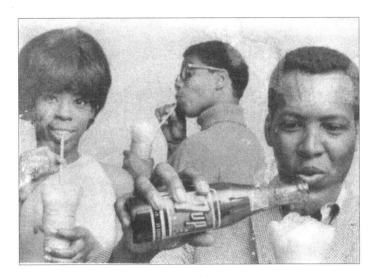

7 UP Photo shoot 1

7 UP Photo shoot 2

Photo shoot Kelvinator 1

Photo shoot Kelvinator 2

Katie & Erik in fashion show

IF I CAN'T HAVE YOU

I met her at work, and she was pleasant and very friendly. She was now the manager of this new group I was in. We shared some private moments and we laughed together. She was a nice manager; I shared all the group's secrets with her. I realized that she was moving and would get a job at another IRS. she was going there first and then apply for a position. She had been at IRS for quite some time. I found out that she had a yellow stove and refrigerator that she wanted to sell. She needed the money to move, so I gave her 250 dollars. She wanted five hundred for them. I was to pay the rest of the money when I picked up the merchandise. There was one problem. I could not get any man to help me get the appliances and the one day that I could come was not a good day for her, but she agreed since there was no other way for me to pick up the appliances.

So, we agreed for me to come as early as I could that Saturday morning. She was planning to leave that day. Saturday my helper and I rented a trailer and went to her house to pick up the appliances. I called her and the phone was busy so I assumed that she was home, and I would call her again, before I got to her house. I knew that she was expecting me, so, we were finally on our way. I lived in the west suburbs, and she lived in Southeast Chicago, a good 50-minute drive. I was so impatient. I thought the driver was driving too slowly, I needed to get there and pick up the appliances and get out of her way, since she really did not want to wait for me that day. She wanted to have this done the day before. So, we pull up to her house and I went to ring the doorbell and you could still hear the phone ringing. Then, neighbors came over and asked us what we were doing, and I told them that was between Mary and me. They then told me that Mary died last night.

"What!" They shared what happened to Mary. The father of her youngest child had threatened her for leaving him and he put a gun to her head and pulled the trigger, The girls were not at home. She was the mother of a teenager from her first marriage and a young daughter. Then her murderer jumped in his car and drove home He told his son to see about Mary. He said that he thought that he might have hurt her. His son jumped in the same car and drove to her house. When he got there the police had arrived, and the neighbors told the police that was the car that had left there after they heard the gun shots. The police grabbed the boy. He explained what his Dad had told him, and the police secured his father's name and address. While they were going to his house, the man who killed her was calling her relatives and told them that she would not be coming there after all. As the police was pounding on his door, a shot rang out. When they broke down the door and entered, they found that he had shot himself in the head. He was dead.

I left the area and returned the rented trailer. I was so depressed. Was it my fault that she was at home that night because of me? When I attended her funeral, everyone who knew the story of that next day was pointing at me and whispering. I kept focusing why I came because she was a friend to me. Weeks later, since I had a receipt, a lawyer called me and asked me if I still wanted to buy the appliances, I replied yes, and he stated he would call me back after checking things out since he found a copy of the receipt in her check book. He promised to get back to me, and when he did, he said he was sorry but after going to the house he found that the appliances were gone, even the carpet on the floor. I asked if I could get back my deposit on them, and he said no, she did not have any money.

Then people started coming out of the woodwork to get custody of her children. One would be eighteen soon, on her own; the other child was about seven and many families and friends tried to get guardianship of the girls. I heard that it was resolved. Custody of the girls was given to the woman that kept them whenever their mother was out of town for work. They always stayed with her, which was often several weeks at a time. This' if I can't have you, nobody can" is sick. There are too many women and men in the world. You can always find someone else. I miss her, knowing that she is no longer here. She was a sweet person and had two lovely children who lost their mother needlessly at such a young age.

KATIE, YOU HAVE CANCER

The doctor told me that there was a lump in my breast. I asked him where because I was doing self-examinations and I never felt anything. So, he placed my hand on it. Wow, that was really an aha moment! Now at one time he was not my favorite doctor. The one that helped me bring my son into the world had retired and was now teaching. This doctor purchased his business. The doctor that I loved was a man of color. A friendly and comforting person, he was a popular gynecologist. When I found out my doctor was gone, I really was not sure I would still go to this new white doctor. But how could I have all these different doctors looking up my legs? So I told the receptionist that the doctor was unfriendly and cold, appearing indifferent, but I still made the follow-up appointment.

Well, back to the breast exam. I made the appointment for a biopsy; I drove to this north suburban hospital, had the blood tests before the surgery, and then went for the surgery. There is still a mark on my chest. Just a small cut was made and then I waited. The waiting was awful. I sat at my desk in the office and just cried from the stress of it. Finally, I found out that the tissue was negative. Well, now I am 35 years old and I kind of stopped going regularly to see my gynecologist. One day I noticed that I had not been to the doctor for a regular examination. So, I made an appointment. The doctor did his exam. He took some tissue I was called to come into the office. My son and I went down to discuss the results. He said, "Katie, you have cancer!" I responded "What?" He repeated it. I was in disbelief. Then he said that it was in the 4th stage. I asked for proof. He went into his pocket and pulled out a picture of a slide with red and a black spot. He gave me directions that we need to remove this cancer soon. I left his office in disbelief. My son was asking me questions I could not answer. But I truly thought this would be my end.

I made out a will. On surgery day, my ex-husband was visiting Erik, and I asked him to drop me off at Mercy Hospital on the south side of Chicago. This was where I delivered our son. I was standing back waiting, an elevator and my doctor walked up and was also waiting. He did not notice me, so I said to him" Hello, he said, hello" then I said" you do not know me?" I am here for you to operate on me." He said oh, I did not recognize you," since I normally always see you without your clothes on." I smiled but I did not like it one bit. Well, there I was on the operating table, all hooked up, and they were starting to put me under anesthesia. I said no, my doctor is not here yet, the doctor said I'm here, I asked him if he was feeling okay. He said he was all right except for his hands shaking. Others laughed but I did not think it was funny at all. They immediately put me under. They removed my uterus and a fallopian tube. After receiving the results from the organs they examined. I did not have cancer. The lab results stated that there was no cancer in any stage. Cancer! This doctor told me I was in the 4th stage of cancer! I never made another appointment with him after his last check on the surgery. A keloid started, while I was in the hospital, I was drugged up so I felt nothing when the doctor opened it and awful stuff came out of it and he changed my bandages himself. After that, the area healed up nicely. It is not that I wanted any more children. It is that he lied to me. I would never trust him again ever.

While in the hospital, my Aunts and cousins came to see me. After I was well my cousin asked me repeatedly if I had been pregnant. I had to reassure her I did not have an abortion or a miscarriage. Years went by and she kept asking me that question, thinking I would change my answer. I think she would have liked those reasons better than, the truth. I know what you are thinking. Katie why didn't you get a second opinion? Well, my minister's wife had a lot of faith in her doctor, she referred me to him. I made an appointment. When they saw me in their white world, he took me in an office just behind the waiting area where it was just a table and a couple of chairs. He suggested that I should go ahead with the surgery, no requesting my medical records and no pelvic examination. No cost, he was a waste of my time. Feeling unsure as to what to do, my doctor said I was in the 4th stage so time was of the essence. So, I just had a little talk with Jesus and went ahead. I knew it! Katie did not have any cancer. I received the lab report and there was no cancer in no stage. Thank you God! This is a perfect example of how white doctors mistreat, misdiagnose black people. I considered suing him. There is a video of the operation. But I just let it go.

Katie in Turtleneck sweater

MOMENTS REMEMBERED

I met a doctor who treated me with acupuncture. She left the hospital and had her own office. She had stopped operating but she was selling herbs, using them for health and weight issues. She was treating me for the problem with my hands. We bonded and became friends. She was nice we enjoyed conversations. She told me her story on how she came to America. How her village put money together to get her here because she was one of the smartest in the village. She talked about sitting near water that ran through her village. she would sit there for hours fishing for food for the family meals. She lived in Viet Nam. Well, she helped me with my right hand. Computer use and crocheting had me in pain and the acupuncture helped a lot. I invited her to come to my church for I was the speaker that day. My talk was about the woman at the well.

She and her husband were doing well. They lived in a southwest suburb. Not too far from me. I was at her house several times. Lovely house and family. The children had both left the home and were doing well for themselves, in college. The herbs she sold was a product supported by Arnold Schwarzenegger during his muscle, building days. One day she called me and asked me to drive up to Wisconsin with her while she did a presentation about her herbs. It was over the weekend Friday and Saturday, and then return. She wanted me to help her drive. I decided to go with her; we were friends. She and her husband picked me up in his workstation wagon. We went to rent a car near the O'Hara airport. She rented a nice big car that looked like what a doctor should arrive in. Then off we went to this woman's house who invited her, and she insisted she stay at her house. The family had a beautiful home. One wall in the great room was all windows and she showed the doctor her room and told me to take the couch. Well, that was no problem until she announced that there was a cat there that might like to sleep on the top of the back of the couch. The doctor was scheduled to do a presentation. She answered questions and then we came back to the woman's house. I thought we would stay in a hotel. So, Dr. went to bed, and I was stuck on that hard couch. I was miserable and that cat scared the shite-out of me. no real rest for me. The next day we went to a hotel conference room, and she did an excellent job on her presentation, but I was exhausted. I told her how unhappy I was on that couch. Dr. had this great big bed. She was a very petite woman the bed was gorgeous, and she invited me in her room, and I laid down and off to sleep I went. I did hear the woman of the house knock on the door and ask me to leave the bedroom because she had the couch ready for me, but Dr. told her never mind, that she told her I was asleep and that she did not want to wake me.

Well, the lady still was insisting that I leave the room, so the Dr. could have her privacy, but the doctor did not open the door and insisted that we were all right. I don't think I moved at all that night, and I felt very rested. That morning the lady of the house suggested I use the shower in the basement. She said her son lived down there. The shower water was silky and very refreshing. While I was in the bathroom a man tried to enter. I had to tell him" I'm in here." He was the woman's son. He said he did not know I was in there; the water was running, and the sound of it did not let him know I was in the bathroom. But, he saw nothing, but I was unhappy that she did not tell him someone was using his bathroom. Of course, I was the only one that was asked to use the facilities that were in the basement. They made coffee for the doctor, and we left. I was one happy girl. This trip was over and all we had to do was get back home.

It was all right for the Vietnamese Dr. to sleep in her guest bedroom, but not me. Our host's friendly looks and smiles for me left her face. But we were leaving, and I did not care if she was unhappy about me sleeping in there. The doctor's husband came to the rental car store and picked us up and drove me home. She thanked me for going with her. She did not say anything about that bedroom situation. I bet she told her husband. So many of the guests at the presentation came to me and thanked me for helping the doctor get there, but I was not worthy of a decent place to sleep. being born black, and all. But what was wonderful to look at besides feeling the draft from all the windows were watching the deer that came out of the woods that first night.

THE FAKE JOB INTERVIEW

I was working at the I.R.S. but I still had an interest in modeling. I loved fashion, so I started looking at the want ads. My John Roberts education was over. And I wanted to have something more fashionable to do as a career. The job ads attracted me to a position that was being managed by a job agency where I could model bras when buyers were selecting the products. The young lady that gave me the address and got my measurements was satisfied that I could get this position because I had good typing skills and job experience and i had attended modeling school. I was excited. This would give me the experience that I needed to do more modeling. I also could pass a typing test and filing test. I wore an attractive outfit and went to the appointment. Why you could see the building from the El station. I was allowed upstairs, by a security guard there was a very long hallway that had a view of the El station. There was a metal chair sitting in the hallway, I waited for quite a while.

Finally, a heavy-set Caucasian woman came down the hallway, heels clicking on the marble floor. She approached me. She was carrying a tape measure I stood up.. She was not open to conversation, she said nothing but made a gesture with the tape measure for me to raise up my arms I raised up my arms she put the measure across the back of my body and like a rope and then she did not try to determine what my measurements were actually. I thought how strange. She isn't even trying to find what my actual measurements were. She did the same thing to measure my waist. She then turned around and left. As she walked away, she said that will be all, as her heels clicked down the hall back the way she came. I left, when I got to the El station, I used the public phone to call the agency that sent me there. She said she just got off the phone with the company and they were upset that she sent me there.

What! She apologized for my experience. She said that she did not have anything else in the area I was looking for. We hung up. Maidenform made the bras. I never bought another one of their bras again. It was so obvious that she did not want to touch me. So I felt the pains of racism. I thought their white bras would look good on me with my skin color. Their loss. I wonder if the security guard knew what I was in for, as I waited. He was a man of color and he was positioned to watch the whole thing.

DON'T TELL ANYONE!

I was working with a special project, filing some forms that were on black microfilm tape with white writing,. It was a highway use tax that needed to be collected. Six employees were assigned to put these forms in alpha order. They were extremely thin and slippery, and they easily stuck together this project had to be done expeditiously. The managers resented any conversation at the table, but we were facing each other every day. I admit I like to talk, a lot. There was some laughter. Which did not mean that we were not working. This lasted a week, and then several of the other ladies were told to return to their desks. The task was insurmountable. Eventually I was left to file these forms alone. While on this assignment I noticed that I was feeling that I had dry eyes, and my eyes felt tired, strange. That night I decided that when I went into the office I would refuse to work on this project. All of the other five employees had been recalled to their desk. I had a feeling I was being punished. I went to my desk and did not go up front to where the excise taxes were.

My manager came to my desk to instruct me to return to filing those forms. I informed her that I was not going to file those forms today, I wear glasses, and I am having problems with my eyesight. Those documents were straining my eyes. I said I would provide a statement from my eye doctor if she preferred. I was called into the office. I thought I was being warned about the fact that I had refused to continue filing those documents, I was preparing my reason that I could not do the filing for 8 hours due to the fact that I was now having eye problems and I was willing to provide a doctor's statement, to prove that fact. Or go and file a complaint with the union.

Much to my surprise, that was not the reason I was called into the Chief's office. I was told that I had been selected for a promotion. I was to start the beginning of the next week. I had applied for that job previously. He told me the title of the job and gave me the address. I was instructed to not tell anyone. about this promotion" What!" not tell anyone! They thought that they could stop me from sharing my good news, a promotion, they only told me at the last moment, that I had the job. so there would be no celebration in the unit for my promotion. I was really happy to leave that unit because the management for that unit was not really an equal opportunity employer. If you are white, you are right, but if you are black, stay back. There were always problems with the personnel of color. We were not treated fairly. I left his office and told all who would listen; "I am out of here." One of my experiences there with my immediate manager: she would follow me into the bathroom every time, When I came out of the toilet, she would be waiting there. Pretending to fix her hair. I finally asked her why are you in the bathroom every time I was in there, she said she was told to follow me. I told her that I would not want her job. As I walked out. The women's toilet was not a sweet-smelling experience.

THE SOUND OF MUSIC

I had a first date with a fellow who was a security guard at the place where I lived. So, I thought maybe that would be fun. He came to escort me to this club. Of course, he did not have his own vehicle, so we jumped in my Volkswagen bug and went to this lounge on the southeast side of Chicago. While I was pulling up to a parking spot, he pulled out a gun, and said nothing. He opened my glove compartment, and I do believe that he caressed the gun as he placed it inside. Oh, Lord, what have I gotten myself into? We went into the lounge and sat down. It was about 10 p.m. the place was dark and really only in fair condition. I ordered a soda, he bought himself a drink. We listened to the music from a disc jockey, and it got boring fast. I sat there for an hour, then I was really ready to go home. All of a sudden, people started coming in and it got crowded soon, five young boys came to the front of the room. (there was no stage,) and they started playing guitars and singing:" A B C it is easy, as 1 2 3." Wow, they were good. We all jumped up and danced and sang along. I even stood in my chair so I could see them better. I was there longer, than I had thought I would have stayed. I found out that I just saw the Jackson 5 at the early stage, of their career, since they came to this dump to perform. I would have left before the group arrived if it had not been for that gun in my glove compartment. After we left the club, my date said for me to just drive myself home, he would walk where he had to go. I thanked him for the good time. I did not know much about him. A few days later he showed up at my door. To let someone in the building, you would respond to a buzz of your apartment, but he just appeared at my door. I peeked through the door peephole, saw it was him, and did not answer. He said." I know you are there; I can see your feet." I still did not answer. I did not want to go out with him again just based on that gun he caressed. Not that I did not have a nice time, but he was someone I did not want to repeat dating or allow in my house. His gun was intimidating. Until I wrote this, I had almost forgotten that I had enjoyed singing with the young Michael Jackson, with the Jackson five. He was so cute as a young performer. To this day I enjoy his music.

My friend Paula invited me to go with her to see Nancy Wilson. Her date was unable to attend, so I got invited in his place. I had another wonderful time. Nancy was wonderful. I really enjoyed her style, and her performance was magnificent. She was so lovely in those elegant gowns.

My boss had two ticket to see a play. He had asked several others if they wanted the tickets; the play was for that night. For "fences" with James Earl Jones. I was asked if I would be able to go." Of course." I called Mama and told her she and I were going out to see a play. We got there early and stood around in the lobby, and there was James Earl Jones. I told Mama,'" that is James Earl Jones, Mama." We heard someone call him Jimmy, so Mama said" HI, Jimmy" to him, and he came over, reached for her hand, kissed her hand, and asked her" Where do I know you?" She gave him a beautiful smile and said she was a fan. She was so lucky; I wish I had tried that. The play was so exciting, we had great seats. She and I really had a good time. This night was wonderful. Thanks, boss!

I had a friend at work that said she could sing. "Of course, you can." I did not really believe her. One day she said she had a ticket for her husband and he said he was not coming, so, she gave me two tickets and Mama and I went to an Opera. And there she was, right in front of an orchestra, and she opened up her mouth. She was wonderful;

it was beautifully done. I learned to appreciate opera. I was so happy that she gave me the opportunity to hear her sing so beautifully.

Every payday, every other week on Thursday, IRS employees would go across the street to the First National Bank of Chicago. We would hurry there because the lines would get rather long. Many wanted to cash their checks at lunch time; my friend was in front of me cashing her check. I saw her take some of her money and slide it into her bra. After I got my check deposited, I saw her talking with her husband; he was counting her money. He told her "You better give me all the Money." I felt so sad for her; he was embarrassing her. She reached in her bra and gave him the rest of the money. The next day she came into the office with a gorgeous little girl. She was trying to keep her at the office all day while she worked. I told her she could not keep the child there. She said she did not have a babysitter. She also said she did not have any money. She allowed her daughter to sit in an inter-view office and closed the door. Of course, an employee went to use that office and he got her from her workstation. She was told she had to leave the office; she could not keep the child there. I do not know what happened to her, but she was full of talent. She may have gotten suspended or let go. I did not see her again.

I met this guy who was in the play Shakespeare's "Othello," the Moor of Venice. The star of the show had lost his leg to cancer. While he was in the Army. At the time I did not know the tragedy of Othello's story, but it was interesting and a sad love story. My friend refused to wear his prosthesis. The fact that he had only one leg did not distract from the play. He was excellent in the play. The college plays I attended were always excellent.

FEAR AND HATE

I was sitting at my desk at the Kedzie office when a woman hollered out to me. There was a phone call for me, she was sitting in the Taxpayer Service area, which served taxpayers requesting information for return preparation. I, very unprofessional hollered back. Please transfer the call to my desk." More exchange, she said, "I can't. You have to come over here to take the call." I went to her work area. On her desk was the phone. I was hoping it was not a bill collector calling me at work. "Hello," I said. Then I heard my estranged husband's voice. He said hello. Katie I was quiet, he said ,"I want you to do me a favor," my thoughts were, what the hell does he want from me? I was still quiet. He asked me to call his mother, and I said well, can't you do that? He said he could not. He again asked me to call her and tell her that he was in jail. I told him I did not have her phone number with me and he obviously did not have the number handy either. I agreed, to call her after I got home from work, for it was in our phone book at home. "What do you want me to tell her?" Just tell her that I will call her as soon as I can. "O.K." I said. Then I asked him, "Why are you in jail?" I am being held because, now I turned by body to the wall since there were a lot of people standing around the counter. It appeared that they were trying to hear my conversation. "Because I killed two white men!" My response, "What!" He quickly said it was in self-defense.

I knew he had secured a new position; he had flown out of town for an interview for a job as a pharmaceutical salesperson. I agreed if the interviewer called me and asked me if i was going to join him later, I would tell them yes that my son and I would join him after he got established and found a place for us to live. He further explained that he had pulled over in a residential area, parked the car with both front windows open, and was opening his mail when two men came up to his car and started harassing him, calling him the" n" word and threatening him. They did not move on, he responded in kind. All of a sudden one of the men reached into the car. Lamont did not have his seat belt on, and the intruder actually succeeded in pulling him out of the window of the car. Lamont had his letter opener in his hand, and a fight with both of them ensued and with his army training, he stabbed both of them.

One of them died at the scene and the other died later at the hospital. Police were called, he was arrested. His employer came and got him out of jail. The inquest was done and there would be no trial. He was released, but he was full of fear because the men's families were not happy about the results. Lamont had no prior records, he was highly supported by his employer, he was a successful lab technician, he was honorably discharged from the Army, and the letter opener was not considered an illegal weapon. Immediately after he was released, he was moving that night because his address was announced in court.

Both of the families were there, and he was concerned about retaliation from the families. Hate raised its ugly head that morning and it could have left our son without a father. I called his mother, Charlie Mae Wallace Lee she just said hello and I told her what he had asked me to say, she asked no questions, I repeated what I said, again, she said nothing. I said goodbye.

My personal opinion of my mother-in-law was that she felt like a below zero day in Chicago i wonder why I was hoping for a Ruth and Naomi relationship, which was not possible. I learned more about my mother-in-law after she died. She was born November 11, 1919. She married Hubert W Lee in January 1938 she left this life December 1996. She was active with her church and loved by her 12 children.

AIRPLANES AND AUTOMOBILES

It was a great day in September, the sun was shining, I was in a good mood, and Mama was at home, enjoying her day. I was driving to work, from Bolingbrook il to Schaumburg, il. Of course, I was driving in the left lane of the I 90 expressways going just a little over the speed limit, my cd was playing my favorite music, and the sky was clear. I have always loved sunny days. Today I was due to be in the office, at 9 a.m. It takes about 38 minutes to get there since it is all expressways. Today seemed no different from any other day. Robert had left earlier for work. I never took the toll road, so I did not save time, taking the I- 90 to I- 355 to work. When the 90 merged into the 355n, the traffic stopped cold. Oh, no, this is going to make me late for work. I hated to be late for work. There is a stigma. My life is much better when I arrive on time. I looked ahead and saw a parking lot of cars just sitting there, and then I saw airplane after airplane going into land at O'Hare Airport. You often saw airplanes take off from O'Hare because that expressway was not far from the airport. But this was extreme. What is happening? My mother called me on my cell which is unusual. She asked me where I was and I told her I was on the expressway; I had not arrived to work yet. She asked me to call her later and she suggested that I turn on the news. Since we were inching forward, I felt I needed to keep a watch on my driving, hoping no one would hit me from behind.

I had never seen so many airplanes landing at O'Hare airport one after another. Whew, I finally made it to the office. I noticed there were few cars in the parking lot. I wondered if they had been caught in the same traffic I was in. That is when I found out that the twin towers had been hit by a plane loaded with passengers, and another plane had hit the other tower. This all happened on the 11th day of September 2001.

What horror!

AT LAST

Well, I met him on a Sunday before church started, I was waiting at the entrance of the room we call the library where the elders gathered before the service. We gather there to greet each other and to prepare

I had scheduled an elder meeting which I held at my house, I invited him to come, only a few Elders came to the meeting. You should have seen his expression on his face when he walked into my house. Mama and I have set up the meeting on the back patio with my wicker table and chairs. Tablecloth matching plates and silverware all elegantly set up. Mom had prepared the food and as usual everything was delicious. We had a good time said prayers, planned training for the Elders. We were getting to know each other. After that Saturday afternoon he asked me to go to lunch with him after church services. We went to Baker's Square a restaurant that served great pies. We talked and talked he shared his life with me. Telling me of his girls, his wife's, his work. He was the Executive Director of a not-for-profit ministry. After a few lunch dates I knew his entire life story. His youngest children did not live in the state so that was a plus for me. He had visitation rights for the youngest two, I thought this could be fun, we became great friends. He invited me one August day to go to the Zoo with him and his girls. The two youngest and the two oldest was going. But I had a date that weekend with my Daddy we was celebrating my birthday. We were going to Medieval Times. While there they took pictures and served us a 4-course meal, with no silverware, it was fun being with

268

Daddy. The joshing was exciting but I thought of that new friend I had who was at the Zoo. But I was glad that Daddy and I was spending time together. During their visits one evening all 4 of us was together at my house the girls brought over some brownies, that they made

I brought out the Uno cards, we sat at a small dining room table and played cards. I thought we were all enjoying the game, when all of a sudden the youngest girl who was sitting close to me kicked me, I noticed she did not appear to react to hitting me, it hurt, but I did not say anything because I thought it was a accident so a few minutes later she kicked me again, and this time she did it with more force, her foot landed on my shins. This really hurt and her face did not change, I jumped up my chair fell backward and I was ready to ramble. I accused her of kicking me, my date was surprised, I told him this was the second time she kicked me. My date apologized. The game was over and she did not admit kicking me, they got ready to go and I told my date to please take the brownies with them. After my experience with her I did not want to even try to eat them. Since I had offered them some of the brownies and they refused. I was invited to ride with him when he took his daughter back to meet their mother which he said was a little more than halfway to Nebraska we met at a Hardy's restaurant. He got out of the car and took them to their mother and I waited in the car a few minutes later, one of the girls came back and apologized for their actions. They performed in the back seat of the car, several times he threaten to pull over. He didn't pull over and they didn't stop.

We begin talking about getting married and his oldest daughter tried to talk us out of getting married so quickly, we had not known each a year. But we had planned to get married after almost a year. His daughter could not talk us out of getting married and she spent the entire time as we traveled to pick up his 2 youngest daughters. To change our minds.

He lived in the lower level of a church. We were listening to music, when he brought in a small gift bag and gave it to me and then while I was looking in it he got on his knees I was sitting on the couch he asked me to marry him. A white bear was holding the rings. I of course, said yes. We put the ring on and hugged and kissed. The next day we were in church and he stood up during joys and concerns and said that he had a joy, that he and I were getting married in the very near future. Later, we scheduled the wedding with our minister for May 17th, 1997. We went to several different kind of marriage classes, one was a weekend class, a re-marriage class, and a class with our minister. We talked with his daughter about them making a commitment to marry especially the oldest one. She felt that she did not want to get married yet. She had been with her boyfriend for quite a long time. She talked with her Dad and me and she finally decided to marry. One daughter married in April, we married in May and the oldest daughter married in August we sent invitations to our wedding to all of his girls, he invited the oldest to be his best man (person) I wanted my son to stand with me as by man of honor. (smile) they both accepted. We asked his second oldest daughter to read a poem from the book, the prophet Kahlil Gibran. The groom planned the entire wedding. I asked him to sign a pre-nuptial agreement, that a lawyer had prepared for me. He signed. I felt secure having that agreement. Since I had the most assets. I knew he was my true love and my best friend. But I had to be careful with my assets.

The wedding was beautiful we walked down the aisle together holding hands, several of our friends sang for us as a gift it was beautifully done one couple wrote and sang a song especially for us. The mother of Robert's oldest girls was present and her husband took the wedding pictures for us. My son purchased the cake and it was beautifully done and so good. He paid for tuxedos for himself and his two boys, who served as candlelighters. I had no ushers, I really felt that people could sit wherever they wanted, but one of the youths at church asked if she could be an usher so I said yes. The attendees were segregated, the groom side was sparse. But I had more brown, black, and white sitting together. One of the special things at the ceremony was that we served communion to our guests. Another was the music my niece Mitzi and her friend Steven Ellison sang a duet. Greta and Earl Bichel wrote and sang a song especially for us. Rev Howard Kennon sang beautifully "In This Very Room." The groom had invited a woman who was a reporter who authored an article about our wedding in her area paper, which was kind of cool, except for the error in the article.

After the ceremony, my son placed a decorated broom in the aisle and After the minister declared us married and the groom saluted the bride we jumped the broom (an African custom), into the sea of matrimony. The men's group gave us several cases of prepared ribs they were served also fried chicken wings my mother prepared. With various salads. And finger foods.

During the new year holidays, the girls were visiting us. So I planned a new year's day party and invited the minister and his wife, who were the first to arrive. As they came into the house and was removing their coats. Her father asked the youngest girl to take these coats upstairs and lay them on the bed. He reached the coats to her and she said, "What am I, the slave." He took her aside and gave her another lecture. I wondered what he said to her. Later that evening she complimented the chili I had made and asked for another bowl full. I was still not happy with them. When they left I found my sheets they used on the couch stuffed in my overflowing closet full of pee. I was told it was my fault because I let them drink soda late in the evening. But if someone had said that would have happen, I would have had no problem saying no! Since the washing machine was in the basement why not put them in there? I was glad that they did not live in Illinois, it was clear that I was not going to be taken as a friend for the girls since I had the impression that I could win them over. I made them a dress, since they did not have any dresses to wear to church, it was a nice dress, knit fabric with a mock turtleneck a shift, with short sleeves and a solid color, after I made them the older girl did not want to wear it. So I just gave up. But their Dad made them wear it and the girl pulled it up really short too short. But I did not say anything, since they were leaving any day. So it would not do any good. So, I just thought I would "forget about it." Before they left we decided to go to the Pizza Hut as we waited for our food. The girls started a contest, every time one of them kissed their dad, the other one would kiss him too. Then each one was either kissing him or waiting to kiss him, the other customers noticed it each time they kissed him the girls would look for my reaction, i tried not to express any feeling until I just got tired of this game. I asked their father to ask them to sit down. He seems to enjoy himself. I was really embarrassed. Being a mixed couple was enough attention for me. But this was really silly.

My dream of having a young daughter as a friendly friend had died. After they went home, it was said that they had to see a counselor who told them that they did not have to come to visit him anymore. It was too much drama for them. For them? I could not believe it, but they stop coming. Which worked out for me. Because they were not going to give us any peace. They had told my mother that they were trying to break us up, I was surprised that children so young, would think of doing such a thing.

LIVING

I was an Audit aide for I.R.S. Examination Division. This was a great sounding job. you get to travel, and the work is done in the field at the corporation's office. This was a pilot to see if an assistant to the agent would help speed up the examination. We were to wear office apparel, our assignments would be typing, or copying and filing. This was a great opportunity. I owned a Volkswagen Bug. Travel and parking fees are reimbursed. We were reimbursed by the miles travel from home whenever we were not at our home office. The downtown office is where I was assigned. The business I was assigned had meters on one side of the street, and there were parked cars all along that area. I found a park that did not have a meter. After entering the building, I asked for the Officer that I was assisting, and the secretary took me to a storage room that was not well lighted, sitting in there was the man I was to assist. First thing he asked me to do was to have a seat at the table behind him, where there was a collection of newspapers. So, I started to read them. He never gave me anything to do. I sat the entire day without him saying a word.

There was something very strange going on. I occasionally heard a meow. Next day, same thing. Then he decided to talk with me. I asked him if he heard a cat and he did not respond. I was bored. He would ask me if I thought a woman needed a good sock, occasionally. This puzzled me, but to get through the day, I answered "Yes." Now, I was thinking of the Jackie Gleason show when Jackie would say to his wife," One of these days, Alice, "to the moon." But his conversation and the meows was a bit much so I asked our manager, "May I have a desk outside of the supply room?" He requested one, and the secretary at the business showed me a desk I could use. The agent gave me one of his reports to read. I was not aware of Tourette syndrome at that time. Being the only person of color in that office, all the employees knew I was from the I.R.S. so They did not talk with me, except once when I asked for the restroom. Now to give you an idea of how I looked I thought I looked professional, but I admit I was different in skin color and hair, I wore a large afro wig. Since my own hair was not tall enough to my liking.

Every day I was there I went to the lady's room. This day a woman from the office came into the lady's room which had several stalls. I was bent over washing my hands. I looked up when she came in and that woman put her hands in my hair and wiggled her fingers. I was beyond angry the nerve of that white woman! She speedily walked into a stall and locked her door, I am glad now, that she did that, for I would have been fired for what I wanted to do to her. I stood around near the exit because I had heated words for her, but she remained in the stall. She put her filthy white hands in my hair. I wanted her to regret she ever even thought of doing this to anybody else.

I enjoyed going to Carson Pirie Scott stores, and while I was downtown Chicago, I would go over there at lunch time. This day I was going into the basement to look at the sale jewelry. There was a wide escalator going down, and an elderly white lady approaching the moving stairs begin carefully to select the right stair for herself. I stepped around her to the farthest side allowing plenty of room and I stood still this woman addressed me and she said, "Everywhere I go, I see one of you." I commented in respect for her, "Everywhere I go, I see one of you." I never forget the warm greeting of white strangers. One of my first assignments when I worked in IRS at the desk of the Collection Division, I was covering for a secretary who was sick that day. I was assigned to answer the phone and this lady, I knew she was white right away, she asked me specific questions about the letter IRS sent her. I answered her questions correctly and advised her of the next steps she should take. I had to repeat them to her twice. I was very patient. At the completion of the call this woman said, "I am so thankful that I did not get one of those colored people that works there." Thank you," she said. My response, "You are welcome." I hung up the phone and laughed.

Robert and I took my Mama and Grandson to a restaurant. My Grandson followed the hostess. Then Mama and I, then Robert, followed. A white woman was sitting in a booth as we passed. She was watching as we came down the aisle to our table. She looked at us, and when she saw Robert (who checks the white box) she said loudly, to the white woman sitting across from her, "What a waste." Then the other woman looked up at us, and I busted out laughing. Currently, often when Robert and I are shopping, I notice that after we enter the checkout lane and Robert is putting the things on the counter and then I move up, the white checkers always ask if we are together. He's standing off from us and I am the one standing at the credit card reader preparing to pay. I want to say, "No, we are not." I just want to pay for his groceries.

On my way to work one morning, {in Chicago traffic}, I was entering the merge lane to join the others on the Dan Ryan expressway I was driving a small Volkswagen Bug. As I continued in the merge lane, there was a driver who thought I was not supposed to get in front of him. He failed to honor the Yield sign. But since my lane forces you in, he decided that it was not worth the trouble to hit me. So, after getting in his lane, I immediately moved to the left, in the almost middle lane. I was aiming for the far-left lane, where you can move rapidly. There was a car that was beeping at me on my right when I looked. There was a young white man with his window down, hollering at me. My window was closed, so I did not hear what he said. Then he had the audacity to give me the finger. I was surprised at his actions. So, I gave the finger back to him with an up-ward action that was extreme. Then the road rage really kicked in and our immature actions stepped in. I changed lanes. He followed me still honking and shouting out of his car at me. I jumped from lane to lane, and he followed, his passenger appearing to be trying to stop him from having an accident finally, he no longer was following me. It was more racist than road rage. How dare I get in front of him, and how dare I say to him what he said to me! I made a promise to not react that way again, because life is too precious to waste it acting foolishly.

We were working in the downtown IRS office, and I had been friendly with the lady that was acting supervisor. I asked her if I could take the rest of the day off, for I had a doctor's appointment. My gynecologist was expecting me. She said O.K. since I had plenty of sick leave. As I got my things and was walking to the door this woman decides to harass me. She asked me what I was going to do when the doctor tells me that I was pregnant. I just could not believe that she said that to me. Thinking to myself why, is she doing this to me? And on top of that, other people could hear her. I said, "Well, Ruth, if the doctor tells me that I am pregnant, I will just call your husband, and tell him that we are going to have a baby." Her mouth fell open and she asked me repeatedly to take that back. I let the door close behind me.

I had to see this doctor. This was a white doctor, and he was very distant and as far as I was concerned, I was not sure I wanted to see him again. He had terrible table side manners,. Considering the places on my body he was assigned to treat medically. When I left that office visit, the secretary asked me about my experience, and I told her how cold and indifferent he seems to be. Well, he got better. He had an office downtown in walking distance from my office right off Michigan Avenue, so I made my next appointments there. This way I did not have to spend my time in his Southside office waiting. That place was always crowded. I used sick leave for my appointments to see the doctor without using my personal time to see the doctor. Well, I am sitting in his office, and I am the only one of color waiting. I did not think about any of it until after my appointment and the appointment clerk tells me to make my appointment at the south side office. I told her I did not want to go to the south side office. That office was close to me, but it was smaller and always crowded. I told her I wanted to come to this office. She seemed disappointed, but she made my appointment there. I will use my Insurance and my money where I want to go. The doctor did not say anything to me about my presence in his downtown office. You can believe I did not sit in the waiting room long

The Kedzie IRS was a boring place, but I was so glad to get that job as a Group Clerk. The job was a Group Secretary in the Examination Division. I wore a large natural hair style at the time and when I was interviewed for the job the person that was the supervisor was not present, a white woman and a man of color interviewed me. He drilled me the roughest, asking questions about childcare and my being able to be at work. Anyway, I got the job. My first day at my new job I was sitting right in front of an accessible area. There was another lady working there; she was group one, and I was group two. Letters sent out to the taxpayers gave information on what to bring to the audit and what group their case was assigned to. Our desks was arranged straight across, with a long table In between us. Each of our desks had a sign hers group one, and mine a similar sign group two. When approaching the Exam side of the office, you could see my desk clearly, and when you entered the office, you then could see the other desk.

The white lady would have a line formed in front of her desk. They would not come to my desk, no matter how long they had to wait for her to take their letters. On the other side of the room was a small sitting area. She would read the letter and walk over to me with the appointment letter. It was amusing, but it takes all kinds. I think she should have handed the Group Two letters back to them and tell them to give that to the person on my right. But she did not. She would walk over to me, and I would take their letter, pull their account out of the file, and take the folder to the next available auditor. The people that came into this office were about 99% white.

One day during the filing season the office manager came to my desk and told me that he received a call from a person who was angry that they had a n word- sitting in front of that office. He told me to be careful. I figured I would watch as well as pray for my safety. One spring day I decided to get some air, so I left the building and walked east to just enjoy the weather that day. I noticed a store, so I decided to maybe buy myself some candy. While looking through the candy, I saw a magazine rack. I loved looking at magazines. I stood there and reviewed all the women's magazines and then purchased some candy.

That was a nice break from the office, so I did it again. The same man was at the counter. Whenever a new version came in, I would purchase it and maybe buy some candy. This time while I was there, I was checking out the magazines when another man came into the store to make a purchase of cigarettes. Looking at me he asked the store clerk if I lived near here and the clerk said he did not know. This exchange was loud enough for me to hear their conversation. I listened and pretended not to notice. The clerk said that he did not know if I lived there, but he added that I have come into the store several times.

No other words that I could hear were said. After the card-carrying hate customer left, I got out of there and walked swiftly back to the office and committed to never go to that store again. I decided to buy my magazines in my own neighborhood. I admit that when I am happiest after work is to be in my car blasting my music on the radio.

I enjoy singing with the artist and having the best time I could have all by myself.

This Friday as I pulled off immediately behind me was a police officer who put on his sirens and signaled for me to pull over. I immediately turned off, the music and went for my purse, and cursed to myself. I was near a bus stop and there were a lot of people standing there, waiting for transportation. The white officer asked for my license. I gave it to him, and he told me to pull up farther from the bus stop. I figured his car was in the way of the bus stop, so I moved my car forward. He moved also, he then came back to my car window and said that he could give me a ticket," For what?" I thought. He wanted to know if I would go out with him, and we could go dancing. As he was handing me back my license, I told him No thanks, I must go home to my family. He said we can go out some other time. I did not say a word. He said I could go but be careful.

One day I walked down to where I parked my car. and there were several men there that worked at that car repair place, they were watching me, as I approached, I noticed that they moved my car right next to the fire hydrant. I had not parked that close to that hydrant. I knew that there were many people that resented the competition from the VW. But when I bought that car for me, it was affordable, there were people not happy that this foreign car was a hot seller, and I was teased about it. I was told I should have bought American; I told my harasser that I bought this car in America, and I paid American money to a white man who appeared to be American, who sold it to me.

The next week that same police stopped me again this time I was on the on ramp to the Dan Ryan. When I saw it was him, I was terrified, because there were no witnesses. He approached my car and asked me out again, Just in case he did not hear me the first time, I told him my husband does not allow me to go out with other men. Once again, he saw me walking from where I parked my car, He hollered out of the police car for me to wait a minute while he turned around. I broke out and ran with the wind, even though I had heels on. When he turned around, I was nowhere to be found. I know he figured out that I worked in the IRS building which was above the bank.

I do not know if you would believe this one; after being unemployed for about 6 months, I wanted to go back to work and the white gentleman that had been my boss, said that there was no opening for me in his unit. I felt he would not want me back, because when I was pregnant, I would eat at my desk which was one of his directions, do not have food at your desk. that I did not follow, having only 30 minutes for lunch I did not have enough time to buy lunch and sit down and eat it. So, I ate out of my desk drawer.

One of my associates told me that there was a vacancy at the office that was on the west side that was on the borderline of Oak Park, Illinois. I knew the man that was the manager of that office. I called him, and he arranged to interview me. I met him and we talked, and he gave me the job of a Reports Clerk which was a little more than I was previously making. Now the person I would be working with was not a part of that process. The white girl that was leaving was not at all pleased to show me the ropes, so I gave myself a little talk and said "Katie, if she could do this, you can do it too." She gave me her last report and I sat there and figured it out. Now the first day that my current manager came back. he came up to me and asked me "Who are you?" I said, "I am Katie," the new Reports Clerk. He went to the manager of the group, the brown skinned man that hired me, and there were no doors to their offices and the dividers were glass, so you could see them, and he appeared upset. Then he went to the Office Manager, being overly dramatic. But their voices were low. There was no privacy in that office. I knew and everyone in the place knew that this man did not want me in his group. I was the unwanted black girl in his group. He found out that they could not fire me, I had previous employment at IRS, and I had exceptionally good evaluations. I also past inspection and the only way he could get rid of me was if I quit.

This man's life ambition was to make me quit. Now if you know me, that was not going to happen. He started sitting on the desk behind me watching me over my shoulder, checking my reports and could not find anything to complain about, also knowing that the previous clerk was only there one day before she left. Whenever I went to the lady's room, he would come and stand outside the rest room and call me to come out. Anyone else in there would tell me, Mr. Jim Crow is calling you Katie, "My response," "I know it and I am sure everyone in the office could hear it too." When I would not come out, He would yell "Katie, I know you are in there." When a woman would come into the lady's room, I would be just be standing there looking in the mirror. They would just smile; I would not come out until he left and stop calling me.

The next week he started asking me to smile for him and let him see my teeth. If I did not respond he would just keep asking me. I know the Bible says not to call someone a fool, but sorry, this man was the biggest fool I had the pleasure of meeting in my life. I went in to talk to the manager that hired me and shared with him all my experiences dealing with this supervisor. He told me," Katie, just hold on; they are going to move this office." He did listen to everything I had to say but gave me no solutions. "This shit had to stop."

I felt compassion for my supervisor. His daughter had mental problems where she would always need to be in the care of others. When I did not bow to his antics, he started sharing his miserable life with me. He told me when he was in school, he would hurry home to sit in his mother's lap and suck his mother's breast. I never commented or looked him in the face. I kept my head down and did my job. Often wondering "Why me, Lord?"

While at the Kedzie office there was a Revenue Officer that I knew from a previous office that I worked in, and when he came into the office, he would pass my desk and of course I would speak to him "Good Morning Mr. XX," and he would stick his tongue out at me. I thought that I was seeing things so the next time I saw him I stopped him and asked him, "Why, when I speak to you, do you stick your tongue out at me?" And this man told me that he thought that I liked it. I could not believe this. I told him I did not like it and I will never bother to speak to you again

My supervisor called me into his office and asked me to meet him in the supply room. I asked him for what and he told me he would show me when I got there. I did not go into the supply room. Another times he called me in his office I brought a note pad to write down my assignment, and he told me about his son who drew a picture of the family His picture did not have two legs, so the teacher called the parents in because of the drawing. The Parents laughed and then told the teacher that he did not always wear his leg around the house. He lost his leg in some war. The phone on my desk rang so I left his office and after the phone call stayed at my desk. Again, he called me in his office and started folding up his pants leg, to show me his artificial leg. I got up and returned to my desk. I made no comment. He also started invading my space, reaching over me and then he called me into his office since I never came into the supply room as he often requested. He opened the center drawer of his desk and had one of those magazines that had a woman with her legs wide open in a sexual position. When I saw that, I just walked out of the room. There were not any doors to the offices, just half glass partitions. I was horrified. He left for lunch, and I begged the other clerk to look at what he showed me.

She finally was convinced to come and when I opened the drawer the magazine was gone. I wanted to nail his ass.

The Manager called me into his office on another occasion and told me that he was planning to get a hotel reservation and give me a key, telling me I should meet him there. He thought that my silence and my just leaving his office was a sign that I agreed, and it was expected to just be with him because he was my boss. Since I did not keep records, I believed him when he said that nobody would believe me.

You know God is Good and there was information going around that the Kedzie office was closing and moving to Skokie Illinois across the street from a mall. I did not want to work for him anymore, and I needed a way out because he told me that I had to go to Skokie with the group. This was so much farther to get there then I wanted to drive daily. Having a small child, it would be a traffic nightmare in the mornings and the evening daily traffic. What if he needed me? I would be over an hour getting home. So, I was told by the union that I should write a note to the manager of Examination Division stating that this move would create a hardship for me and request to be reassigned to a position in the Chicago area. I went to my new office and this place had doors to the offices, and to me that was not a good thing. The union also told me to leave home my regular time as if I was going to the Kedzie Office which most of the people going there lived closer than I. So, I was late, when I arrived, I was greeted by my boss telling me I had an interview at the downtown office as soon as I could get there. He was angry since he did not expect me to not move with them. I was sure when I saw that door to his office that I would catch hell from him since he was so bold. I thought that I should have reported him and kept a calendar of his sexual aggressiveness toward me, but I had so much on my plate that I just did not.

While working there, during the filing season, I was in a video handing out forms for the IRS. I never saw the tape, but others told me that they saw me on TV. In 1976 I purchased a house in Maywood Il. It was a sided house located on 2nd Avenue. 1715 South I was so excited the house sold for$ 30,500.00 I made a $500.00 down payment. The lawyer that was working for the seller said that he would take care of everything. The only thing that spoiled it for me was that the finance company wanted a statement from my ex-husband that he would continue to send me the $100 a month child support, which he signed and gave to me. When the closing was over, the lawyer turned over a key to me and then asked me if he could keep the key to my house I took the key out of his hand and left his office.

Soon after we moved,my Mama wanted me to drive her to the west side of Chicago so she could attend the church that she used to attend. She was not used to public transportation to Maywood yet, so I drove her to her church I found I was un-familiar with this area. After dropping her off I was searching for the way back to the main street where I can get on the expressway back home. When I found that street and noticed that I could not make a left turn I thought of driving across the street to enter the gas station and then turn into the main street but looking around I did not see a police car. That route could still get me a ticket. So, I just turned left anyway. Breaking the law, anyway, and to be pulled over by two white policemen, my thoughts were how much is this ticket going to cost me. To my surprise the officers approached us cautiously. The one on the passenger side, I saw him unbuckle his gun. My son was turned to watch the policeman on the driver's side approach us; he had his hand on his gun. I was afraid for my life. I instruct-ed my son to not move. Be still. The policeman on the driver's side asked me where I was going, I said home he asked me where I lived, I lived in Maywood Il, He then asked me for my driver's license. Of course, my license was not showing my current address. He told me my address was in Chicago. I told him we recently moved, and I sent the DMV a change of address letter. I said I was trying to get to the Congress expressway. I mentioned that I was not familiar with this area. He said that he stopped me because we fit the description of someone who committed a robbery. He gave me my license back and told me to be careful. Then they left, and I was relieved they pulled off before me. It took me a minute to compose myself. This was not the only time the police had stopped me, but it was the only one that I was fearful. For our lives.

There was a day at the Call site when I came in early, and I drove my cousin's car because she could not get the window down and she did not have a garage to put it in. So, we ex-changed cars until she could get the window repaired, so I only had the Saab for a day or so, when this white guy in the group saw the car and I was the only one in the office he loudly slammed down his briefcase and declared how defeated he felt because I was coming to work in an expensive car. Usually, you knew by the parked cars who was in the office because you knew what car they drove. I thought it was hilarious that he would have a hissy fit about what I came to work in.

When my son started driving, I invited him to sit down and we had a talk about how you address any police who stop you I advised him to be respectful of the police it did not matter who had the uniform on. Be polite and follow their instructions to the letter do not complain. Do not try to run away. I told him that if he ran from the police they will shoot you and if you do not have a gun on you, they will put a gun in your hand as you lay on the ground dying and there is nothing I can do about it but bury you. Driving while black gave him many opportunities to be stopped by the police. One policeman in Maywood gave him 5 tickets and then arrested him and slapped him and broke his glasses, my son was to pick me up at the El station. When I went to the station and asked why this policeman hit my son. The Captain took me in another area and threaten me if I complained I would not receive any help from them and I would be sorry if I complained. The police officer that wrote the tickets appeared to be Spanish, the captain was African American. I realized that he had the upper hand and there was no God in him because of his threat to a woman. I said nothing, he gave me my car keys and I went home.

GAY

After I was divorced, I would say that I was a "gay divorcee," using this phase a lot. I soon found out that it had a different meaning Than the one I was using I pulled out the dictionary and noted that my definition was considered dated. To me it meant that I was lighthearted and carefree, on top of the world. It did not mean that I was a girl who wanted a girlfriend, romantically. I was finally free from my disappointment in my selection of a life mate. Legally divorced. To show friends that I had shaken off the feelings of rejection and knowing that I did not desire to stay or be depressed, I had a coming out party.

My son and I would move forward together. My nephew Jeffery He is a born entertainer. He attended St. Stanislaus Kostka School. They presented a musical, "The Wonderful World of Oz." Jeffery played the scarecrow, and he was a part of the choreographers for the songs "Ease on Down" and" Slide Some Oil to Me" "You Can't Win." Also, "A Brand-New Day." He was the only choreographer for that number. The play was wonderful. This was done while he was in the 8th grade. He is an artist gifted in dancing and singing. We are immensely proud of his accomplishments. He starred in "Metropolis." He played Marco. I have an 8 track of his show while he worked as a dancer, singer, and choreographer on the cruise ship Holland American. He made a great interpretation of Tina Turner dancing and singing "Proud Mary." My brother told me that Jeffery shared with him that he wanted to marry a man but years later, when my brother brought it up in conversation, Jeffery denied ever saying it. Jeffery decided that he preferred to be called Happi. He currently lives in California. He has given dancing lessons to some of the stars' children. He also recently graduated from National University with a master's degree in Human Behavior; he earned his BFA from Columbia College in Chicago. He is working toward his doctorate in Education. He currently is working with youths who are interested in dance and singing He came from California to attend his grandmother's funeral, and he sang beautifully, "His Eyes Were on the Sparrow." I asked him to sing because Mama said that she wanted him to sing at her funeral. My nephew is a wonderful person, and we all love him. He is a same gender loving person.

My son had a relationship with a young girl he met at church. She was the grandchild of a member of the church. I was not happy with their friendship. She lived far away from us, and he ruined things for me with these enormous phone bills. He was very selfish with the phone, and he did not give a damn that I had to pay for the calls. And on top of that, he hid the phone bill. He also knew that I needed a phone on at home for my Mama was home alone. They managed to get themselves pregnant and I was so disappointed. He knew about birth control and celibacy. But they had other ideas. He had to take the train to Joliet to be with her, and he missed the last train to return home one day. Her mother called and explained what happened and said he would be home the next morning. I was not born yesterday. It all was a set up for them to be together. They conceived a child. I had mixed emotions. I had talked to my son about who is the responsible party. I reminded him of the lesson I gave him about what men should wear, and he said the girl did not want him to put on one. Red flag. I worried because he was legal, and she was not. Of course, he said he did not know that she was as young as she was. News, she had a miscarriage. I thought the drama was over, then her mother called me again and asked me to pay for a D & C for her daughter. I advised her that she should talk with the responsible party.

I was not going to pay for anything of this matter, she was wasting her time talking to me. They were determined and conceived again, and my son wanted to marry the girl. I told him that was not all right with me. "You do not have a job, or savings, or a place for your bride to live. So how can you get married?" He said she could live in the basement with us. "No, son, I am not taking care of any extra people." "Well," he said, "Can we get married, and me stay here, and she stay with her Parent?" I said, "If you are married, you will move out of my house and support yourself." Well, he left and lived with her in her Parents' house. He got a job and worked. But he moved back home soon. He said he was a father of a little girl and wanted to go to the hospital and visit them. I was not available to take him. When we visited, it was after receiving the birth announcement. Alycea Wallace was born August 6th. We visited the child and her mother. But we were not allowed to see the child again until she was 18 years old, when she was graduating high school. She invited us to attend her basketball game. It was a fun evening. It was a high school basketball game to which we were invited. So, we came to the ballgame and the graduation. She got a basketball scholarship for college. While in college she posted her relationships with other females. She was one of the LGBQT. Currently she is married, and she and her wife are happy together. And they have a son now 2 years old.

My cousin Herman was a petite boy when he was in school. I did not see him often, but one day he was riding the streetcar that I got on. It was good to see him. He had those light brown eyes. Which was natural and they were so expressive. He had been drawing some women's fashions, and we discussed his designs and during that conversation we pledged that he would draw the designs and I would do the sewing. We really enjoyed making our plans for our future. Then it became time for me to get off the streetcar. We bonded on that ride, But after that I never heard from him for many years. I heard through the grapevine that Herman had moved to California and he had a sex change operation. She changed her name to Gwen. I also heard that she had been beaten badly and her mother Thelma Wilson left for California to be with her. On August 25th, 1990, I planned a trunk show. "Escape the Ordinaire." "Sweaters and Things II". The show was at Sharko's Restaruant, 1 West Roosevelt Road, Villa Park, IL. I invited other entrepreneurs to show their wares. There were a jewelry table, a nail technician, a children's corner with books and toys. I also advertised exercises. "shape up" wardrobe planning, a fashion show, other entertainment provided by Stairway to the Stars, skin care classes and breakfast cooking. The tickets were $5.00 The restaurant provided the best hors d'oeuvres. The ticket sales and the exhibitor's charges full paid all the expenses of the event. I heard from Gwen after I sent out flyers to advertise my trunk show I sent one to her mother Thelma. Gwen called me on the phone, but she did not identify herself as my cousin Herman. We just talked about her sewing business. She stated she made fur coats. She said she was going to come to my trunk show. I was disappointed. When she did not show up. I thought I knew who she was. I wanted very much to see her again. The show went off well. Quite a few people came; they looked at my collection. I sold one sweater. We were in the restaurant's balcony; I had this rattan trunk with 12 sweaters I designed and crocheted. May 30th, 2005. I received word that her mother Thelma Wilson died Ann my cousin and I went to the funeral. Thelma was well loved by her congregation. We went up front to express our sympathy to the immediate family. I heard a voice under a large, veiled hat say, "Katie it is so good to see you." I returned the hug an moved on through the rest of the family sitting on the front row. I could not see the face of the relative that knew me. After sitting down and thinking about it, my cousin Ann asked, "Who was that woman who called your name? "I told her that used to be Herman "What that was Herman?" "Yes" The obituary said that my cousin Thelma had two girls and a boy. I knew she had two boys and a girl Gwen was busy after funeral and I stood behind her while she talked with others. I never got a chance to talk with her again. While

I was waiting to speak with her, I got the impression that she was avoiding me.

So I left. Later I called the phone number she had given me but it was disconnected. Thelma Wilson my Mama's niece, her mother Johnnie Ethel Stamps Williams. I inquired with the immediate family whether any of them had a picture of my Aunt. I also thought of her as the families long lost sister. After leaving Mississippi and settling in St Louis, MO. Thelma Wilson was born in Anguilla, Mississippi, and she was the daughter of McKinley and Johnnie Ethel Stamps Williams. Thelma passed May 30th, 2005.Two years later I found out that Gwendolyn Flakes (GIGI) died on the same date his mother died. Her sister never told me how she died. So, I did not question her. She mentioned how difficult it was to produce an obituary for her. I advised her to just have her name, date of birth, date of death, and a prayer," The Lord is my Shepard," which is what I used for my Mama and I requested a copy, I advised her I would not be able to attend the services. I wonder if she was ill or depressed due to the death of her mother. Thelma's death may have left her without the support system that she needed.

I asked my Grandson if he was gay. He said "Grandma. What does the phrase gay person mean to you?" "Well, it means that a person who is gay are attracted to a person that is of the same sex." "No Grandma, I am queer." I thought my question was not answered if I understood his response. We changed the subject and spoke of other things. I told him about a memory I had of him at his preschool graduation. When a graduate was leading the song. "This Little Light of Mine." The girl's voice was so soft, even with the microphone. Suddenly my Grandson took the microphone and really belted out the song with the help of the young choir. The parents and I cheered them on. The sweet young ones were so cute and happy in their blue graduation gowns. After my conversation with my oldest Grandson. I went to the dictionary app on my phone to determine if I had the correct understanding of the word "queer" or "peculiar." Queer came to be used as a pejorative, against those with same-sex desires or relationships. In late 19th century.

My Grandson is still the joy of my life; he is talented and smart. We enjoy each other's company. He is also making his stand in the world and has been in magazines and books He even tried to get me and Robert to pay for him to attend John Robert's Modeling School, the one I went to when I was young. We did not commit in paying for his modeling education. He and I spent a lot of time together as he was growing up. We even took a course of Fencing together; it was fun.

Erik II has done a lot of traveling for his performances. He traveled to Berlin, Germany; London, England; Stavanger, Norway; Stockholm, Sweden; New Orleans, LA ;Austin Texas; and New York, NY. After he lived in New York for about 18 months, we were happy that he came home to Chicago, IL. as his base. If you would like to check him out, he prefers to call himself Mr. Wallace. You may use Futurehood.net to check out his songs including "It Girl" on this site. He is on the cover of the book Cause and Effect, Issue 2, and also on the cover of the magazine "Covers" and he was in the "New York Sun Times" Spring Fashion Booklet, modeling. He has produced a CD. He is interesting and enthusiastic about his status. Family and friends love him.

Alycea and Tomesha Wallace

Herman Wilson

Erik L Wallace II

THEY CALL IT
SWEET ALABAMA

As I leave my home early in the morning, I find there is no one outside. And I travel toward my appointment. Just a few feet from my house I turn the corner. A truck turns left on the divided street, I notice this huge flag attached to a pole that is attached to the back of this truck. It is blowing in the breeze. This flag strikes fear in my heart. I decide that I will not turn my head to look at the driver. Who has his drivers' side window down and resting his arms on the window door, out of the side of my eyes I checked to see if he is pointing something at me. He looks at me, and that huge flag with the stars and bars, waves.

Relief took away my fear. My window was closed but he spoke not a word I could hear, and I watched him from my rear-view window, hoping he did not turn around and follow me. He did not turn at the next street opening, he kept going. I exhaled.

These are not the best of times. Racism is raising its ugly head. Hate is holding rallies. Reconciliation is needed now. We have Hate groups growing in numbers. We have people not just speaking objections to the skin colors and religious objections but being violent, and carrying military type weapons, at rallies, using cars to run down people. That flag is just fabric but the reason for it scares me. Why can't we love one another? In 2020 there were 20 Hate groups in Alabama. Some are difficult to obtain information about. They are migrating on-line. There are 838 hate groups in this country. Will love overcome hate?

IN THE MIDDLE
OF THE NIGHT

I listened to her. The labored breathing was making me feel if only I could pray or just touch her, she would be healed from this pain she must be feeling. Her chest was rising and falling, as if she was running. I listened from my bedroom on the baby monitor that I had put in her room. I could not just lie there, I got up and sat with her. I picked up her hand, does she know I am here? I thought, oh, Mama, I know this is hard on you. You were the last one in your family. All of the others are gone. All 9 of her siblings. I gave her some drops of the pain medicine. She moved her lips and took it in. When I saw that, I thought she might open her eyes, but no other movement.

My husband came into the room and put his hands directly on my shoulders to comfort me. He said nothing, that I remember and then he left the room. I called the hospice hot line and a man answered. he told me to just give her some drops of the morphine. I told him I had to drive my son to work. He told me to stay there, I did not listen, I wanted to run away. I was up all night; I knew I would be right back. just gone for a few minutes. My son was ready for work. My husband had already left. I wondered why he did not offer to drop him off, they worked in the same area. Erik could not lose that job. So, I jumped into yesterday's clothes and left the house. I quickly drove him to work. Rushed home, and there was something different in the air of the room. I didn't hear her heavy breathing. I rushed upstairs to her room, and she wasn't breathing any more. I touched her and she was warm to the touch. Oh God, she's gone, oh no, why did I leave? Oh no, I have to call hospice, I called them. The same man answered he said he would notify her case worker who would be right out. I called my brother, crying in the phone, "Mama's gone, James, she is gone," he said he would be right over, I called my Daddy, and told him. He got off the phone really quick, I called our Pastor Roger. Then I called Robert and told him to go get Erik from work. I called Mitzi my niece and Erma my sister-in-law, asked them to tell others. My niece Mitzi came over first. She brought her husband Albert. She was helping me, just by her being there. I told them what happened.

I just left to take Erik to work. Oh, why did I leave? I felt so bad that I was not there to hold on to her hand. to offer some comfort. did she know I wasn't' there? Mitzi said, "Aunt Katie, let's just sit down and let us mourn now," she wanted me to cry. I couldn't do it. I just started laughing, and then I couldn't stop laughing. My heart ached for my Mama; I just could not shed any tears. People came over, Mitzi made some waffles. My nephew and his mother were there. My dad and brother came in the door, I was moving closer to my brother. When his oldest son rudely pushed me aside and hugged his dad. I just did not understand why he would do that. Then tears just flooded from my eyes, my brother's wife kissed my cheeks, I was shocked. I was unhappy that she showed me the compassion that my mother and I never experienced from her. He previously told me that he would not bring her around. They went upstairs to see my mother, and I remained downstairs. My dad, my brother, Pastor Roger, then the man from the funeral home arrived all had come downstairs. He asked if all the people there would gather away from the front door, we gathered in the kitchen. We all held hands and Pastor Roger led us in prayer. Again, I could not hold the tears back. I walked away and saw the funeral director carry my mother out the front door, she was in a black zippered bag. I thought goodbye Mama. My nieces Angela and

Mitzi, her Granddaughters went through Mama closets to select an outfit for her. We selected a white two piece suit a jacket and skirt. I pulled out a red kufi for her head, and some red shoes that was in her closet. I also wanted her to have a bible I gave her. The small compact one I had, because the one she used was well used some of the pages were tattered. It had been well used. She had some pills that she was supposed to take thrown under the bed and there was some money there too.

I spent the evening receiving calls and several friends came by to see me. I was tired but not relaxed to sleep. I went through the pictures that we would post on the board of the funeral home. We only wanted a wreath for the coffin. We had a picture of mother on a stand, and after about 45 minutes they begin to close that coffin, and my brother and I looked upon my mother's face one last time. I spoke at the funeral, her Grandson and Granddaughter sang, and her niece, it was all very well done. The members of our church was well represented and they all sat in the back Robert's side of the family was well represented. It was nice that they shared the service with us. After walking away from the grave, I did not know what I would ever do without her.

Mama was such a big part of my life. We laughed together, cried together, faced challenges together. She was a wonderful Mother and a great friend. We were all blessed to have her in our life. Her love was unconditional. My son and husband walked me back to my car. My Grandson Erik was driving the car with Taylor and Tyler, my youngest grandchildren sitting in the back seeing Mama's casket put in that hole, was so hard to believe what I was seeing. My beloved Mama born April 25th, 1916, she passed November 29th, 2005. I love you Mama!

Ida Buckingham
in the U.S., Find A Grave Index, 1600s-Current

Name:	Ida Buckingham
Birth Date:	1916
Birth Place:	USA
Death Date:	2005
Death Place:	USA
Cemetery:	Chapel Hill Gardens West
Burial or Cremation Place:	Oakbrook Terrace, DuPage County, Illinois, USA
Has Bio?:	N
URL:	http://www.findagrave.com/cgi-...

Source Information

Ancestry.com. *U.S., Find A Grave Index, 1600s-Current* [database on-line]. Provo, UT, USA: Ancestry.com Operations, Inc., 2012.

Original data: *Find A Grave*. Find A Grave. http://www.findagrave.com/cgi-bin/fg.cgi.

Description

This database contains an index to cemetery and burial details posted on Find A Grave. Corrections and additions to memorials can be submitted on the Find A Grave site. When viewing a record in this database, you can navigate to the corresponding memorial on Find A Grave by clicking "Go to website" or clicking on the Find A Grave URL. Once viewing the memorial on Find A Grave, corrections can be submitted by clicking the 'edit' tab. Learn more...

Ida Buckingham Find a Grave index

Parents

EUGENE
STAMPS
1880–

Edna CASTON
STAMPS
1878–

Children (2)

Jeffery James Price   B: 1934

Katie Price   B: 1940

Ida Stamps Price
B: 25 Apr 1916 in Utica, Mississippi
D: 29 Nov 2005 in Chicago, Cook, Illinois, USA

James Price
B: 02/01/1916 in jackson Mississippi

Ida Stamps
in the 1920 United States Federal Census

[**Detail**] [Source]

Name:	Ida Stamps
Age:	3
Birth Year:	abt 1917
Birthplace:	Mississippi
Home in 1920:	Utica, Hinds, Mississippi
Street:	Utica Tallahalah Road
Residence Date:	1920
Race:	Black
Gender:	Female
Relation to Head of House:	Daughter
Marital Status:	Single
Father's Name:	Eugene Stamps
Father's Birthplace:	Mississippi
Mother's Name:	Edna Stamps
Mother's Birthplace:	Mississippi
Occupation:	None
Neighbors:	View others on page

Household Members	Age	Relationship
Eugene Stamps	40	Head
Edna Stamps	37	Wife
Mary J Stamps	18	Daughter
Isiah Stamps	17	Son
Katie M Stamps	15	Daughter

1920 census Ida Stamps

300

WILL YOU KNOW MY NAME

Daddy and I talked every morning after he was sent home from the hospital. They told his wife they were releasing him and she failed to come and get him until the next day when she could have some help; they said that they were unable to do anything for him. My brother called me and told me to wait until they called me, before coming to Chicago I did not understand, why? At what point of his deterioration were they going to call me?

I needed travel time from Alabama to Chicago. I really wanted to be there now. I sent him a plant that was rather expensive and Lois, my Daddy's' wife, told me she left it at the hospital. She mentioned that she had enough to do to bring him home, so she left the plant. This made my blood boil. Since Daddy was in hospice, I asked Lois if I could speak to the hospice nurse. She gave me her phone number, and the nurse and I talked about Daddy's condition. I wanted to know how serious his condition was. Did she think that he had enough time for me to wait to come to Chicago? Of course, she could not say that everything depends. She concluded our conversation telling me that I could call her anytime. This felt more reassuring. After I talked to the nurse, Daddy called me and was upset because Lois told him that I talked to his nurse, as if they were not telling me the truth about his health, which was not the case. So I just let him spew and correct me. When he finished talking, I told him o.k. But I knew since my Mama was on hospice care that the nurse was there to help the whole. family. I had to agree with Dad. Dad tried to get Lois and me to cooperate with one another. After about 45 years, our relationship never worked. As I was growing up, he told us while the three of us were on the phone that he loved us both.

Somebody did not recognize that there is a difference in the love for one's daughter which is different from a love for one's wife. This time when I called Daddy's cell phone Lois answered and told me that the nurse was with Daddy, she also told me that she wanted to take Daddy to the bank and i told her that you can't do that! He is in hospice," he can't go to the bank, in his condition." She didn't say anything else and told me Daddy will call me back. Daddy had a bank account that he told James and I that he wanted us to divide that money up between us, when he was gone, I told him that he would have to make that known at the bank, or prepare a will, he told me he told Lois and she will give it to us, I told him that will not work. When I see you in heaven, Daddy I will be telling you that Lois did not give us that money.

We laughed it off. Daddy called me and told me to come to Chicago. I was not invited to stay with him or my brother. He told Lois to send me a check for $500.00, enclosed was a note that read: This is the money you asked your father for. Well, what is this ? I did not ask Daddy for any money. I just disregarded the note and told my son, i was going to Chicago to see Dad, he was living in Texas. He decided to take the bus to Alabama and ride with me to Chicago, since my husband was not planning to go with me. So, I waited an extra day for Erik to get here, I let him have an evening of rest and early the next day we left for Chicago. We had a great time riding and talking together on the road. I did all of the driving to get there. I asked my Grandchildren's Grandmother if I could stay with them, she told me that we were welcome to come and stay with them.

When we got to Chicago, my Daddy was really weak and thin but he still had that great charm. It was good to see him and at that point he was not eating and we encouraged him to eat he said he wanted a burger from McDonald's. So, we got one for him, then we watched him eat it. I even took pictures. He was carried in a regular chair to the table. I felt sad inside because I knew he was leaving me. But I was glad I did not wait for this mysterious call from my brother and Lois. We stayed around most of the day, Lois went and brought back packaged dinners. Which we enjoyed. She seemed really nervous and we left telling Dad we would come back tomorrow. The next day, I called my brother and asked him what time was he going to be at Dad's house, we agreed to meet there. When we got here James came out of the house and told us not to stay long, that Lois did not want us to be there long. This upset me, but I went in and talked with Dad a while. When I came out of his room, Lois threw a folder at me while I was seating at the table it landed on the table. It was his hospital report, Dad had 4th stage kidney failure. There was no treatment for him. He was 94 years young, when we left that day Lois walked us to the door, I was the last person to exit and Lois placed her hand on my back and pushed me out of the door. I grabbed the banister and decided that this woman has to be crazy. After James told me that Lois said I could only stay a few hours that I had to go, I decided to go home, since the reason i came was to see Daddy, so I told Daddy I was leaving that day. He was sitting on the bed and i told him i was leaving to go home and I kissed him on his checks and told him that everything was going to be alright. Lois came in the room sat down next to Daddy and asked me to kiss her too. I could not believe she was going there. I did as she requested in front of Daddy.

I walked out of her house and my son and i went home. I heard that she was talking about me in the kitchen and Erik did not tell me exactly what she said but he was upset about what was said. I told my brother, that when Dad died that I did not want to hear it from Lois, will he call me please, Daddy and I still talked every morning. He told me that he did not think that he will be able to beat this thing that he had, I asked him if he was in pain. He said no, but he wished he were, he felt just weak. He asked to speak to Robert and told him something about marriage, Daddy requested that Robert take care of his daughter. Robert did not really tell me what Daddy talked to him about. Daddy also said that he believed in God and was not afraid of what was happening to him he told me he loved me. We hung up. When I called the next morning, he answered he said he did not feel very good and that he would call me tomorrow, he told me he loved me and we said we will talk tomorrow. The next morning, I called and Lois answered his cell, she said that the nurse was in with him and she would have James call me because James was on his way over, I knew then that Daddy had died. Within the hour James called me and told me that Dad had died.

Well in-between one of those days he called me to tell me that there was no money for James and me, he had given us what he wanted us to have while he was alive, he wanted me to understand this, of course I said, I understood I knew he was retracting his promise to us. James, most have mentioned it to him. James called me and told me that Lois's sister wanted information so she could write the obituary he told her he did not know what his father's mother name was or any other information he told them they had to ask me. He gave me Daddy's sister-in-law's phone number, I called her. She asked me to write it and text it back to her, so I wrote it, she added that Daddy had joined this church, which i did not know about. Daddy was born 2/1/1916 died 05/14/2010, Lois and Dad married in 1955, i did not include the child he had while still married to Lois.

I did not think it mattered. He was in prison. My half-brother's mother asked me to send him an obituary, so I did, he had a concern when he got it, he said Lois knew about him, Daddy told me that he told Lois about the child, the reason he told is because I told him that I did not want to be the one to explain this to Lois, before his demise. He told her and she did not speak to him for weeks. But they stayed together.

Daddy told me if Lois wanted him to leave their house, she had to give him 50,000. At that time it would have been half the value of the property. When I arrived at the funeral home, Lois was waiting outside she came up to me and hugged me and then pushed me away. How strange. After the funeral we lined up to take Daddy's body to the cemetery, as they lowered the body, i picked up 3 of the beautiful red roses i kissed one and threw it in the grave, i kept the others brought them back to Alabama with me and it lasted a long time.

Daddy had a sister that lived in Mississippi, they did not want to tell her about Daddy, because Lois did not want her to come up there. So, his sister Fannie was not told according to my cousin, until after Dad was buried. Sometimes I wish I could pick up the phone to call him. My Mama's first and only love. Oh how I miss them both. A time after I returned home, Lois called me and asked me for information such as Dad's mother's name, I thought you have been married to Daddy 45 years, and you do not know your husband's mother's name. I told her I would call her back. I called her back with the information I had, she got the money out of the bank and asked my brother what he thought of her if she did not put a marker on Daddy's grave. She wanted the money to fix the water problem she had in the basement for the last time. Of course, James did not have any objections, I wished she had asked me. I would have had plenty to say. After the funeral in a conversation with my brother he told me that he had a glimpse of our sister. What I did not know I had a sister!

Lois sent me a check for $50.00 and wrote that she knew that my Daddy would have wanted to give me a gift for my birthday. I was 70 years old. This act brought tears to my eyes, even now as I share it with you, water leaked out of my eyes.

STORMS

After moving to Alabama we got an apartment. It was a 2-master suite but it was small for me and I still wanted to live in a house. We found some new homes just across the highway to rent. I was happy. We also found a Disciple of Christ Church not far from us. We joined that congregation. I started working with the chairperson responsible for a monthly assignment to provide a hot lunch hey used a different church that had a large kitchen and was open for use.

Our members were responsible for preparing food and serving it by the schedule. This particular day was sunny with beautiful white fluffy clouds. I noticed it when I left, The Month was April the day was the 27th the year 2011. April 27th, 2011 The ladies from the church had served lunch and cleaned up the kitchen and we all left for the day. Happy that we could help so many that came to be served.. I went home exhausted and sat down in my easy chair and turned on the television. A few minutes after relaxing the television went blank. My first thought was I had paid the bill for both the electric company and Charter Communications. I got up from my seat and went outside to see if anyone else had electrical problems. When I stepped outside, I noticed that my neighbors were outside and pointing north. I looked in that direction, I saw a big white spinning tornado. I ran in the house but I really did not know what to do, I sat down in my chair and prayed.

Later I found out that over 300 people died across the deep south and Alabama was hit the worse. The church where we served lunch just about an hour after I left was completely destroyed. I think they were able to locate some of the large cans of vegetables in the rubble. That was a scary experience. So many stories after that storm, stories of miracles and death. There was another storm that affected my heart when my beloved brother was in the hospital he had medical issues for quite a while. He endured pain and he told me that he had lost a lot of weight. Being just the two of us we were close. I know how he hated hospitals. When he said that he could not swallow, He also added that he was tired of people telling him what to do. I thought, after our conversation to leave a message on his answering machine insisting that he go to the hospital I explained that they can help you and feed you intravenously. Also control your pain. Later that day I got a call from a doctor who was attending to my brother and he shared some of his medical conditions, he said that there was a hole in his chest and that they could not operate because of the blood clots in his heart. If they tried to operate on him he will die on the table. He wanted me to reach out to his children and he asked for one of their phone numbers, I gave him James', oldest child phone number since she lived close to that hospital. When I was able to talk to James he told me "Do not come here" I knew they had a no visitors mandate. He added "Do not waste a trip here." He knew how stubborn I could be. James also said in his usual humor "You cannot get in or out of this place."

The storm in my heart was whirling and whirling and I kept trying to reach out to my brother, my person. Our last conversation with him he said "Katie I cannot hold the phone it is too heavy." We said, "I love you" and we hung up. A day after that moment the doctor called again and told me to sit down he had bad news. My brother had a massive stroke in the brain with a blood bleed and there was nothing else they could do for him but keep him comfortable. The next day January 3rd, 2022, my brother died. I received the information in a text from his wife. I was so glad that 3 of his children got to see him before he closed his eyes for the last time. You know people; when events happen like President Kennedy was assassinated, Bobby Kennedy was assassinated, Martin Luther King Jr was assassinated. James was not the President of United States or the one who was running for a political office nor a civil rights activist. The lost you feel. It is so deep, because he was my person. The last time I saw him was in 2020, after attending our cousin Ann's funeral, in Chicago, After Aunt Estella died James announced that he would not go to any funerals. Of course, he was at Mama and Daddy's services. My brother worked for the Chicago Transit Authority as a bus driver, he worked for our Daddy at his gas station, he also worked security in one of those high-income properties until he got the job at NBC, he told me he helped Dolly Parton get out of her limousine his arm and hand was in the Photo it was in the paper the actor that was scheduled to be there was missing so James got the part. He retired from N.B.C. after working 15 years. After the storm rip through me After the tears slowed down, after the dark clouds moved I understood something clearly at last a new day, filled with hope for tomorrow and faith that one day we, the Price family will be able to join together with no tears just joy for the Grace and love God offers us. This book is In honor of Jeffery James Price Jr., October 25/28th, 1934 - January 03, 2022.

"The greatest thing you'll ever learn is to love and be loved in return" from the song "Nature Boy", composed by Eden Ahbez.

Celebrating Jeffrey James' retirement

Daddy, Mitzi, James and Angela

Family of Angela Freeman, Mitzi Ekekhor, Jeffery J Price Jr, Takijah Murphy, Kizza Harris

Brother and Sister Katie and James

James and Katie 2020

BIOGRAPHY

I was born in Mississippi and raised in Chicago, my brother and I had all we needed to survive. The necessities provided by our Mama. I enjoyed learning, especially being around other people. I attended school until I finished High School. For the I.R.S. I took college courses in accounting. I was trained as a facilitator, Toast Mistress, Union Stewart, Computer trainer for Revenue Officers. I was an instructor for many of the IRS programs. I also held managerial positions. My top position with them was a Tax Collector of small business.

My interests lead me in modeling, fashion shows fashion designing, making clothes, crocheting, cooking and discovering family history and keeping information on family that had passed on. I collect and take family pictures and have over 1500 photos, in albums. Recently I said to my niece "You mean you were in the same room as my son and neither one of you took a picture!" I try to attend all the events my Nieces and Nephews and Grandchildren invite us to. I reach out to my cousins that are open to have conversation with me. I am planning a family quilt with the faces of each member on a square. I am also planning to downsize my collection of fabric, patterns and yarn, in the very near future.

I belong to an open book club, I attend church, I previously held various positions with the congregations, I currently study with a Bible study group, I follow my young extended family on Facebook, since I live very far from my Chicago roots. My husband and I have family in Illinois,

Nebraska, Kansas and Texas. We have 7 children and 25 grandchildren, 6 great grandchildren. I heard this somewhere "I am a Chicago girl living in an Alabama World." I want to thank several people that I have met here in Alabama. Sydney Sparks, a friend who designed a cover, Nancy Campbell, friend and Editor, Jeffery James Price, brother and contributor, Erik L Wallace II, Grandson and contributor, Debbie Kellogg, Sister-in-law and Ancestry researcher, and Robert K Davis, Husband and contributor. I appreciate you all.

CPSIA information can be obtained
at www.ICGtesting.com
Printed in the USA
BVHW020826120922
646801BV00006B/174